A Boy Named Sue

A Boy Named Sue

Gender and Country Music

Edited by
Kristine M. McCusker and Diane Pecknold

UNIVERSITY PRESS OF MISSISSIPPI
JACKSON

www.upress.state.ms.us

The University Press of Mississippi is a member of the Association of American University Presses.

Illustration credits: Pages 6 and 20, courtesy of the Southern Appalachian Archives of Berea College, Berea, Kentucky; pages 30, 33, 91, 102, 109, and 127, courtesy of Country Music Hall of Fame and Museum; pages 47 and 54, courtesy of R. A. Andreas/Bear Family Records; page 73, © Ernest C. Withers, courtesy of Panopticon Gallery, Waltham, MA, US; page 137, courtesy Longbranch Entertainment Complex; page 159, photo by Harry Langdon. used by permission of Sony Music Nashville; page 170, photo by Russell James, used by permission of Warner/Elektra/Atlantic; page 188, courtesy of Bloodshot Records; page 191, photo by Dale Stewart, design by Grant Alden, used by permission of *No Depression*.

12 11 10 09 08 07 06 05 04   4 3 2 1

Library of Congress Cataloging-in-Publication Data

A boy named Sue : gender and country music / edited by Kristine M. McCusker and Diane Pecknold.
    p. cm. — (American made music series)
Includes bibliographical references and index.
ISBN 1-57806-677-8 (cloth : alk. paper) — ISBN 1-57806-678-6 (pbk. : alk. paper)
    1. Country music—History and criticism. 2. Femininity in popular culture.
3. Masculinity in popular culture. I. McCusker, Kristine M. II. Pecknold, Diane.
III. Series.
ML3524.B68   2004
781.642'082—dc22   2004007354

British Library Cataloging-in-Publication Data available

Contents

Foreword

Muddying the Clear Water

The Dubious Transparency of Country Music

DAVID SANJEK

However familiar their destination or the landmarks encountered along the way, some expeditions of the imagination seem to be repeated generation after generation, as if the very itinerary was hardwired into our genetic makeup. Like Orpheus or Ahab, we hunger after our private Eurydices and white whales, betting that the reward at journey's end will compensate for all the confusion and consternation that came before. In the context of American popular music, one of the most traveled paths leads to the satisfaction of an insatiable appetite for authenticity. Confronted by globalization, cross-media merchandising, and the vertigo-inducing transfer of entertainment properties between an ever-shrinking number of conglomerates, many people yearn for something unsullied by deal making, debt ceilings, and demographic surveys. Something that, notwithstanding its transformation into digital bits and bytes, will retain upon its broadly disseminated lines of code uncontested evidence of the sweat and spirit that led to its creation.

Inevitably, that appetite remains evanescent through and through, for it encourages the belief that the need to be compensated for any creative enterprise reduces that activity to nothing more or less than mercenary labor. We attach our investment in unvarnished communication to an ideological currency that invariably proves to be counterfeit when we separate the spheres of musical meaning from money making. As Joli Jensen pointedly observes, "Cultural products are not like shoes and sausages, and imagining their production as handicrafts that become tainted by industrial or market forces is nostalgic and simplistic."[1] And yet, agonizing over authenticity and yearning for a sphere of activity free from institutional or monetary constraints enters the cultural dialogue year after year, even though these notions constitute some of the most contested concepts in our entire cultural vocabulary. The hankering after evidence of some kind of creative purity continues, therefore, to lead any number of people on any number of quests, however chimerical their object might appear.

In the context of country music, that quest can be traced back to the body of recordings made at Bristol, Tennessee, in 1927, which history has come to regard as maybe not the birth but then the formal ascendance of the genre. If it is possible to put either Eck Robertson's or Fiddlin' John Carson's earlier efforts out of mind temporarily, one can subsequently engage in the kind of originary mythologizing that accords the work supervised by Ralph Peer on this occasion as a kind of initial efflorescence. Many historians of the genre have gone even a step further and taken the efforts of the emerging stars of the episode, the Carter Family and Jimmie Rodgers, and assigned to each of them the two principal tributaries that constitute the range of stylistic expression in country. With the former, all the material and mindset associated with the sentiments of stability and tradition; the home place and the hearth. With the latter, the transient proclivities of the rambler and, with them, the stylistic predisposition to nibble away at generic boundaries that led Rodgers to record with such a range of artists, from Hawaiian guitarists to Louis Armstrong.

It doesn't take a great deal of thought to recognize the gender dynamics at work in this construction, assigning to the feminine habits of constancy and tradition while the masculine becomes associated with a predisposition for impatience and innovation. So straight-jacketed are these definitions that country performers for many years were expected, if not coerced, to toe the line. When Kitty Wells responded to Hank Thompson's ode to the honky-tonk life, it was a demure, almost polite performance. What would the history of the genre be like if, instead, "It Wasn't God Who Made Honky-Tonk Angels" were recorded by Rose Maddox, or Jean Shepherd for that matter? The dubious notion that the female side of the genre did not begin to kick up its heels until a number of years after Wells's rise to stardom held sway for quite some time. It took the groundbreaking efforts of Mary A. Bufwack and Robert K. Oermann in *Finding Her Voice* to trace the substantial contribution of women to country.[2]

Efforts that include this volume follow in the wake of their work and begin the complex task of analyzing and appraising the body of performances to which they brought attention. My own small effort, illustrating the fact that rockabilly was not solely a masculine enterprise as well as the fact that its female proponents could trace their roots to women who stomped their boots in the honky-tonk mode, added to this exercise.[3] Still, gender categories continue their rigid hold upon even the critical consciousness about country, if not the whole of American music. Even so thoughtful and broadminded a work as Richard Peterson's *Creating Country Music*, in its operating metaphors of "hard core" and "soft shell," employs a discourse with gendered qualities, though he admits that the categories are far from firm and members of either gender can be assigned to each type of performance.[4]

Another odyssey that seeks to locate authenticity in the country of country and trails gender language in its wake comes in the opening of the concert documentary *Down from the Mountain*, shot in 2000 at the Ryman Auditorium in Nashville. It features performers from the soundtrack of *O Brother, Where Art Thou?*, written and directed by the Coen brothers. More than simply an unadorned transcription of a public event, the film commemorates the successful marketing of this material as an antidote to what some believed at the time to be the stranglehold upon the record charts by mainstream pop and gangster rap. Sales of the soundtrack have exceeded six million to date. That achievement may not have led to a wholesale commercial renaissance for the kind of music featured in the film, but it did demonstrate that the ears of a significant portion of the American public were ready for a change from the artificiality of pop and the anger of rap. The concert, the tour that followed, as well as comments about the material made by the soundtrack producer, T. Bone Burnett, in a number of media amount therefore to a cultural argument in the form of a commercial enterprise. The Coen brothers brought to life in their film a vision of the Depression South that bypassed the historical record in favor of a mythic recasting of everyday life, while Burnett conceived of the soundtrack as part of a more elaborate effort to reconfigure the unvarnished, nonelectrified, emotionally direct veracity of American vernacular expression at the core of commercial music.

While *Down from the Mountain* does not explicitly embody a wholesale diatribe about the corrupt status of commercial music, one can discern a distinct point of view implicit in the structure of the documentary. It appears most notably in the manner in which the filmmakers—Nick Doob, Chris Hegedus, and D. A. Pennebaker—begin the film in the guise of a journey. This narrative gesture draws attention to the geographical separation between the rural sphere in which country music first took hold and the metropolitan world where that material is packaged and promoted. As the film opens, we find ourselves behind the wheel of a vehicle that travels the route between the back roads of rural America and the rain-streaked streets of downtown Nashville.

No voice or set of features identifies the driver, yet we are led nonetheless to identify with the shift in perspective that this individual traverses as being a matter of more than geography alone. As much as anything, the less than subtle impression comes across that the music we are about to hear arrives from a far away place, distinct from and implicitly superior to the metropolitan environment most of us inhabit and where the concert itself will take place. The implicit biblical tone of the film's title lends as well a sense of country music being somehow spiritually superior and a necessary tonic to more worldly forms of creative expression.

This perspective parallels the point of view that has dominated much mainstream commentary on country music in recent years, most notably in the well-received but conceptually questionable *In the Country of Country* by Nicolas Dawidoff. Earlier analyses of country music addressed to a general readership—Paul Hemphill's *The Nashville Sound* comes to mind—made an eloquent case for the genre by undermining the unexamined yet widely held assumption that the genre was little more than sentimental and simple-minded claptrap composed by untutored hicks.[5] Hemphill and others ushered in the now undisputed belief that country lyrics embody some of the most potent use of the poetic potential of vernacular expression. Dawidoff accepts this perspective, yet he associates it primarily with a limited and narrow body of artists almost altogether from the past of country music and argues that their material acts as an ideological counterpoint to the anxieties of the present age. In contrast to the "ear candy" promulgated by contemporary Music Row, the repertoire that he circumscribes as country remains limited to material that "is simply worded, string-driven melodic music concerned with subjects that are both quotidian and universal; faith, love, family, work, heartbreak, pleasure, sin, joy, and suffering."[6] How much one can detect in Dawidoff's language echoes of that gendered discourse spoken of earlier. The form of country music he values throughout his book resembles the feminine strain of the genre, as if only those subjects, as listed above, that bear upon the complexity of domestic life could hold any weight or substance.

Dawidoff adds that, "The best country was always proudly devoid of affect," for it, in effect, dowses its listeners with the cold water of actuality, not the makeshift matter of triviality.[7] As if a secular form of sacred oratory, "Country forced you to wake upon on Sunday morning and confront your life."[8] Unlike the juvenile attractions of pop and rap, this is "raw stuff for grown-up people who aren't getting any younger and know something about disappointment."[9] In our neoconservative present day, the kind of language Dawidoff chooses makes country bear an uncomfortable resemblance to the ethical scorekeeping advocated by moralists like William Bennett and Rush Limbaugh. It makes listening to country music more of a corrective than a creative experience.

While the initial episode of *Down from the Mountain* appears simply to parrot Dawidoff's association of country music with a morally superior universe, certain details of local geography that the camera's point of view picks up do, thankfully, complicate the presentation. Most notably, the rural scenery comes across as less than pastoral. Instead, tumbledown factories attest to the fact that the process of industrialization that tore apart the agricultural homestead has itself succumbed to the insatiable appetites of globalization. The appeal to the virtues of the home place take on a different character when that locale is no longer pristine and protected, except in memory or the imagination. Some of the quotidian and universal subjects Dawidoff memorializes have become tarnished, if not torn apart. The "raw stuff" that the present rural working class faces is the reality of downsizing, outsourcing, and the replacement of family farming by agribusiness.

At the same time, the introductory sequence reinforces longstanding clichés about the perils of modernization and how country music acts as an antidote to the diminishment of tradition. This is illustrated through architectural images of the urban metropolis. As the vehicle approaches downtown Nashville, we see the imposing skyline of this very cosmopolitan locale. The presence of numerous skyscrapers and forms of contemporary architecture call attention to the recent reinvigoration of the city's long abandoned inner core. In one curious shot, the Ryman Auditorium is made to seem a less imposing structure than it is to the naked eye when poised by the camera against the dual towers of the Bell South offices that dominate the city's skyline like the twin peaks of Batman's cowl. Having this corporate edifice overshadow the Ryman visually brings across the feeling that at any moment it might engulf and devour the older structure. It also endows the long time home of the *Grand Ole Opry* with the kind of sacral dimension that Burnett and the performers endeavor to ascribe to the music. However much, the film appears to argue, the city fathers scheme to bring Nashville further up the hierarchy of urban centers, the cultural as well as ideological baggage attached to the Ryman will endure.

Despite the attention and honor lavished upon the Ryman, the opening sequence manages curiously to excise any direct reference to the local residence of the record industry, Music Row. To do so would deliberately complicate the argument being made about the authenticity of country music and take away the opportunity to use the genre as a foil for all that is considered ersatz in the cultural sphere. The fact that business interests attached themselves to the genre almost the minute it began to be recorded in the 1920s was mitigated by the fact that for many years the offices assigned to monitor and market these artists were housed in unassuming domestic spaces. To travel down Music Row was to encounter a residential neighborhood given over to cultural exchanges. It managed somehow to combine, consciously or unconsciously, the two strains of gender discourse attached to country: the masculine sweat of commerce housed in the feminine-tinged structures with porches and neatly manicured lawns. This setting reinforced as well the homespun dimension of the repertoire and the familial quality of the relationships between managers and musicians. Whenever newcomers arrived in Nashville, their anxieties were allayed, even if only in the ideal sense, by the feeling that they merely had to knock on the industry's front door in order to be invited in to pick a tune.

Nowadays, those encounters increasingly occur in structures that to the naked eye might as well house insurance brokers or commodity traders and where the music that changes hands could easily possess just about as much personality as a balance sheet. The inclination to cover over the exigencies of industrialization by endeavoring to remain domestic and down-to-earth becomes much harder when visitors to corporate offices must pass by security guards and receive identity badges. The earlier glad-handing was a pose as much as a policy, yet it followed from the genre's unfailing effort to keep from public view all the hierarchical relationships that drive the commercial marketplace. What Burnett and likewise the *O Brother* troupe try to keep in place is an investment in making transparent a set of roles and rituals that remain as elaborate and potentially entrapping as those involved in any other form of human communication. Even the backstage banter in the film constitutes a means of making these successful individuals seem like jes' folks. Emmylou Harris's anxious checking of national baseball scores on her palm pilot or Gillian Welch wishing she did not have to change from her street clothes into a more formal dress: these and other gestures, like the buildings on Music Row or the sacralization of the Ryman, draw attention to the effort to keep a complex set of cultural values bound up in the banal behavior of our everyday lives. Or, to return to gendered discourse, to keep it feminized: domestic, down-to-earth, and not daring to be extreme or outlandish.

Much of the recent scholarship on country music has made an effort to collapse this separation of the authentic and the ersatz. It alerts us to the demands of making sense of something we love rather than simply demonizing whatever it is we do not like about how it conducts its affairs. Barbara Ching reminds us that whatever transparency country music might possess is a matter of our choosing. Instead, she argues, it behooves us "to listen for complexity when we think we hear simplicity."[10] We need to recognize the role of signifying practices in the construction of a form of communication that works feverishly to obscure the labor it entails. "It's important to take this music figuratively," Ching argues, "to grant its makers the power of figurative and complex speech that is routinely granted to artists and other people we take seriously."[11] As much as anything, the manner in which a number of country artists are customarily referred to by their first names—Dolly, Willie, and Waylon among many—attempts to erase their unique identities and bring them closer to those who consume their material. What becomes forgotten in the process is how these artists have worked as diligently and deliberately in creating both those personae and that catalog of songs as their fans have in determining how those particular singers stand out from the "imposters" about them.

The essays in this collection encourage the dissolution of the purported transparency of country music by attending diligently to the role of gender to which I have alluded throughout this introduction. As stated earlier, ground-breaking writers like Bufwack and Oermann have enumerated how many women have been left out of histories of the genre or examined how roving vagabonds were contrasted with maternal Madonnas. The more demanding work that remains to be done is tackled by these writers: investigating how gender operates throughout the whole constellation of images, attitudes, and operations attendant to country music, from fan publications to dance styles to the repertoire broadcast over radio. Beverly Keel indicates this dynamic in artists of the present hour, while Kristine McCusker dwells upon patterns in the past. The stories told by Beverly Keel and Emily C. Neely indicate that the dilemmas and detours perpetrated upon someone as well known as Shania Twain bear parallels with a vital figure like Charline Arthur that history has benched unceremoniously upon the sidelines. Others bring attention to the gender dynamics present in the careers of male stars. Peter La Chapelle goes beyond the tabloid headlines of Western Swing star Spade Cooley's killing of his wife to show how his public image of trouble-free domesticity was a strain upon his psyche. Michael Bertrand takes us beyond the customary narrative tied to rockabilly and its regal leader, Elvis, and intimates how the "flaming creatures" that lit up the airwaves and jukeboxes of the 1950s challenged our sense of what it was to be a man. Joli Jensen reinforces the need to never forget how all star images are constructions, and not ones with single dimensions. The perspective given to the career of Patsy Cline by her handlers, her fans (past and present), and the woman herself were far from synonymous, as Jensen illustrates, leading to an array of Patsys rather than a stationary portrait. Diane Pecknold draws us back to the business culture of country and the role of women in the management of artists' careers, particularly when fans adopted professional responsibilities before the business culture of Nashville unceremoniously took over the making of careers. And, finally, Jocelyn Neal takes up a subject that has been too little examined in all realms of American popular music, dance, and shows how gendered are our roles even when we shake our tail feather out on the dance floor.

In conclusion, the fine writing to be found in this collection reinforces that whenever we overlook the complexity and contradiction in country music, we simply encourage the desire Joli Jensen eloquently dubs "purity by proxy"—the insistence that "other people and forms manifest and maintain virtue for us."[12] Such a wish is a luxury we can no longer afford. Instead, we must continue to recognize and document how country music, and all American music for that matter, is a muddy and turbulent mix. Otherwise, whatever expeditions of the imagination we might take will only land us in the ditch or stuck in detours that keep us from ever arriving at our desired destination.

Acknowledgments

Even books that seem to be the work of a single author are usually a group effort in one sense or another. That collective effort is, of course, more obvious in the case of an essay collection such as this. We would therefore first like to thank our contributors for their enthusiasm, hard work, and good will as we put the collection together.

We would also like to thank Middle Tennessee State University, which supplied Kristine McCusker with release time to allow for preparation of the manuscript. We are very grateful to the Gustave Reese Publication Endowment Fund of the American Musicological Society for the publication subvention without which we could not have illustrated the book.

This collection was conceived as a result of a panel presented for the 2001 meeting of the American Studies Association, and we would like to thank that panel's audience and participants, whose engagement encouraged us to pursue the project. The organizers of the 2003 International Country Music Conference gave the editors and several of the contributors a valuable opportunity to get feedback on the project from a delightful and collegial group of country music scholars before we submitted the final manuscript. Colleagues at Middle Tennessee State University, especially Louis Haas and the History Department's Women's Work Group, provided support at critical moments during this book's evolution. Our editors at the University Press of Mississippi, Craig Gill and Anne Stascavage, were both gracious and helpful when we encountered the inevitable complications that emerge with any book.

A number of individuals and institutions provided photographs and other permissions for the essays and we thank them for their assistance and generosity. They include Harry Rice at the Southern Appalachian Archives of Berea College; Grant Alden at *No Depression* magazine; Michael Gray, Dawn Oberg, and Denny Adcock at the Country Music Hall of Fame and Museum; Nan Warshaw at Bloodshot Records; Richard Weize at Bear Family Records; Paul Quigley at *Southern Cultures;* the editors of *Southern Folklore;* Shelle at the Longbranch Saloon in Raleigh, North Carolina; and the staff at the Panopticon Gallery.

Clark Johnson, Katie Lou McCusker, and Larry Puzzo lived with this book from its inception and they are pleased (albeit for entirely different reasons) that it is finally done. We also thank Grace Puzzo and Lily Johnson for timing their births around our deadlines.

Finally, one of the great advantages of writing about country music is the endless supply of good song titles that fit the text perfectly. That the title of this book is borrowed from Johnny Cash's hit rendition of Shel Silverstein's song "A Boy Named Sue" takes on added meaning, though, in light of the recent deaths of Cash and his wife, June Carter Cash. We will certainly not be the last to draw inspiration from their music and their lives.

Introduction

KRISTINE M. McCUSKER AND DIANE PECKNOLD

In February of 1969, Johnny Cash recorded "A Boy Named Sue," his ode to masculine adventure and fatherly transgression, at a concert for the inmates of San Quentin prison. The song's dark humor and references to drinking, fighting, and rebellion struck a particular chord with the crowd, who cheered the protagonist's attempts to murder his father, the man who dared to name him Sue. Of course, the song's resolution—in which the long-absent father tells his son the shameful name "helped to make you strong," just as he had planned—promised that even wandering and cantankerous fathers could still fulfill their paternal responsibilities and teach their sons about manhood. The song's irreverent play on masculine gender conventions held obvious appeal for an all-male audience of inmates whose own experiences must have borne out the lyrical assertion that "the world is rough, and if a man's gonna make it, he's gotta get tough," and who might have sought reassurance about their personal identities as absent fathers, estranged sons, and men. But it also found a much larger audience, eventually reaching number one on the country music charts and number two on the pop music charts. That more diverse audience made its own uses of the song's gender confusion. For some, the song might have resonated with or satirized the gender-bending politics of hippie youth culture; others may have found in it simple comic relief; and still others heard in its lyrics the comfort they needed to face their own tribulations of challenged masculinity.[1]

The performance and popularity of "A Boy Named Sue" highlight the underappreciated role gender has played in defining country music's identity as a genre. Gender has always been critical to the production and consumption of country music. It has demarcated the kinds of sounds and images that could be included within the genre's boundaries; it has helped to determine the songs and artists audiences would buy or reject; and it has shaped the identities listeners could make for themselves in relation to the music they enjoyed. Gendered imagery has been used to defend and preserve country's "essence" and to radically redirect its development.

This book is an exploration of the impact of gender on the artistic and institutional development of country music. We use gender here not as a code for "women" but in its more encompassing theoretical sense, to describe social constructions of masculinity and femininity, and to emphasize the way those constructions are used to create shared meaning. While gender made an early appearance in country music scholarship, much of the work to date falls into what Joan Scott has characterized as a descriptive mode, an approach that acknowledges gender without explaining how or why this particular method of categorization has structured meaning, or with what consequences.[2] Descriptive accounts have been critical to the project of restoring women to the country music canon, but gender can help us to understand much more about country music than just women's experiences. Class boundaries, cultural tastes, institutional hierarchies, performance styles, and appropriate roles for audiences have all been constructed partly through the invocation of gender.

We view gender as one of the central dynamics of country music history and culture; gender codes are a remarkably flexible way of making meaning, and their uses have been far less predictable than the somewhat rigid dichotomy between male and female cultural domains that has characterized past scholarship on the subject would suggest. This collection of essays shows that social prescriptions for men and women, as they were performed in country music, have evolved over time in response to the changing web of relationships between performers, the industry, the audience, and larger historical forces. Gender has also helped to structure those relationships. In particular, it has been used to establish and defend the stylistic and institutional boundaries separating country music from pop, rock 'n' roll, folk, and other genres. Indeed, these essays suggest that gender imagery has been a site for stylistic innovation throughout the course of country music's development, inseparable from more commonly recognized arenas for creativity such as instrumentation, lyrical content, or performance style.

When gender is brought to bear in this way on country music's conventional narrative, it challenges important features of the now-familiar story first outlined by Bill C. Malone in his authoritative history of the genre, *Country Music USA*, and forces us to question traditional understandings of country music's important commercial moments and transitions. It shows us that women, who have been underrepresented in the story of country's development, actually played critical roles in its evolution as a form of commercial entertainment, whether as performers, producers, or audience members. It also calls attention to the genre's reliance on specific definitions and performances of masculinity for its appeal, and complements an already rich body of work on class in country music.[3] Finally, a gendered analysis changes our understanding of country music audiences, bringing into sharper focus a diverse national listenership composed of a variety of local, regional, and class groups.

The contributors to this collection come from an array of disciplinary backgrounds and apply a number of different methodologies and approaches to their work. Insights from the fields of history, communication studies, cultural studies, sociology, and musicology, among others, offer a holistic view of the production and consumption of country music that allows us to trace the connections between lived social roles and the ways those roles are represented through popular culture. The articles are organized chronologically to emphasize the evolution and impact of gender roles over time. The essays also represent a wide range of inquiry that encompasses many of the styles that have been gathered under the moniker of "country and western music."

Even so, the collection is exploratory rather than definitive. A systematic treatment of gender in each subgenre of the varied and expansive country field is beyond the scope of this collection. Thus, there is little here about bluegrass music, for example, or about the commercial country music of the 1970s and 1980s. Readers can find out more about the role of gender in specific subgenres by consulting the works noted under further reading. The collection also reflects the relatively slower development of masculinity studies as compared to women's studies. We have only begun to suggest the importance of examining how men's careers and personas have been affected by the politics of audience and industry gender expectations.

Several central themes recur across the essays. The contributions of Kristine M. McCusker and Joli Jensen emphasize how the complex relationship between gender and class has shaped the country tradition. McCusker challenges the conventional wisdom that equates women with noncommercial folk music by showing how the invented persona of Linda Parker, the embodiment of an idealized vision of southern womanhood, expanded the commercial appeal of the *National Barn Dance* by revising the class identity of country music during the depths of the Great Depression. Jensen examines the differences between contemporary and posthumous images of Patsy Cline and finds that a romanticized gender identity has become an increasingly significant part of the Patsy legend, in spite of the fact that Patsy herself minimized her role as a woman in favor of other identities such as class. Jensen suggests that it mattered little that ideological feminism was unimportant to Patsy Cline during her career. As fans and critics remade her for their own uses, they drew on her lived social role as a strong woman to create a posthumous image of her as a protofeminist.

Essays by Peter La Chapelle, Michael Bertrand, and Jocelyn R. Neal reveal how constructions of gender expressed through country music are nested within the social relations of production and consumption that bind performer, industry, and audience. In his reading of fan culture in postwar Southern California, historian Peter La Chapelle finds the contested terrain of women's domesticity mapped onto country music, and explores the tensions between the different gender ideals espoused by magazines, artists, and fans. Michael Bertrand examines the common origins of honky-tonk and rock 'n' roll in the white experience of rural-to-urban migration, and explains how a young generation of white men found in Elvis Presley's invocation of urban black masculinity a new model for carving out their own space in an unfamiliar environment. Musicologist Jocelyn R. Neal uses the gendered rituals of the contemporary country dance hall to show that, notwithstanding popular fears about homogenization, local communities still shape the consumption of country music. These essays begin to untangle the roles male and female performers and fans have played in constructing as well as contesting restrictive gender identities in the contexts of their own lives.

Several essays explore the way gendered discourse has been used to fix country music's place in the cultural hierarchy, to represent the low-other status that is one of the genre's defining features. Literary scholar Andreas Huyssen has described how modernist aesthetics in the nineteenth and twentieth centuries proposed a binary formulation that presented high culture as masculine while equating the corrupting influences of mass culture with femininity.[4] This collection reveals the recurring adoption, even by those immersed exclusively in a mass cultural milieu, of modernist notions of gender and cultural hierarchy. Diane Pecknold shows, for example, how such notions suffused the country industry's claims to professional respectability in the 1960s. Executives in the country field deftly manipulated postwar gender tropes as they worked to achieve full membership in the white-collar fraternity of the music business and to recast the genre's class image for advertisers. Barbara Ching demonstrates that discourses of masculine critical authority versus feminine cultural corruption continue to define the cultural position of country music in new ways, showing us how alt.country's retro machismo and anti-commercialist critique of mainstream country remain rooted in modernism's aesthetic assumptions.

Finally, articles by Emily C. Neely and Beverly Keel remind us of the unstable nature of male gatekeeping in the country industry. In her account of the career of Charline Arthur, a female honky-tonk artist who achieved only limited popularity in her day, Neely demonstrates that the unwillingness of female fans to identify with particular representations of gender may have limited the repertoire of acceptable gender roles for the genre's stars as much as chauvinist assumptions within the industry. Beverly Keel describes both the commercially successful revolution wrought by the emergent feminism of Nashville's female stars in the 1990s and the continuing limitations on acceptable images for women in the country field. Reading the stories of Charline Arthur and Shania Twain side by side suggests that the industry has been willing to encourage, and profit from, rebellion against traditional gender roles as much as it has reinforced them.

Together, these essays offer persuasive evidence that a full understanding of the development of country music cannot be achieved without a comprehensive examination of the role gender has played in shaping the genre. The collection is meant to be both an extension of and a revision to several decades of meticulous work on men and women in country music. We hope it will challenge features of the traditional narrative of country music, uncover some of the reasons for that narrative's continued dominance, and point to new possibilities for creating a more complete story.

Bibliography and Further Reading

Bufwack, Mary A., and Robert K. Oermann. *Finding Her Voice: The Saga of Women in Country Music*. New York: Crown, 1993.

Ching, Barbara. *Wrong's What I Do Best: Hard Country Music and Contemporary Culture*. New York: Oxford University Press, 2001.

Cohen, Norm, and Anne Cohen. "Folk and Hillbilly Music: Further Thoughts on Their Relation." *JEMF Quarterly*, 13 (Summer 1977): 50–57.

Fox, Pamela. "Recycled 'Trash': Gender and Authenticity in Country Music Autobiography." *American Quarterly*, 50 (June 1998): 234–66.

Grundy, Pamela. " 'We Always Tried to Be Good People': Respectability, Crazy Water Crystals, and Hillbilly Music on the Air, 1933–1935." *Journal of American History*, 81 (March 1995): 1591–1620.

Henry, Murphy H. "Come Prepared to Stay. Bring Fiddle: The Story of Sally Ann Forrester, the Original Bluegrass Girl." In *Country Music Annual 2001*, ed. Charles K. Wolfe and James E. Akenson. Lexington: University Press of Kentucky, 2001.

Leppert, Richard, and George Lipsitz. "Age, the Body, and Experience in the Music of Hank Williams." In *All That Glitters: Country Music in America*, ed. George H. Lewis. Bowling Green, Ohio: Bowling Green State University Popular Press, 1993.

Lomax, Alan. *The Folk Songs of North America*. Garden City, N.Y.: Doubleday, 1960.

Malone, Bill C. *Country Music, USA*. Revised Edition. Austin: University of Texas Press, 1985.

Miles, Emma Bell. *Spirit of the Mountains*. Knoxville: University of Tennessee Press, 1905, reprint 1975.

Morris, Kenneth E. "Sometimes It's Hard to Be a Woman: Reinterpreting a Country Music Classic." *Popular Music and Society*, 16 (Spring 1992): 1–11.

Oermann, Robert K., and Mary A. Bufwack. "Songs of Self-Assertion: Women in Country Music." Somerville, Mass.: New England Free Press, 1979.

Ortega, Teresa. " 'My name is Sue! How do you do?': Johnny Cash as Lesbian Icon." *South Atlantic Quarterly*, 94 (Winter 1995): 259–72.

Peterson, Richard A. "Class Unconsciousness in Country Music." In *You Wrote My Life: Lyrical Themes in Country Music*, ed. Melton A. McLauren and Richard A. Peterson. Philadelphia: Gordon and Breach, 1992.

Peterson, Richard A. "The Dialectic of Hard-Core and Soft-Shell Country Music." *South Atlantic Quarterly*, 94 (Winter 1995): 273–300.

Sanjek, David. "Can a Fujiyama Mama Be the Female Elvis? The Wild, Wild Women of Rockabilly." In *Sexing the Groove: Popular Music and Gender*, ed. Sheila Whiteley. New York: Routledge, 1997.

Saucier, Karen A. "Healers and Heartbreakers: Images of Men and Women in Country Music." *Journal of Popular Culture*, 20 (Winter 1986): 147–65.

Scott, Joan Wallach. *Gender and the Politics of History*. New York: Columbia University Press, 1988.

Wilson, Pamela. "Mountains of Contradictions: Gender, Class, and Region in the Star Image of Dolly Parton." *South Atlantic Quarterly*, 94 (Winter 1995): 109–34.

A Boy Named
Sue

"Bury Me Beneath the Willow"

Linda Parker and Definitions of Tradition on the National Barn Dance, 1932–1935

KRISTINE M. McCUSKER

"Bury Me Beneath the Willow"

My heart is sad and I am lonely
Thinking of the one I love
I know that I shall never more see him
till we meet in heaven above
Then bury me beneath the willow.[1]

On WLS Chicago's *National Barn Dance,* Linda Parker seemed to be the image of tradition embodied. She was born in Kentucky and, like many in her audience, had migrated to the industrial areas around Chicago. But Linda was special: Her knowledge of old Southern ballads from Kentucky and "the plaintive note, so typical of mountain music," as WLS's 1934 *Family Album* noted, seemed to be tradition in all its glory. She had learned to sing "just as her mother and her grandmother sang, artlessly, but from the heart," and her repertoire included traditional old ballads and tunes such as "I'll Be All Smiles Tonight," and her signature song, "Bury Me Beneath the Willow." Listeners latched onto her ability to sing traditional tunes and, perhaps, soothe their fears of living in the present. As one listener wrote:

> There is something poignantly appealing about Linda's songs . . . something that takes us away from the cares of mundane strife and the daily chores of the big city . . . something that sweeps the smoke and the heat,

Originally published in *Southern Folklore* (1999), v. 56, no. 3.

or intense cold away. . . . the worries and the cares of the day [disappear]
when Linda begins to sing her songs in her own sweet, inimitable way.[2]

When Parker died young from peritonitis in August 1935 (she was twenty-three), the *National Barn Dance* cast and its audience were devastated. One listener wrote to *Stand By!*, WLS's fan magazine, "It is with deep regret and sorrow that I write this letter concerning that beautiful little sunbonnet girl, Linda Parker, my favorite feminine performer." Her manager, John Lair, told audiences that her pallbearers were her backup band, the Cumberland Ridge Runners and that, in a fitting tribute, she had been buried beneath a willow, which wept continuously over her early death.[3]

Linda Parker was clearly a moral, middle-class woman, but Jeanne Muenich, the woman who performed as Parker, does not seem to have been as wholesome or as virtuous as Parker was. It has been difficult to reconstruct Jeanne Muenich's life or her experiences portraying Parker because she played the character so well. What is clear is that she was born in Indiana, not Kentucky, may have been an illegitimate child, may have been a juvenile delinquent, and was probably singing in nightclubs when Lair discovered her. And, most grievously, a weeping willow does not stand guard over her gravestone.[4]

The way that Jeanne Muenich and her manager, John Lair, outlined Parker and the ways the audience reacted to her suggest that there are significant problems with country music historians' most cherished assumption: that Southern, commercial music was (and is) solely the language of working-class men and women.[5] In the heyday of the barn dance, an urban-based radio genre that broadcast constructed images of a rural past nationwide, characters and music attracted a much broader audience than a strictly working-class constituency. Stage performances that combined images and metaphors referring to both middle- and working-class experiences enticed a broad section of Americans to tune in from the late 1920s to the late 1940s. Indeed, if one especially examines the female images such as Linda Parker, one finds a distinctly middle-class presence on stage that fed into a large middle-class audience for the genre.

It is crucial to understand the class differences on barn dance stages since it, first, fostered the growth of a mass audience, and second, hid the tensions implicit in unconventional women such as Jeanne Muenich, rewriting their lives to be media's idealized women such as Linda Parker. The barn dance genre is important to this discussion because broadcasters linked their construction of a traditional Southern past inextricably to women. They constructed a nostalgic, romanticized image of the Appalachian South as a place where tradition stood intact. At the center of that nostalgic image were women who performed as the sentimental mother (as Linda Parker did) or various versions of this character. They exemplified and inscribed separate spheres ideology on stage, a middle-class ideology that determined, at least in terms of what Americans believed, appropriate social roles for women and men. Thus, on the *National Barn Dance*, it no longer mattered who Jeanne Muenich was; Linda Parker seemed to be the middle class's ideal woman whose music, voice, and character tamed a world out of control from her radio microphone, who provided a sanctuary for her listeners.

I will discuss three points in this chapter. First, I describe how my approach and methodology differ from previous attempts to analyze women's experiences in country music, and how they lead to the argument that the middle class had a significant place in the barn dance genre. Second, I explain the genre's constructed image, which built on mainstream ideas of a traditional Appalachian South, and the ways those ideas were reframed to meet the needs of its audiences in the 1930s and 1940s. Finally, I focus on Linda Parker, the ways her character represented the ideology of separate spheres on stage, and the manner by which John Lair and Jeanne Muenich constructed—and in the process erased those facts from Muenich's life that were inappropriate for—Linda Parker.

Historians' analyses of women in country music have been too superficial and simplistic to account for female performers' actual experiences on stage and the manner by which those experiences instituted the middle-class ideology of separate spheres over the airwaves. There are typically four assertions made concerning women. First, there are those who, using definitions of participation based on men's experience, especially in the recording industry, argue that few or no women sang on country music's stages. With their heavy emphasis on commercial success in the recording industry, where men outshone women, no dramatic commercial success equals no women in the industry in these scholars' terms.[6] Second, there are those who argue that women did sing, but their numbers were few, albeit overtly significant, and

"Girl" singer Linda Parker showed off her legs while her stage chaperones, the Cumberland Ridge Runners, showed off their musical instruments.

their influence was extraordinary.[7] Third is the oh-woe-is-me narrative in which scholars bemoan the lack of opportunities available to women in the industry.[8] Finally, there are those who argue that any woman who crossed boundaries into the "men's" industry was a protofeminist, bent on starting a new women's movement.[9]

The basic problem lies in scholars' acceptance of a middle-class ideology that women's historians call "separate spheres" or "the cult of true womanhood." As the United States began to industrialize in the early nineteenth century, middle-class Americans constructed an ideology that decreed that men belonged in the public sphere of work and politics, and women found their "natural" place in the home. The home, under a woman's tutelage, became a sanctified haven nurtured by her, and a place where a man could find refuge after a day braving a harsh public world. For country music historians who have bought into this ideology, their analyses manifest its assumptions: women were either at home or were breaking out of their "natural" world, imagining a revolution.[10]

As women's historians have pointed out, however, how Americans talked about women and what women actually did were two separate, albeit overlapping, entities. Moreover, women's historians have found that this ideology tends to hide women's public activities because they do not fit society's accepted norms.[11] With this in mind, they ask different questions. It's not, why are not more women on stage? but, where are they and why? These questions should force scholars to turn away from recorded music to barn dance radio, where women began to appear as "girl" singers in the early 1930s. It is also important to ask *why* they appeared there with increasing frequency, rather than to chart their popularity and commercial success.

What made girl singers increasingly popular on stage was the constructed image of the South that the barn dance genre began to feature in the late 1920s. Barn dances, based on a rural tradition, the Saturday night dance party, tended to appear on stations in industrial areas such as Chicago, Los Angeles, Cincinnati, and Nashville where Southerners had migrated in the 1920s, 1930s and 1940s. By 1949, there were some 600 shows nationwide.[12] Performers utilized popular images of a supposedly traditional Southern past rooted in the Appalachian mountains, an image that repackaged ideas of Appalachia that had existed in American culture since the late nineteenth century. As historian Henry Shapiro argues, Northern groups redefined the area and its people as anachronisms during an era of tremendous industrial change and innovation. Whereas the rest of America embraced the "civilized" paraphernalia of a modern industrial age, Appalachia's isolated, primitive people lived in hovels and espoused violence (particularly in the form of family feuds) and other socially deviant behavior that seemed part of an earlier time.[13]

While outsiders such as Columbia folklorist Dorothy Scarborough, called Appalachians "contemporary ancestors," paradoxically, they lauded the region's isolation since it had kept modern technology from corrupting

Appalachia's repository of music and other cultural material.[14] These contemporary ancestors seemed to promise that pure, unadulterated ideals of family and community—of tradition itself—had existed intact from colonial times. That purity, that community spirit, seemed a counterpoint to the sterility and artifice of a modern industrial culture based not on family values, but on consumption and greed. Adherents both on stage and off, Southern and Northern alike, clung to Appalachia as a repository of all that was good and true and honest about being American in general.

At the heart of these mainstream ideas concerning the Appalachian South was a vision of Appalachia and its isolation, especially in regards to its music, that construed specific parts of the mountain South as either female or male, a construction that barn dance broadcasters and performers instituted on stage. Some early writers, such as Tennessean Emma Bell Miles, called string band and square dance music men's music since both were fast-paced, intense, and public music. Ballads seemed to be the province of women since ballads were slower, more melodic, softer, more tragic, and sung in private. Hence, they were feminine. Emma Miles displayed the divided nature of Appalachian music—and of ideas of Appalachian culture itself—when she wrote,

> The man bears his occasional days of pain with fortitude such as a brave lad might display, but he never learns the meaning of resignation. The woman belongs to the race, to the *old people*. He is a part of the *young nation*. His first songs are yodels. Then he learns dance tunes, and songs of hunting and fighting and drinking, and couplets of terse, quaint fun. It is over the loom and the knitting that old ballads are dreamily, endlessly crooned [by women].[15]

The first *National Barn Dance* performer who used these popular concepts was Kentuckian Bradley Kincaid, and it was Kincaid who was primarily responsible for their prominence at the beginning of barn dance radio's commercial age in the late 1920s. A Berea College graduate, Kincaid migrated to Chicago to work for the YMCA, and then joined WLS's staff in 1928. Eventually billing himself as the Kentucky Mountain Boy with his Houn' Dog Guitar, Kincaid touted himself as an expert on "old time" or traditional music, and used his connections to the Kentucky mountains—as well as his ties to Berea College—to create a role for himself as an expert on mountain music.[16]

Kincaid's use of Appalachia was apparent in a series of radio addresses he broadcast, probably in 1929, in which he erased what he considered the more immoral implications of Appalachia's image, especially its working-class orientation and the hillbillies who seemed to dominate it. In doing so, Kincaid turned the region into a distinctly middle-class metaphor appropriate for on-air broadcast while preserving the elements that benefited him the most. It is difficult to determine whether it was his new stage job or the missionary zeal he learned at Berea and later used in his YMCA work that influenced his stage persona the most. Perhaps it was his perception of himself as a middle-class Southerner that prompted him to search for new metaphors, particularly from his home state, that fit his on-stage character. What is apparent is that his reconstruction of the South exploited this significant feature of American consciousness for his own benefit.

In his 1929 radio addresses, Kincaid attempted to resurrect the image of the mountain South while simultaneously attempting to retain the characteristics that defined mountain music as traditional and moral. To combat the image that all mountain folks were hillbillies who were poor, for example, he argued that the region had a highly developed class structure that was similar to other regions. Some inhabitants were, he said, "wealthy, highly educated, progressive, others are poor, are not well informed, show little evidence of progress from year to year. . . . Some individuals and some families are lawless, but the great majority are peaceable and law-abiding."[17]

Kincaid highlighted other components of a middle-class, modern lifestyle that Appalachian residents adhered to, namely nice houses, fashionable dress, modern conveniences, and beliefs in scientific thought. Yet, while they were in some ways quite modern, mountain Southerners had a tradition that outsiders did not have: a vibrant culture studded with noble music that modern commercialism had yet to sully.

Women were at the center of Kincaid's vision of Appalachia as he outlined both its modern and traditional qualities. He featured a Southern woman who was everything that her Northern sister was: graceful, charming, well dressed, and in charge of the housework. She was also a mother who sacrificed her personal ambitions for the welfare of her offspring so "that the best of her blood and her family ideals may be perpetuated."[18] Kincaid's Southern woman was, however, many things her Northern sister was not. While other, more modern (read: Northern) women worried about "family budgeting . . . careers outside the home . . . diets for people who are reducing, or professional advice about childbearing and child-rearing," Kincaid argued that the mountain woman followed a long line of successful parents, rearing her kids to be "stalwart, dependable children" so that the "country may enjoy the benefits of her parental love and pride."[19]

While her preservation of traditional gender roles and ideals was crucial, so, too, was her skill as an artisan. Kincaid accentuated her ability to make artistically designed household goods that had been, he said, "woven by hand on ancient looms made by pioneer hands of long ago. Some of these articles bear evidence of rare skill and artistic taste in the women who make them."[20] This Appalachian woman also preserved, sang, and taught her family songs of "surpassing sweetness" which had been brought "by early settlers across the sea." Mountain women "loved to sing these old ballads and songs while they are doing the housework. It drives away lonesomeness. They sing as naturally as the wood thrush sings and for very much the same reason."[21]

Kincaid's wife, Irma, was the embodiment of tradition in his act. A trained musician who arranged the music for his published song-books, Irma doubled as the quintessential homemaker and mother. During his heyday on the *National Barn Dance*, for example, she gave birth to twin daughters, Barbara and Allyne named for Kincaid's signature song, "Barbara Allen." Pictures of Irma, Bradley, and the twins graced his songbooks with Bradley facing the camera and Irma's benevolent smiling face tilted toward a picture of the twins.[22]

It is clear from Kincaid's surviving mail that listeners embraced his gendered image of tradition. When he angered fan Emma Riley Akeman, she questioned, in a letter she wrote in April 1931, whether he had made his mother proud. His mother, according to Akeman, "prayed before she went to bed for help and strength that she might rear her son to the highest plains in the world of whom she may rightfully be proud. . . . Ah [and] how her heart aked [ached] when she saw from some heavenly place her strugles personified?"[23]

WLS broadcaster John Lair began to utilize this gendered image of Appalachia as well, imagining it in the same middle-class terms that Kincaid did. Lair and the *National Barn Dance* regularly invoked Appalachian tradition using ballads, string band music, and "hayseed humor," but modernized it to account for radio technology, to satisfy the many advertisers who sought to sponsor barn dance programs beginning in the late 1920s, and to meet the needs of the audiences who tuned in to listen.[24] To build his audience of middle-class listeners, Lair imagined the Appalachian South as an aural refuge from modern times for both urban and rural people.

Lair's barn dance programs seemed to provide therapy for an audience plagued by the Depression and other modern ills. They provided, first, a refuge from the present, using memories of the past. A native Kentuckian who had migrated to Chicago in the 1920s, Lair's shows featured memories of his Kentucky home, but stated them in such broad terms that his recollections could be conduits for all kinds of listeners to journey back in their own minds. This was an easy task because radio was not a visual medium that hampered listeners' highly individualized journeys. According to Lair's scripts, past Southern life was always better and more wholesome than current urban living. Shows performed that pastoral picture using references to a singer's fictitious front porch or to a play party peopled with good friends and music. Phrases such as "Remember how . . ." and "I wonder where she is tonite" were typical in scripts. The emphasis on the past as better was explicit: there was a purity in past lives that modern ones did not have, and the musicians lamented its loss. "Them was real days an them was real folks," Lair told his listeners.[25]

That refuge also seemed to be a cure for homesick Southern migrants who desired home and, more broadly, desired the familiar. The song "Back to Old Smoky Mountain," for example, prompted Lair to tell radio audiences this in the early 1930s:

> When we wuz goin over it while ago back there in a back room gittin ready to come on the air it jest struck us all in a heap how doggoned homesick we wuz. We got to talkin old times over an we jest decided all at once to throw away the program we'd bin workin on an come out here an kinda relieve our feelins some by tellin everybody about it.[26]

Music was, in the case of this quote, literally a release of feelings of loss ("kinda relieve our feelins"), albeit a public one shared with listeners. A Christmas show was another tinged with a nostalgic longing for home.

Doc Hopkins sang "Steamboat," and Lair told his audience, "Wish we was all on that old boat with Doc an headed South. This Chrismus business getsa feller all stirred up an thinkin of home."[27]

Shows were more than therapy for homesick migrants or those who desired a more familiar time. They were also a refuge for folks faced with modern concerns. This manifested itself on many barn dance shows. Cousin Emmy's music on St. Louis's KMOX, for example, seemed to tame a modern world out of control. One writer said, "Every morning the notoriously noxious air of St. Louis is purified by the natural twang of real mountaineer goings on."[28] Advertisers such as *National Barn Dance* sponsor Alka Seltzer told listeners that those modern ills such as colds, stress, and upset stomachs could be cured by listening to the barn dance—and by buying some Alka Seltzer. WLS *National Barn Dance* programs, published in 1936, told audiences that performers were just "home folks" who strove "to lighten your cares by bringing you wholesome fun and entertainment."[29] "Get Well, Keep Well," said an ad for Alka Seltzer, poised beneath a group picture of the *National Barn Dance* cast.[30] The performers on the *Renfro Valley Barn Dance*—a Lair barn dance show broadcast in the late 1930s and early 1940s from Kentucky—mimicked their Chicago peers, portraying rural situations they thought might help city residents. The following is from a Monday night program:

> Homer: Mister Ler, them city folks aint gonna want to fool with plain old cider. They'druther have chamm pain an' things like a't.
> Lair: Aw, Homer, you believe all the tales you read in novels an' magazines about life in the cities. Mostly it's a lot of hooey.[31]

In another broadcast, Lair stuck a mike out the window (or so he told listeners) so that city residents might hear the therapeutic sounds of katydids:

> Folks shut up in a hot, noisy city tonight might git a little relaxation an' pleasure outa hearin' the katydid serenadin' frum the coll dark woods surrounding the schoolhouse here. Open the winders wide—everybody git quiet an' less see if the radio will pick it up fer the folks.[32]

Lair was a master at using descriptive language to make his nostalgic images come to life. A show featuring the country parlor, for example, virtually put the listener in that Victorian emblem of civilized society with John Lair as her guide. "Well, while we're here," he told listeners, "less take a look around. Smells jest a little bit musty in here, don't it."[33] Lair also used descriptive language to recreate rural scenes. For example, on one undated show from the early 1930s, he wrote a script that included a description of the first settlers to the "Kintucky" mountains. He wrote,

> It took min [men] of courage an determination to turn back to the North
> an East after comin through The Gap an push back into the dim, misty
> Cumberlands, into the shut in coves an deep valleys where they built their
> rough log houses an begin the struggle fer existence in these hills that has
> never let up. The wolves howled along their trail, the indun always had a
> fire ready to torture their flesh er destroy their homes.[34]

In the early years of barn dance radio, few Southern women graced barn dance stages. Restrictions against working outside the home were probably the main reason why Southern women did not work on stage. Many Southern women did work, but there were few venues that were as public as performance. Moreover, in its early years, radio work simply did not pay, and performers used the medium to advertise local appearances. When advertisers began paying for radio programs, however, in the late 1920s and early 1930s, this ensured many women potentially lucrative and stable jobs, even during the worst of the Depression.

Why did broadcasters hire women with increasing frequency? First, because they feared the intrusion of public voices into the home, especially ones accompanied by advertisements, broadcasters may have hoped that their incursion into that sanctified space would be mitigated by women's voices. Traditional Southern women seemed to have civilized the radio waves because they supposedly did not brave the harsh public world and thus seemed to control the potential artifice of advertising. Second, in imagining barn dance radio as therapeutic, broadcasters gave the shows a decidedly feminine cast. The qualities of refuge and therapy had long been associated with the home and women by the middle class. Thus, in the first explicit depictions of Southern women, the emphasis was on mothers who stood on stage singing to their listening audience as they would to their own children. It was precisely because they could represent separate spheres ideology on stage that women were able to find decidedly nontraditional work as performers.

At first, Southern women were simply metaphors on shows such as John Lair's programs for Chicago's WLS *National Barn Dance*. The programs Lair produced featured a new gendered image of tradition based on a Northern, middle-class musical trope, the sentimental mother. The sentimental mother was a Victorian idol who was the mistress of the home and the moral guide for men.[35] Following the elegiac tradition in music that dramatized children's separation from mothers, the sentimental mother came to represent, at least on barn dance stages, migrants' real separations from their homes and families. Lair remolded her into a distinctly Southern idol by portraying her as the traditional mother left at the rural, Southern homestead while her children migrated—geographically, to new places and mentally, to new modern times.

By combining a Northern metaphor with a Southern past, Lair was able to create a broad character that both Southerners and Northerners recognized while tying her to his shows' themes of nostalgia, refuge, and homesickness. He wanted to reproduce images that his Southern audience found familiar, but in order to build a mass audience, he needed to mute more overt Southern characteristics, such as a nasal twang, to make them seem less alien. The point was, after all, to entice the listener to stay tuned for the sponsors' ads, not to make them turn the radio off.

This feminine metaphor fit well into Lair's nostalgic image of the past since separate spheres ideology decreed that women, in general, should provide a refuge from public worries. In portraying women as providers of sanctuaries, Lair exploited assumptions concerning women's preservation of cultural material, especially music. Mothers were traditional, constant, and incorruptible, even when the outside world changed rapidly. That made the music that they preserved equally pure and unadulterated, even when they sang it on barn dance stages. Contemporary definitions of "authenticity" reinforced the image of women as refuges. Appalachian folk music in American culture was stable, uniform music that did not change even as modern America embraced new technology like radios. Since women were the keepers of the South's oral tradition, they were its "genuine" and authentic singers.[36]

This metaphor manifested itself in scripts Lair wrote in the early 1930s. In one, for example, he wrote, "[I]t was the women who really kept them

[Old English and Scotch ballads] alive—the men didn't seem to find much time for such things . . . but I used to listen by the hour to my great-grandmother and grandmother reciting some of those old ballads in a sing-song voice."[37] He touted these women as the keepers of the past, as the true curators of tradition. Tradition was a woman's responsibility, part of her domestic duties that she nurtured alongside her children, husband, and home.

Lair's Civil War show contained a typical reference to the sentimental mother. Discussing antebellum controversies that preceded the Civil War, Lair said, "Nobody could talk about anything but the war and its attendant heartaches," but, he stated,

> It's always the wimmin that shed them [tears] in times like this and mighty few wimmin either North or South was made outa that kinda stuff. Northern mothers sent their sons with aprayer fer their return an Southern Mothers done the same. Motherhood aint m ch diffrunt, no matter which side of the line they're on.[38]

Later, it was her name that dying soldiers cried out as they writhed in pain on battlefields across the South. Lair attempted to recreate a Civil War battlefield, interspersing his comments with music that bolstered the image he sought to build in his listeners' imaginations.

> Thousands of dying boys cryin out in their last precious minnits fer Mother, like this boy [Bob and Mack sing, "Break the News to Mother"]. An Mother heard. Don't think she didn't. No matter how fer apart they were. Here's a song about one Mother who knew her boy would never come whistlin up the lane agin never smell the honeysuckle coverin the old palin' fence around the yard, never see another sunset acrost the pasture field nor sing around the farm with the joy of livin.[39]

Music, in this case "Break the News to Mother," reinforced the assumption that women were sanctified mothers whom young men sought to protect in the Civil War. In keeping with his desire to develop a character that referred to both the North and South, Lair bestowed the sanctity of motherhood on both Southerners and Northerners, an easy thing for him to do since the sentimental mother combined elements of both regions.

On other shows, Lair used this musical trope to acknowledge that many migrants found it difficult to go home. Whereas cold water and the reliance on oil lamps had been a part of everyday rural life before a migrant moved, modern conveniences such as running water and electric lights made these formerly trivial matters unendurable. Thus, migrants may have stayed away from home to avoid those hardships. Others feared that home was not what it used to be. Mother, in this instance, represented the old traditional life of hardship and sacrifice, and Lair reminded his audiences that a migrant had to remain responsible to her or her memory. "Maybe the old place aint the same no more; maybe there's a Stone Neath the Maple Tree at yore old home an Mother aint there to greet you, but aint they somebody there you owe somethin to?" Lair admonished his listeners in December 1930.[40] Listeners could, of course, fulfill their responsibilities by buying a lamp from sponsor Alladin Lamps and sending it to the home folks.

If the sentimental mother made sporadic appearances on Lair's early WLS shows, she was a prominent and common metaphor in the music he wrote and featured on stage. One tune, "Take Me Back to Renfro Valley," a song about one person's desire to return home, included the line, "Mother sang in Renfro Valley." Another song, "One Step More," described one person's desire to leave earth for heaven so that he could unload the heavy burden that earthly matters had given him. Lair devoted the third refrain to the narrator being rewarded in heaven by seeing his sainted mother:

> *Mother's long been over Yonder;*
> *She'll be waiting for me too;*
> *She'll be Oh! so glad to see me*
> *Proud to know that I've pulled through.*
> *She will be the first to greet me*
> *When I enter Heaven's door.*
> *Oh, I'll soon be with you, Mother*
> *For it's only one step more.[41]*

He wrote other music, of course, to fit his show's many moods, but as long as nostalgia dominated, so, too, did the sentimental mother.

Metaphors were all well and good, but radio's assumption that it portrayed everyday life forced Lair to search for a woman who could embody

Lair's constructed image of tradition, who could make the metaphors in radio scripts and music come alive. But, in keeping with radio's demands, he needed to transform the sentimental mother into a more commercial image. Two demands were most pressing. First, radio celebrated the culture of youth which meant that a young woman, not an old one, was more appropriate for the stage. The second demand was a technological one. Microphones required that a singer have a voice that fit its specifications—namely, not too loud, or nasal, as Southern mountain voices tended to be, or boisterous—or else the mikes would be overwhelmed. Someone with a soft, melodic voice, who crooned as Bing Crosby did, was more appropriate for the stage. Thus, to make "Linda Parker," Lair had to transform his image of Southern tradition from an elderly mother worn by her nurturing into a little girl wearing "little ole gingham dresses an sunbonnets." The sentimental mother became the young girl named Linda Parker who waited for marriage and motherhood.

How Lair discovered Muenich and what she was doing before coming to the *National Barn Dance* is unclear. Lair told an interviewer that she was working as a nightclub singer and had come to WLS to do an ad for her act.[42] One historian disputes this, saying Muenich had already been working at the station when she became Linda Parker.[43] However she came to WLS, by February 1932, she was working on stage. Accepting radio work meant Muenich agreed to help make the sentimental mother come alive for audience consumption. She was a perfect choice for two reasons. The first was obviously musical talent; Jeanne Muenich could sing. The second requirement was her physical features. Because of the "rising commercial value of the human face," as historian Kathy Peiss argues, in which Americans valued certain physical features over others, physical beauty was a commodity to be sold, and Jeanne Muenich was certainly a lovely woman.[44] Broadcasters thought shows sold if they included pretty women for men to look at or to imagine from descriptions given over the air. They intended comments such as "and here's pretty Linda Parker" as a means for listeners to imagine their own versions of pretty and beautiful. In this way, barn dance radio continued a theatrical tradition of commodifying and objectifying women's bodies for men's visual pleasure and consumption, but broadened that pleasure to be an aural one.[45]

After he found the perfect woman, John Lair seems to have been the one who chose a new name for Muenich. She first appeared on stage on a Thursday noon program on February 25, 1932, and until broadcast time, according to the script, her name had not been chosen. A list of potential names was typed on the back of the script, a list which included Piney Linville, Dulcie Lewis, and Linda Parker, Linda Marshall, and 15 other last names. The name "Linda" had been typed into the script, and Parker was handwritten in later. Why he chose this particular name is unclear. Perhaps Jeanne Muenich was too ethnic sounding and not all-American enough. Whatever the reason, a name change was necessary.[46]

If the stories about Jeanne Muenich and her stint as a juvenile delinquent are true, then she was a prime candidate for a new background, one that fit the Linda Parker character and Lair's image of a traditional Southern past. No longer was she from Indiana; she now hailed from Covington, Kentucky, a former Southerner who had migrated with her family to industrial Hammond, Indiana. She was also no longer illegitimate nor a juvenile delinquent. And when Lair mentioned her nightclub days, he implied that she had been rescued from that degraded life in order to sing the pure, moral music that audiences desired.

Finally, a repertoire befitting the little Sunbonnet Girl was the finishing touch. Since, as station documents said, Parker put her knowledge of old Southern ballads from Kentucky to good use, she needed songs that fit that category. Lair helped Muenich construct a repertoire replete with songs such as "Mother's Old Sunbonnet," which described the singer's desire for God to care well for her mother.

> There's a faded old sunbonnet
> On a peg behind the door.
> It's the one my sainted Mother used to wear.
> Till one day she hung it up and
> Never took it down nor more
> And since that day we've left it hanging there.
>
> Oh, God be good to mother
> Wherever she may be!
> Please grant her rest and comfort over there.
> And keep her just the same sweet smiling angel,
> She always seemed to me.
> In that old sun bonnet that she used to wear.[47]

When Muenich sang this song, she was the singer who wished her mother a restful place in heaven. Simultaneously, however, wearing her own sunbonnet, she also seemed to be that mother, at least one whose future would be sacrifice and toil for her own family.

It was more than a song's words that allowed Muenich to portray the sentimental mother. It was also the sound of her voice that elicited comparisons to that Victorian saint. She had a lush, soft, melodic voice that fit microphone technology perfectly. Muenich, singing as Parker, sang "Meet Mother in the Sky," "Some Mother's Boy," and "Mother's Old Sunbonnet," using a voice that seemed to whisper soft, sweet lullabies into microphones, an intimate mode of performance that spoke individually to each listener as a mother to her child.

The next step was to place Muenich, playing Parker, on stage within the barn dance context. On her first show in February 1932, Lair asked his listeners to

> [S]hut yer eyes an imagine you kin see a little ole grey log cabin settin back aways frum the bend of a lazy windin river . . . an a long cool front porch runnin the full length of it with mornin glories an honeysuckle climbin around on it. An up on the porch . . . sets a little ole girl in a gingham dress, with a sunbonnet slung over her shoulder, settin there an strummin away on a two dollar gittar an singin a million dollar song. Got the picture? Well, hold it—an lissen to this![48]

Then, according to surviving script material, Muenich stepped to the mike and sang "I'll Be All Smiles Tonight" with the Cumberland Ridge Runners, John Lair's band of Kentucky merrymakers, backing her up. After she finished, Lair told the audience that Parker had moved "all the way up here to WLS" from Kentucky to make music with the Cumberland Ridge Runners.[49] Thus, from the first, Lair created the fiction that was Linda Parker.

Other shows repeated the context that made Linda Parker possible. Indeed, Jeanne Muenich could change everything about herself, but without a backdrop—the music, the scenario—she was meaningless. Programs such as *Play Party Frolic*, the *Hamlin Wizard Hour*, and the *Coon Creek Social*, all sponsored half-hours of the Saturday night barn dance, provided that framework. The *Hamlin Wizard Hour*, broadcast on February 24, 1934, was a typical

Linda Parker, surrounded by the Cumberland Ridge Runners, displayed her traditional sunbonnet and dulcimer, which complemented her modern hairstyle and makeup.

show which the announcer touted as "an imaginary trip down to a cabin in the Renfro Valley of Old Kentucky, there to hear these mountain folks in their weekly gathering—laughing, chatting, playing fiddle tunes, and singing the songs that they love."[50] These "getherings," Lair told the audience, had taken place since 1796 and were slow to change because "these Renfro Valley folks, when they know somethin's good they're mighty slow about changin." One of those traditional folks was Lindy Parker, "frum up on Parker's Creek."[51]

Most shows featured Muenich as the sentimental mother. On a Mother's Day show of the *Play Party Frolic* in May 1932, for example, John Lair said,

> [A]n now, folks, before we break up the party we want to take notice of this bein the eve of a speshil occasion—a mighty speshil occasion—an dedica a number to Mothers—not the "Mothers old an Gray" etc, you' hear hundreds of songs *to* them an *about* them tonight an tomorrow—but to

the mothers who carry the world on their tired shoulders, the workers, the mothers on the farms an the plantations, the backwoods an the prairies, the mothers that wear the badge of sacrificin Motherhood everwhere—a faded old sunbonnet—to your sunbonnet Mother and the memory we dedicate this song. Lindy![52]

Then Linda Parker stepped to the microphone and sang "Faded Old Sunbonnet."

Most listeners seemed to have bought Muenich's ability to become tradition in the terms she and Lair intended. For example, W. DeMont Wright wrote barn dance broadcasters in February 1934 that when Linda Parker sang "I Shall Be All Smiles Tonight," he knew he was truly listening to "old time" music. That was a "song my mother sang when I was a boy," he said, "and if I remember correctly, it was an old song then, one she knew when she was a girl."[53] Another listener wrote, "Linda Parker mirrors fresh breezes . . . mountain peaks . . . tall timber . . . rushing streams. She brings this refreshing and soothing essence into our tiny living room. We always listen to her with nostalgia in our hearts."[54] For listeners, Parker civilized the airwaves and the modern world they represented.

Her character was so real that Muenich's own mother, Mrs. E. E. Muenich, confused her daughter with the Linda Parker image. Although she referred to her daughter by her family nickname, Nenny, in letters written to Lair after Muenich died, she signed them, "Linda's Mom and Dad." She also reminded Lair of her daughter's song, "When I Take My Vacation in Heaven." Mrs. Muenich wrote Lair that her daughter "had told me before she went out on the road this last time that she couldn't afford to take a vacation. Well [a vacation in heaven], that was the only vacation she could afford."[55]

Muenich's death in 1935 fit well with her character because the sentimental mother included a tragic element in that the mother's sacrifice on earth could only be justly rewarded in heaven. Her performance of songs such as "Meet Mother in the Sky" were explicit reminders to her audience that only by dying would the song's main character find peace. Muenich's death thus made Linda Parker more popular since the tragic element in her character was now obvious.

John Lair helped matters by playing up her death. Her pallbearers were her backup band, the Cumberland Ridge Runners, and, in reference to one of her standard songs, "Bury Me Beneath a Willow," Lair told listeners that Linda was buried beneath a willow in Pine Lake Cemetery in La Porte, Indiana. Finally, her gravestone reads, "Linda Parker, wife of Arthur Janes," not her married name, Jeanne E. Janes, as cemetery records do.[56]

Fans were devastated at Parker's death and wrote the station, expressing their grief. They sent letters of condolence to her husband, Art Janes, and to her mother. Those letters also expressed the writers' own grief at the loss of a close friend.[57] Lois Almy, for example, wrote, "Our entire household is filled with sorrow, in fact as much as at the passing of a dear friend, because that is the place she always held in our home. Her sweet songs and beautiful character shall always live in loving memory of her."[58]

Because Linda Parker was a character that could easily be donned by others, she did not really die. Thus, although Jeanne Muenich had died, Linda Parker did not, and Lair continued to use her on programs. For example, WLS compiled a songbook of *100 WLS Barn Dance Favorites* that it dedicated to Parker and included the words to two of Parker's songs, "Bury Me Beneath the Willow" and "Take Me Back to Renfro Valley." The sale of that book financed a new half-hour barn dance show called *Bunk House and Cabin Songs*.

WLS Chicago and John Lair continued to resurrect Parker on stage in other ways. For example, the *Bunk House and Cabin Songs* show staged a memorial to Parker on Muenich's birthday in January 1936, using other popular female performers to sing Parker's signature songs and, for a brief moment, to become Linda Parker. As the Girls of the Golden West sang "I'll Be All Smiles Tonight," Lair reminded the audience that Parker was "always 'All Smiles' around her friends and the boys and girls she worked with, always ready for fun and laughter."[59] When Patsy Montana sang "Take Me Back to Renfro Valley," Lair told listeners to "remember Our Little Sunbonnet Girl—when she was young an' eager for life . . . instead of thinking of her racked with the pain an' torture of those last despairin' days before she left us."[60]

Lair also told listeners that, although they could not send birthday cards to Linda, they could send them to her mother, and he gave out Mrs. Muenich's address over the air. Mrs. Muenich later reported to Lair that she received hundreds of letters.[61] Listeners also wrote the station, thanking them for the commemorative program. Charles Baker, for example, wrote,

> I sure enjoyed the program you announced in memory of Linda Parker. I sure loved to hear Linda sing and carried a heavy heart more than I can find words to express when I heard she had passed away. The boys and girls at WLS seem near to me and as I very seldom tell any one how I feel I must say for the whole staff at W.L.S. is in reality a blessing to hungry humanity.[62]

Middle-class female images such as Linda Parker's sentimental mother were vital parts of the barn dance genre's broad appeal. It was the explicit incorporation of separate spheres that put middle-class men and women on center stage alongside their working-class counterparts. And it was women portraying mothers and providing a sanctuary on stage for their audiences that were the most explicit evidence of this middle-class ideology. Women's ability to tame a modern world, to represent a Southern mountain breeze that wafted over the radio waves to soothe their listeners' worried brows, inextricably tied the genre's definitions of tradition to moral, virtuous women.

"Spade Doesn't Look Exactly Starved"

Country Music and the Negotiation of Women's
Domesticity in Cold War Los Angeles

PETER LA CHAPELLE

Country musicians rarely made the society page, so when the *Antelope Valley Press* asked to interview Spade and Ella Mae Cooley at the couple's massive new ranch home in 1960, the couple easily concurred. Newcomers to the Antelope Valley—an area that was quickly becoming the rural playground of the Hollywood jet set—the Cooleys showed off their 1200-acre ranch and talked about the television bandleader's plans to build a fifteen-million-dollar Disneyland-style water theme park in the area. Although admiring of the surrounding chaparral, the family powerboat, and other toys Cooley and his sons paraded before the *Press* photographer, the newspaper's reporter was most taken with the blissful domestic environment the family created. "Mrs. Spade," the newspaper asserted, kept a "comfortable, attractive, spotlessly clean ranch home of Western simplicity." Although Ella Mae handled the family pocketbook, the paper assured us that she had not abandoned her wifely duty of preparing meals for the family: "Spade," the reporter noted with a nod to the bandleader's once-svelte waistline, "doesn't look exactly starved."[1]

Despite the reporter's efforts to offer readers a candid glimpse of a favorite performer at home, the *Press* story masked more than it revealed. Not four months after the article ran, the Cooley home was grabbing headlines again—this time as a grisly crime scene befitting the plot of a Hollywood *film noir* or a Raymond Chandler detective novel. According to newspaper and police accounts, Spade Cooley, a leading light on the Los Angeles country music scene for nearly two decades and one of the most recognizable faces in

Southern California, had tortured, beaten, and stomped to death Ella Mae in the home—all in front of their fourteen-year-old daughter. The press lashed out at Cooley, proclaiming the easygoing broadcasting persona of the former Oklahoma farm laborer to be nothing more than a ruse, an effective device for hiding a private life of affairs, explosive tirades, threats, abuse and other skeletons. No longer a "ranch home of Western simplicity" in the public mind, the Cooleys' picturesque canyon home seemed more like a purgatory than anything else.[2]

Today the *Antelope Valley Press* piece might be written off as a single instance of sloppy newsgathering or an overall indictment of lifestyle journalism. With its fusion of themes such as domesticity, family, celebrity, and consumerism, however, the article stands as more than a historical curiosity or a reporter's glaring oversight. Home interviews of country music performers, in fact, filled thousands of inches of copy in Southern California fan magazines and regional newspapers during the 1950s and 1960s and, like the Cooley article, tended to focus on the homemaking capabilities of what one publication would later term "the women behind the men." Although few portraits would prove as tragic or as misrepresentative as the Cooley article, coverage of the local scene in *Country Music Report* and *Country Music Life* and in national publications such as *Country Song Roundup* worked in conjunction with larger societal efforts to normalize the role of the suburban stay-at-home caretaker and to discourage women from pursuing outside employment by repeatedly portraying women's homemaking abilities as the key to their star husbands' successful careers. This is not to say that such notions were digested unquestioningly by women. Indeed, ignited by a strong working-class tradition of women's employment and involvement in the local fan subculture during World War II, some female artists and fans contested constraints and pushed the boundaries of women's accepted social, cultural, and political roles.

Building on the debate that has emerged among women's historians such as Elaine Tyler May and Joanne Meyerowitz about the degree of agency American women experienced during the 1950s, study of Southern California suggests that rather than a site that only reinforced social taboos or a site that only fomented rebellion, country music subculture served as a contested terrain in which a variety of voices—feminist and antifeminist as well as modernist and traditionalist—grappled over issues related to women's role in the home and occupational outlook.[3] Women who defied expectations were not always successful in their efforts and often had to contend with an industry system that discouraged even the mildest rumblings. Nevertheless, the cultural politics of local country music mirrored national debates about women's roles in cold war society and laid some of the ground work for later manifestations of female participation in country music.

That the field was so contested should give pause to those scholars who lend support to the popular assumption that country music has *always* been defined by its parochialism or its social conservatism. Southern California country music women, as the reader will find, were seizing and advocating for an expansion of roles far ahead of much of the mainstream and many other sections of national culture.

Meeting the Mrs.

Magazine Culture, Male Honky-Tonk, and
the Domestication of Women's Space

By the mid-1950s, country music had become big business in Southern California. Not only had the Dust Bowl migration brought tens of thousands of new "Okie" listeners from the border South, but local broadcasters such as Pasadena station KXLA played a pioneering national role in the development of the all-country radio format. Local musicians and industry personnel, furthermore, began to receive patronage from the mammoth new automobile dealerships that had begun to dot the suburban landscape—places such as Vel's Ford in Torrance and Cal Worthington's Worthington Dodge in Long Beach. The presence of such businesses as advertisers and sponsors of country music reflected the new economic clout that blue-collar Dust Bowlers had reaped from the higher-paying Fordist wage structure of the local military-industrial complex, as well as the growing cult of the automobile both in their home states and in California.[4] Hailing from an impoverished Okie background, Worthington used his Saturday afternoon *Cal's Corral* television program, which combined country music with folksy "Will Rogers-style" sales pitches, to help make his car dealership the "largest Dodge Agency in the world." Although the gradual emergence of Nashville as the reigning corporate citadel of country music was beginning to persuade local performers and industry personnel to relocate to Tennessee by the late 1950s, Los Angeles was home to several country music television programs and to Capitol Records. Formed during World War II as a jazz and pop label, Capitol quickly spawned a successful country music division and soon established itself alongside the New York giants as one of the four "majors" of the national recording industry.[5]

The emergence of several enduring country music fan periodicals in the mid-1950s and early 1960s was itself indicative of the success of country music in Los Angeles, but it is important to keep in mind that these magazines were building on an already rich, though more short-lived, tradition of fan journalism. Fan journals of the 1940s such as *Top Hand*, based in Hollywood, and *Jamboree Magazine*, based in Ventura, had offered colorful, lucid, but ultimately ephemeral documentation of celebrity news and Southern California country music events, particularly the jazz-influenced western swing style popular among defense workers during the war. Another magazine, Pasadena's *Western and Country Music*, made a brief but unsuccessful effort to drum up readership in the early 1950s by heralding the region as a bastion of "Western" rather than Southern country music.[6]

It was not, however, until the mid-1950s and early 1960s that local fan magazines began to cast an uninterrupted eye on the local scene. Local magazines such as *Country Music Life, Country Music Report,* and *Country Music Review*— all based in suburban Orange County, California—along with an already growing spate of Hollywood-based columns and articles in the national magazine *Country Song Roundup* (headquartered in Derby, Connecticut) began to offer local musicians, fans, and business people a longer lasting and more complete picture of local country music happenings. *Country Music Life,* the flagship of these new local magazines, was a photo-laden glossy whose very title suggested publishing impresario Henry Luce's spectacularly successful *Life* magazine. The magazine, which often featured lengthy transcription-style interviews of major local and national artists, had the longest reign of the locals, running from 1965 to 1969 and paving the way for such tabloid-style 1970s periodicals as Covina's *California Country* and Universal City's *California Town and Country.*[7]

Women played important roles in the earliest days of Southern California fan journalism. During the 1940s, a time when tens of thousands of local women entered the local defense industry as part of a national effort to win the war, several female writers came to the fore. Sunny Ciesla, a former waitress and North American Aviation worker who had come to know the local scene during the war, was perhaps the most prolific of these early Rosie the Riveter–era writers, covering Hollywood country music in a column for the *National Hill-Billy News*, based in West Virginia. Ciesla's columns often took the standard promotional tactic of mentioning artist and club bookings, but she could also turn a wistful phrase, telling in one column the story of a woman stricken with extreme arthritis who had learned to walk, dance, and even find herself a husband by attending western swing performances at an area nightclub. Men such as C. Phil Henderson, a former writer for the jazz journal *Down Beat* who promoted country music, tended to dominate as editors of publications such as *Top Hand*, but 1940s fan journalism remained enough of a cottage industry to allow female fan club members such as Dusti Lynn and small-time female entrepreneurs such as Grace Purdy, who operated a kiosk selling country music souvenirs at local dance halls, to come to the forefront as fan magazine writers. Lynn, a singer of Oklahoma Cherokee ancestry who had served as president of the Spade Cooley fan club, used her column to present herself as the very antithesis of the "backward" stereotype that had plagued Okie migrants since arriving in the 1930s. She informed readers of her visits to elite nightclubs and tony resorts and appeared in her monthly column's mug photo as a glamorous, daintily gloved society woman propped improbably against a film set wagon wheel. So prominent were women in promotional work that by 1946, *Top Hand* not only named a woman, Bobbie Bennett, as its club manager of the year, but ran a poem and article praising Purdy for her selfless efforts to "tell the world about 'Western Swing.' "[8]

During the 1950s and early 1960s, women's pull in local fan journalism began to weaken, however, as the new journals turned to industry professionals and full-time male writers. National magazine *Country Song Roundup* started this trend in the early 1950s by hiring local radio personality George Sanders to write the "Hollywood Hoe-Down Lowdown" column, but before long female writers such as Ciesla, Purdy, and Lynn had been almost entirely replaced by male chroniclers of the new Orange County journals—men such as Bill A. Wheeler of *Country Music Report* and Jim Harris of *Country Music Life*, who had college degrees in communications or backgrounds in the recording industry. There were of course some exceptions. Carolina Cotton, a popular local western swing singer, tried her hand at writing about the Hollywood scene for New York's *Rustic Roundup* during a short stint in the late 1950s, and Devvy Davenport served as a fan magazine editor in the early 1960s, but the majority of the stories about country music and, in particular, about the aspiring new female soloists of the 1950s, were passed from female to male writers.[9]

While limiting female voices, local journals also ushered in a new era of political and social conservatism in their choice of coverage. In the mid-1940s, L.A.'s *Top Hand* had publicized efforts to form a union-like organization for country musicians, had offered space for local musicians to air worker grievances against a local ballroom impresario, and had run a mildly riské photo in which local group the Rangerettes bared legs and midriffs. *Country Music Life*, its successor in the cold war era, however, sidelined coverage of industry politics and generally avoided discussions of divorce and sexuality, a difficult task indeed during a period when frank honky-tonk numbers topped national and local charts. In a rather prim and almost Victorian manner, the magazine pledged in its inaugural issue to "be a clean, wholesome magazine . . . that your children, your friends, or your clergyman may examine without embarrassment to anyone." When photographed, women in *Country Music Life* were conservatively dressed, often wearing full length skirts.[10]

Central to the shake-up of fan magazine style were a series of performer portraits that blended suburban family themes with a new and more conservative gender politics. Marginally focused on the careers of successful husband-performers, the real emphasis of such stories was on scrutinizing how well women performed with an oven, a mop, and a broom. In such stories, which became even more plentiful at the advent of the Kennedy era, country music wives and even their performer-husbands were judged by women's ability to care for the offspring and maintain a clean orderly home. In some, such as *Country Song Roundup*'s regular 1950s feature "Meet the Mrs.," staffers queried the "women behind the men" and assessed their homemaking skills, while others, such as *Country Music Report*'s 1960s "At Home with . . ." series, hyped women's domestic work as paramount to the success

Appearing the archetype of a postwar father, country performer Doye O'Dell "presides over a comfortable Encino home" in this 1963 *Country Music Report* piece. Articles such as these emphasized women's subservience in the home. O'Dell was known for his migration-themed 1947 hit "Dear Okie" and *Western Varieties*, a local children's television program he hosted.

of their hardworking image-conscious men. Although the women described in these articles nary got a negative review, the message was clear: the ideal wife and mother gave up career and other aspirations to stay at home and care for kids and husbands. Working outside the home, the subtext of these articles warned, created chaos in the family and might affect a husband's ability to succeed in the business world. Understanding wives and concerned mothers had no respectable choice but to stay at home.[11]

So adamant about touting subservience and homemaking skills in women were the writers of these pieces that they regularly avoided explorations of potentially revealing tensions between the members of prominent country music families. By soft-pedaling or ignoring rumors of abuse within "the charming Cooley family," the *Antelope Valley Press* was perhaps the most blatant offender, but not the only culprit. Ruth O'Dell, wife of Southern California western music star Doye O'Dell, was the subject of an early "Meet the Mrs." column. Ruth loved "being a housewife" and enjoyed "cooking and baking," the magazine reported, even though she had given up successful careers as a studio publicist, fashion model, and magazine short-story writer. Most importantly, *Country Song Roundup* argued, her husband, Doye, had found solace in the secure and soothing environment she provided in the couple's hillside Studio City home. "One has only to observe that contented gleam in Doye's brown eyes to know how happy his home life must be," the article argued. The writer never queried Ruth, however, on just how happy she was giving up seemingly coveted careers as a publicist, fashion model, and writer who had published in *Colliers*, *Red Book*, and *Screen Magazine*.[12]

The formats and even titles of these new features—"At Home with . . ." and "Meet the Mrs."—stressed a restructuring of the family iconography of country music that had consequences for the role of women. While the Carter Family and local favorites the Beverly Hill Billies, both predominant groups of the prewar era, had emphasized women's active participation in an extended radio family of real and imagined "aunts" and "uncles," the new fan magazines of the cold war era had narrowed that ideal to a male breadwinner and a subordinate female homemaker with offspring in tow. Appearing with great consistency, such column titles suggested that country music wives never begrudged their husbands the limelight, but preferred a quieter and more private existence, either tucked away "At Home" or so removed from the public world that one needed special effort to even "Meet the Mrs."[13]

Large and located in desirable suburban or exo-suburban locales, the homes depicted in such stories were similarly rich in subtext, serving as both monuments to class mobility and testaments to the usefulness of a docile, domestic femininity. On one level, fan magazine writers portrayed such houses as symbols of consumerism and male social status, proof that hard work might allow a poor part-Cherokee migrant such as Cooley or the tough-talking son of a Texas minister such as radio performer Stuart Hamblen to acquire the finer things in life. Such stories invited less prosperous readers to fantasize about luxurious spaces such as Hamblen's large Mulholland Drive estate, a "castle overlooking California's San Fernando Valley" originally owned by film legend Errol Flynn, or imagine themselves amid a forest of consumer goods such as Cooley's luxurious powerboat and purportedly irreplaceable antique instrument collection. Hamblen's "At Home with . . ." portrait even attempted to provoke affinity among ex–Dust Bowl readers by describing the radio and television performer's well-known and rather genteel pursuit of exotic game trophies for his home as merely the handiwork of an average "impassioned hunter"—a figure and activity with which many country music listeners were well acquainted, at least on a subsistence level. Such depictions reflected reality as well as fostered yearnings for consumer goods, suburban homes, and middle-class lifestyles among a listener base that still remained largely blue collar. Indeed, a study of the shift in the locations of area country music night spots suggests that the region's largely Okie fan base was itself moving out of older and more diverse neighborhoods of L.A.'s inner urban core and into more prosperous and whiter areas of the suburban fringe.[14]

More than Okie Horatio Alger tales, however, these artist-at-home stories suggested that the joy of owning a suburban domicile was as much a product of female subservience as male business acumen. While it was women's action in the kitchen and the playroom that ensured domestic serenity, the same women who performed these household chores were paradoxically reduced to objects that epitomized the amenities of their family homes. Ruth O'Dell's suburban Studio City house, "a lovely hillside home with a beautiful view . . . and a large swimming pool," reflected "the warmth of her personality," according to her "Meet the Mrs." column. Artist-at-home articles also emphasized "womanly" virtues such as resignation and perseverance, suggesting that women's endurance of men's indiscretions might ultimately yield unparalleled domestic bliss. Indeed, the home itself might act as a symbol of what might be accomplished if women compliantly stood by their men. The writer of the "At Home with . . ." piece on the Hamblens, in fact, invoked the family's large estate as a metaphor for devoted Susie's years of patience while her husband battled alcoholism and other unnamed "complexities" (i.e., infidelities?) that came with success. "The Hamblen house, 1500 feet above the floor of the San Fernando Valley, culminates a life long dream of Susie's," the magazine argued. "It is a monument in irony to the happiness of Hamblen's conquering of a dismal past." By doing so, the writer equated Susie's stoic endurance with the sublime structure of the dwelling itself.[15]

Occasionally fan magazines deviated from such fare and offered messages promoting some level of equality in chores and household relations, but such efforts were often negated by contrary depictions within the same pages. One of these articles, a 1965 *Country Music Review* piece on Joe and Rose Lee Maphis—billed in the story as "Mr. and Mrs. Country Music"—suggested that it was good and even proper for men to pitch in around the house and

"Mr. and Mrs. Country Music": This 1965 photo of country music duo Joe and Rose Lee Maphis, appearing in a special annual edition of *Country Music Review*, was highly unusual in that it suggested that women *and* men should share domestic duties equally. Most fan magazine depictions of the 1950s and early 1960s focused instead on women's responsibilities around the home.

for women to make their way in the business world. Photographed by the periodical in their Bakersfield kitchen, Joe stooped over to mop while wife Rose Lee stood in a more dominant pose looking on. "No Debate— Household chores are shared in this home, just as breadwinning," read the caption below. The composition of the photo further enhanced the perception of equality and amicable communication between the sexes. While the pair looked thoughtfully into each other eyes, tall Joe's stooping actually made him appear to be roughly the same height as his wife. Although the Maphis article proved that local fan magazines could momentarily envision a degree of domestic egalitarianism, the general tendency to promote a more lopsided division of duties worked to diminish the potentially progressive impact of such messages. This even occurred in portraits of the selfsame Maphises. Placing a new twist on the traditional artist-at-home story, a later *Country Music Life* interview of the Maphises on board their deluxe live-in tour bus celebrated the couple's adherence to conservative gender norms. The article described Joe's main domestic duty as doing the driving. Rose Lee, on the other hand, kept herself busy "sewing, answering numerous letters from fans, or whipping up that favorite dish for her ever-loving husband."[16]

This emphasis on housework and the private sphere of the suburban home as the ultimate setting for country music publicity marked a major departure not just from prewar radio programming and early fan journalism, but from local country music publicity efforts in general. Earlier publicity vehicles, in fact, had almost universally emphasized the great outdoors and tried to link male and female performers to a hardy strain of rusticity rooted in communal land use. Artists and promoters often used such images to play up the "Western" as opposed to "Southern" roots of area country music, but such efforts also bespoke a general sense of awe toward spaces that were open, pastoral, and public. During the 1930s, no less a figure than Woody Guthrie, emerging Left icon and local "hillbilly" radio singer, had championed public and semipublic places such as municipal Griffith Park and Forest Lawn Memorial Park—a palatial combination of cemetery, funeral parlor, art gallery, and wedding chapel— in *Woody and Lefty Lou's Favorite Collection of Old Time Hill Country Songs*, a folio advertising a local program he shared with a female singing partner. During the 1940s, popular country music publicity materials such as *Spade Cooley's Western Swing Song Folio* stressed fictional communal spaces in which neighborly cattle men and ranch women worked together as coequals. The folio pictured Cooley, dressed in a cook's hat and frock, preparing a meal at a fictional western-style backyard barbecue for the men and women of his band. Cooley's propensity to cook was even depicted as being a particularly alluring attribute to women. Photographed squatting next to a deep pit barbecue in one shot, Cooley appeared to be placing barbecued meat on the plate of a standing and smiling Carolina Cotton. "Who is tempting who?" read the caption below. Even into the early 1950s, some room remained for alternative nondomestic forms of femininity, especially those based on rough sports and the outdoors. Carolina Cotton, for instance, was recognized as "Queen of the Range" and an "Honorary Sheriff" in one country music publication, suggesting her connection with an active outdoor lifestyle, as well as past times that were generally associated with men. "She's a crack shot with a .45 or a rifle," the article explained, "and is also an expert at wrestling and judo." By the mid-1950s, however, fan magazines and the local press almost universally eschewed outdoor themes and staged rural photo-ops in favor of portraits of artists in their suburban homes.[17]

Like the largely male-written fan magazines of the Eisenhower and Kennedy eras, male song lyrics sanctioned keeping women in their place. Especially important were the verses associated with local performers of honky-tonk, the punchy new Oklahoma-Texas musical style that had come to replace western swing as the most popular fare in local circles in the 1950s. With their emphasis on tavern life and the tensions emerging within the postwar two-parent nuclear family, the lyrics of area honky-tonk songs not only blamed women unevenly for domestic strife, but argued that chores at home were the only salvation for the scorned or wayward woman.

Quantitative study of honky-tonk lyrics recorded by local artists suggests that when families or relationships fell apart in honky-tonk songs, tavern-haunting women were almost always the culprits. Particularly informative is a survey I conducted of hits recorded by area honky-tonk leaders Johnny Bond and the Maphises; local artist Johnny Horton, who launched a national career in the area; and national stars, such as Hank Thompson and Lefty Frizzell, who established deep or lasting ties to Los Angeles. In a sample of thirty-three chart-topping or regionally popular honky-tonk records made by these six performers during the 1950s, twenty-two songs—two-thirds of the total—placed the woman at blame for the dissolution of the relationship or the male's declining psychological state. By comparison, Woody Guthrie and Maxine "Lefty Lou" Crissman's Depression-era radio song books blamed men and women nearly equally for break-ups—about half each—in the lyrics of their thirty-five unrequited love songs. Of the 1950s-era songs, cheating— featured as the reason for troubles in twelve—topped the list of reasons for break-ups caused by women, followed by drunkenness and carousing, abandonment, lack of affection, and lying.[18]

On a more qualitative level, the consequences of bar hopping, "honky-tonking," or enjoying, as one song put it, "the gay night life" were also unequally divided between men and women in this sample of lyrics. When men honky-tonked, they generally lost brain cells and sleep. When women honky-tonked, they generally lost families and homes. By speaking of the prices that honky-tonking—a presumably public activity—exacted on women's lives, male honky-tonk music questioned women's freer access to formerly all-male institutions and aligned itself at least tentatively on the conservative end of national debates about whether women should retreat into the private realm of the home or maintain a balance between work, fulfilling public lives, and responsibilities at home.[19]

Media and expert pressure on women to contain their sexual urges during the postwar era—as described by historians such as Elaine Tyler May—further contributed to the conservative tendencies of cold war honky-tonk narratives. Allowed too much freedom in their leisure activities, women, such lyrics argued, might turn to sexual indiscretion where they risked being tagged with one of an ever-growing list of honky-tonk epithets: abusers, cheaters, home wreckers, two-time traitors, heart breakers, or as one Frizzell hit put it "the root of all evil." Part of the misogyny apparent in male honky-tonk originated in the style's infancy in the 1930s when, according to eminent country music historian Bill C. Malone, the honky-tonk tavern was "essentially a masculine retreat . . . The woman who went there alone generally was not respected, even if her affections sought." By the 1950s, however, even so-called "respectable" women were regularly attending Southern California taverns by themselves, but their presence remained an issue of at least subconscious contention. Joe and Rose Lee Maphis's "Dim Lights, Thick Smoke" was particularly instructive, placing guilt on women, as some experts of the era did, not just for carousing, but for spending too much time away from a house "filled with love and a husband so true." Perhaps most devastatingly, the antiheroine is finally advised in the final chorus that she is trading her "home and little children" for "the club down the street."[20]

"Women Ought to Rule the World"
Female Performers and Fans Strike Back

Although efforts to lionize country music June Cleavers and berate women for hitting the town made inroads among listeners of both sexes, female fans and performers often negotiated and contested the same constrictions. Some local performers went so far as to pit themselves against the "good ol' boy" industry network and call into question the very foundations of patriarchy, while others toiled metaphorically against other constraints such as the lack of women in political office and the sexual double standard. Rather than being passive and undiscriminating consumers of popular culture, female fans appear not only to have been aware of the strictures placed on female artists, but to have linked personal notions of liberation, in some cases, with the rising careers of local female soloists.

Such independent behavior was not entirely new to the region. Los Angeles and California, in fact, had served as homes to such early iconoclasts as Patsy Montana and Rose Maddox, who billed themselves as rugged cattle women and touted unorthodox formulations of femininity as early as the 1930s. Born Ruby Blevins in Hope, Arkansas, Montana had come to Los Angeles at eighteen and found work on local radio in 1931. Though Montana later left the region for Chicago's *National Barn Dance*, she began to develop the rough-and-tumble cowgirl image that characterized her later career while in California. Her signature recording, the jazzy yodeling hit "I Want To Be a Cowboy's Sweetheart" (1935), told of a young woman's desire to lasso and ride horses along with the men. Although the song defined its female protagonist according to her relationship with a man (she was, after all, a *cowboy's* sweetheart), Montana saw herself as encouraging young women—especially girls—to pursue careers and outdoor activities that had once been restricted to men. In a 1959 interview program on Los Angeles radio station KXLA, she told the audience that she was trying to create a kind of girls' culture—a kind of country music answer to the Girl Scouts—in which women were encouraged to present themselves as the equals of men.[21]

In the 1940s, Rose Maddox embraced an assertive and flamboyant form of femininity rooted in working-class musical style, comedic stage antics, and ostentatious cowgirl dress. Originally from Alabama, Maddox migrated to California's Central Valley as a young girl during the Depression. Rose fronted the Maddox Brothers and Rose, a raucous hillbilly-style band composed of her brothers and other male musicians. Though technically based in Modesto, the sibling group spent much of its time in Los Angeles, recording on Southern California's Four Star label and appearing regularly on KFVD, the radio station that helped spawn the careers of Spade Cooley, Stuart Hamblen, and Maddox family friend Woody Guthrie. Touted as "The Most Colorful Hillbilly Band in America" for their dazzling outfits, the Maddoxes also effected a certain individuality in their music by borrowing heavily from African American styles such as boogie and singing songs about strong female characters. Maddox's band not only recorded class protest numbers such as Woody Guthrie's "Philadelphia Lawyer (Reno Blues)" to which they added studio gunshots, but also songs alluding to gender equity such as "I Wish I Was A Single Girl Again," a public domain song in which a housewife chafes at gender role assignments and complains about the drudgery of domestic chores.[22]

Southern California performers continued promoting unconventional and confrontational forms of femininity in the early 1950s despite social and business conditions that made it difficult to do so. Jean Shepard, perhaps the most prominent local female soloist from the early Eisenhower era, not only sang pithy honky-tonk numbers that bemoaned the behavior of the honky-tonk man, but even suggested that through collective action women could uproot the very foundations of patriarchy. Born in Oklahoma, Jean Shepard moved to California's San Joaquin Valley with her sharecropping parents after World War II. Shepard began performing in coastal San Luis Obispo in the late 1940s and by 1954 had moved to the San Fernando Valley. There she recorded for L.A.'s sole industry giant, Capitol Records. Among Shepard's earliest singles were numbers that decried the masculine excesses of the honky-tonk, songs made possible because of a more open attitude toward female artists and themes during the late 1940s. Some singles, such as "The Trouble with Girls" (1952), argued that the real problems facing women were men who refused to do household chores and took their relationships lightly, while later tunes criticized the male sports culture's propensity to produce household discord: "It ain't no fun trying to be his wife when Baltimore ain't winning." Such songs were much in line with the bereaved homemaker image extolled by national country music figures such as Kitty Wells, but, rather than simply bemoaning infidelities as many of those songs did, Shepard's songs began to propose solutions and address the inequities within social roles and the division of labor in the nuclear family.[23]

Although Shepard hit pay dirt in early 1953 with "A Dear John Letter"—a weepy Korean War–era duet in which a stateside woman writes her military sweetheart to inform him she has left him—her most feminist recording came later that year. Paradoxically written by a man, Shepard's "Two Hoops and a Holler" railed against a double standard that sanctioned men's fighting, cursing, smoking, drinking, and cheating, but heaped public opprobrium on a woman who "drinks or smokes or tells a joke." The song went on to suggest that women's duties were more cumbersome than men's and that women could only resist these injustices by acting together collectively and politically:

> *If all the gals would stick to me,*
> *We'd change the world around.*
> *We'd make the men walk on their knees*
> *And sleep out on the ground.*
> *What I'm really trying to say*
> *And I know you'll understand*
> *Is that women ought to rule the world*
> *Because the men ain't worth a—*
>
> *Two hoops and holler*
> *They're the lowest thing in town.*

The recording served as an early and cogent challenge to the underrepresentation of women in positions of authority and presented its listeners with the vicarious satisfaction that oppressive men might ultimately be brought to justice. Despite great promise, "Two Hoops" failed to place on the charts. Although some contend that the song failed to hit the charts because it was too shocking for public tastes, Shepard biographer Chris Skinker argues that the most likely reason for the song's failure was that disc jockeys, a group that was almost entirely male, were offended by the unrepentant lyrics and failed to give it ample airtime. Whatever the reason, Shepard appears to have followed up by withdrawing from outright challenges to patriarchy in her music and began featuring a more ambivalent assertiveness. Often these songs took men to task for their failings and indiscretions, but failed to pose the political transformation offered by "Two Hoops." Shepard blamed men for lying and cheating in "Girls in Disgrace" (1955), as well as ruining women's reputations and ignoring their needs in her answer songs "The Root of All Evil (Is a Man)" (1960) and "Second Fiddle (To an Old Guitar)" (1964), but not again would she insist that women ought to rule the world.[24]

The resistance Shepard faced in getting airplay for more ardently feminist recordings and her subsequent transition toward less controversial song lyrics was part of a larger dilemma facing women in country music in the 1950s.

Yet there appears to have been public support for many of these recordings. The *Grand Ole Opry* and the NBC radio network banned Kitty Wells's tamely-feminist 1952 recording "It Wasn't God Who Made Honky-Tonk Angels." The song eventually became a hit only through live audience response and juke-box play. On a local level, the change from live to disc jockey formats further hindered women's aspirations. Although women such as Maddox and Carolina Cotton had hosted their own live shows locally in the 1940s, the switch to largely or all-male disc jockey staffs in the 1950s ensured an environment more hostile to iconoclastic female performers. By 1963, Long Beach's KFOX-AM-FM, the area's leading country radio station, even attributed its sales and national prominence to its all-male disc jockey lineup, advertising in *Country Music Report* with this slogan: "KFOX does it with MANPOWER!" [25]

More feminist offerings such as Shepard's early 1950s platters may have been ignored by radio programmers, but local performers did pave the way for aspects of the coming sexual revolution to make a mark in local country music culture. Sometimes billed as "the female Elvis," Wanda Jackson broached the almost Victorian social and sexual norms of the country landscape in the mid-1950s with her country and rockabilly songs. Born in central Oklahoma and living briefly in Southern California in the 1940s, Jackson returned to Los Angeles to sign with Capitol in the 1950s and cut compositions that tended to feature sexually assertive young women who often seemed more sensually sophisticated than the men they were courting. Her most lyrically and musically daring recording, "Fujiyama Mama" (1958), was originally recorded as an r&b number. Jackson eschewed the original, however, and added growls, shrieks, and soft deep-voiced interludes to the song. The lyrics equated the female libido with the volcano and the atom bomb:

> *I been to Nagasaki, Hiroshima, too—*
> *The things I did to them baby, I can do to you,*
> *'Cause I'm a Fujiyama mama, and I'm just about to blow my top. . . .*
> *And when I start eruptin', ain't nobody gonna make me stop*

Despite its potential to raise ire from Japanese survivors, Jackson's rendition paradoxically became an overnight smash in the Pacific nation, but failed to chart in the U.S. "The American people in the '50s weren't ready for a female rocker," Jackson later told one interviewer. "They sure weren't ready to accept a girl screaming and rocking and rolling."[26]

Jackson eventually returned to singing less startling honky-tonk and gospel numbers, but others took up the mantle of sexually assertive lyrics. While Shepard's vision of political independence and a feminization of the world political system continued to face hurdles, the more overt sexuality displayed in Jackson's late 1950s recordings slowly became safer terrain. A rising star in the late 1960s, Barbara Mandrell, another Texas-Oklahoma migrant who started her career in Southern California haunts, scored her first number one country spot with "The Midnight Oil," a composition she described as "a sultry number about two people seeing each other in the middle of the night." Mandrell's hit proved that it was becoming more acceptable for women to sing candidly about feminine desire.[27]

Although female performers experienced mixed results in their efforts to broaden horizons for country music women, an examination of members of the Southern California fan subculture suggests that female enthusiasts did not fully embrace the subservient domestic ideal promoted by fan journalism and male honky-tonk lyrics. Interviews of fans who attended a series of multiartist "package" country music shows at the Long Beach Municipal Auditorium in the 1950s suggest that the subculture that developed among show attendees may have actually even encouraged female fans to contest the June Cleaver model and develop more liberated ideas about women's role in society. Shirley Desy, a self described "teenage country music lover" who finagled her father into driving her to the Long Beach shows before she was old enough to drive, felt a strong sense of identification with the show's female soloists, women such as Shepard, Wells, and Skeeter Davis who were just beginning to make a name for themselves in country music. Desy sympathized with the ups and downs of these vocalists' careers, linking them with her own struggles as an adolescent and teenager. In a 2001 interview, she said her contact with the shows led her to realizations about the bias female artists faced and allowed her to cultivate a sense of pride at the obstacles these performers were forced to overcome. "Women were not given the freedoms that men were given—anywhere—not just country music," Desy remembered. "There was probably more of the good-ol'-boy concept in country music than anyplace else. I was really proud when women started making things that were good . . . because I thought that they were all talented and I thought they deserved it." With their focus on economic struggle and gender bias, Desy also felt that female country music vocalists had something more important to say about the struggles women faced in the postwar period than the female pop vocalists who were more explicitly marketed to her generation.[28]

Ultimately, Desy found that her experiences as a fan made her a more assertive person because they taught her the value of standing up for her own tastes and beliefs. She said she felt a sense of community with the intergenerational Long Beach audiences, but by the mid-1950s her love for country music put her at odds with her high school classmates. "I felt like an outcast to my peers because during that time rock and roll was the type of music the kids loved," she said. "I tolerated rock and roll and kept my likes to myself in order to avoid criticism." When she later relented and went with a boyfriend to some rock events, she even felt a slight pang of guilt. "I was so dedicated to country," Desy remembered. "I felt like I was being disloyal." Such attachment eventually led her to resist the temptation to hide her affinity toward country music. Being "country when country wasn't cool," she said, eventually led her to be more confident and—if need be—more confrontational about her preferences and her relationships.[29]

Conclusion

Taken at face value, the proliferation of artist-at-home articles in the 1950s and 1960s might suggest a cut-and-dried case for the misogyny of Southern California country music—proof that the musical subculture largely shaped and sustained by the hundreds of thousands arrivals from the Dust Bowl extended the fabled social conservatism of migrants to debates about women's roles at work and in the family. The famed conservatism or "plain-folk Americanism" of the Okie migration, according to this view, had reared its ugly head yet again, contributing to a working-class version of the ennui that Betty Friedan so aptly described in *The Feminine Mystique*.[30]

The real track record, however, was much more ambiguous than that promoted in fan magazine literature. Southern California country music fans of the 1950s and 1960s were confronted with a variety of models related to women's behavior. True, fan magazines and the growing male-dominated honky-tonk industry offered relatively conservative messages about women's roles in society and in the family, but local female performers were successful— at least temporarily—in countering such depictions and offering new images of a more independent womanhood that in one case threatened to place a woman in a world-dominant position. Female fans, as Desy's story suggests, delighted in female artists' successes, deeply affected at times with the independence these performers appeared to display. The country music culture of Southern California in the 1950s, then, must be seen as a site of active dialogue over competing notions of acceptable women's behavior as well as a contested terrain upon which audiences selectively processed the symbols, messages, and ideologies they encountered. Conservative fan magazine writers, male disc jockeys, and misogynist lyricists enjoyed a great deal of control over what political messages might reach fans, but female performers and fans exercised a substantial, if somewhat underestimated, role in establishing their own notions about women's capabilities and the role they should play in society.

Charline Arthur

The (Un) Making of a Honky-Tonk Star

EMILY C. NEELY

"She was a woman before her time" is the oft-repeated phrase used to describe Charline Arthur and her flash-in-the-pan career as a honky-tonk singer. In the early 1950s she was a charismatic, rising talent who sported an individualism unique to female country performers. She released singles through RCA, performed at choice venues, such as the Louisiana Hayride and the Grand Ole Opry, and toured with the big names in honky-tonk, all the while maintaining a bold and assertive stage persona. By 1956, though, Nashville and the country music audience had lost interest in her. While Charline was an anomaly in many ways, it is important to recognize her as a woman of her time when considering her inability to attain country music stardom. She and her personal experiences were grounded within a social and cultural context peculiar to the early 1950s. In this regard, Charline does not simply represent a martyred feminist felled at the hands of record labels preserving their status within a patriarchal establishment; while some chose to reject the assertive persona that Charline portrayed in her songs and on stage, others chose to support her, or at least give her a chance. The Nashville country music industry, despite its reputation for being "the tail of the dog . . . the most sexist of all the entertainment industries," as Nashville producer Wendy Waldman said in 1992, was less an obstacle for Charline than were the popular fan media and the female listening audience.[1]

Like most of her honky-tonk contemporaries, Charline came from modest origins. She was born Charline Highsmith, the daughter of a Pentecostal,

Originally published in the fall 2002 issue of *Southern Cultures*, required reading for southerners and those who wonder what makes the South the South.

relatively poor couple in Henrietta, Texas. Her parents were both amateur musicians, and from an early age music and performance seem to have been the central motivating forces in her life. In 1945, at the age of fifteen, she left home to travel with a medicine show, and in 1948 she married Jack Arthur, who managed her early career and also played bass on several of her recordings. Her debut in Nashville came in 1952, when, during a stint as a disc jockey and singer at KERB in Kermit, Texas, Colonel Tom Parker, the man best known for his role in bringing Elvis Presley to RCA Records, introduced her to Hill and Range Publishing Company, which in turn led to a recording contract with RCA-Victor Records.

In early 1955 Charline appeared to have made it to the top. At RCA she recorded under the production direction of two moguls of Nashville, Steve Sholes and Chet Atkins. Country disc jockeys voted her second best female country performer (Kitty Wells being first) in a 1955 national poll.[2] On tour she performed with Johnny Cash, Jerry Lee Lewis, Elvis Presley, Marty Robbins, Lefty Frizzell, as well as other country legends. After recording for just three years, though, Charline's progression toward country stardom came to a screeching halt; her contract with RCA-Victor expired, and she did not receive another offer. Thereafter she spent her days performing in small, local clubs and recording for some minor record labels. When she died in 1987, she was surviving on a monthly disability check.[3]

In 1986 the German label Bear Family Records released *Welcome to the Club*, a compilation of singles that Charline had recorded between 1949 and 1957.[4] It passed largely unnoticed. During the early 1990s, however, a rising interest in women's participation in country music sparked her rediscovery. In 1991 Bob Allen, a journalist who wrote the liner notes for the Bear Family release, composed a one-page article about her for *The Journal for the Society of the Preservation of Old Time Country Music*. Historians Mary A. Bufwack and Robert K. Oermann's massive 1993 work, *Finding Her Voice: The Saga of Women in Country Music*, also included a segment on Charline's life, in which they concluded that, "Charline fought for the right to become country's first truly aggressive, independent female of the postwar era. Ultimately she lost."[5]

Why did this charismatic and talented performer, who mingled with the stars of honky-tonk, slip so quickly into obscurity? Generally her failure is attributed to two factors. Like other women aspiring to honky-tonk stardom, she had to maneuver within a notoriously chauvinistic music industry. Country music, like other spheres of postwar life in the U.S., could be a confining space for women. Between 1945 and 1955, for example, female vocalists participated in less than ten percent of country albums that charted in *Billboard*.[6] In 1952 Roy Acuff actually warned Kitty Wells's husband Johnnie Wright, "Don't ever headline a show with a woman. It won't ever work, because people just don't go for women."[7] An arguably related issue for Charline is that by the time she and Chet Atkins parted ways in 1956, she had acquired a reputation for being quite difficult to work with, inclining other producers to shy away from her. As she herself put it, "I just felt [Atkins] didn't have the right substance for my vocal style, but he was the top dog and there was nothing I could do. I remember the last time we recorded together, me and him had it out good and proper. I was crying so bad."[8] Without a doubt, as a woman Charline faced obstacles from within the music industry as she sought the bright lights, and her fiery personality (including, for example, a reputation for sometimes heavy drinking) may have contributed to her eventual alienation from Nashville producers.

Yet neither the workings of Music Row nor her personal experiences and relationships there fully account for Charline's inability to achieve country music stardom. Though she clashed frequently with Chet Atkins over his backup guitar style and choice of songs, what is notable is that Sholes and Atkins were initially receptive to working with her. In other words, RCA felt that Charline's music would appeal to the country music audience despite, *or perhaps because of,* its message of female assertiveness that so distanced her music from that of other up-and-coming female performers. Further illumination as to the industry's stance on Charline can be found in her rankings as runner-up to Kitty Wells (1955) and then third place the following year in the "Best Female Singer" category of a national DJ poll. Charline had "arrived" according to many of her fellow DJs, her *peers*. She had apparently cleared gates that typically excluded women from the business. Despite the increased visibility that came with the RCA contract (e.g., promotions and better bookings), however, the public failed to purchase her albums. An overlooked cause for Charline's short-lived career was her inability, created in part by a conservative media, to secure a substantial fan base among female listeners.

Charline's music was largely influenced by, and representative of, the honky-tonk tradition, a genre that defined country music during the early to

While Charline's female contemporaries tended to model their style on the very feminine look of Kitty Wells, Charline's more masculine wardrobe harkened back to the attire of 1930s and 1940s cowgirls like Patsy Montana and Texas Ruby.

mid-1950s. Honky-tonk began to develop as part of a southern, working-class bar culture in the 1930s. After World War II, though, it metamorphosed into a national, commercial enterprise as rural southerners in search of work migrated to northern (and, to a lesser degree, southern) cities, which rapidly concentrated and expanded the country listening audience. In the postwar years, honky-tonk themes often focused on feelings of displacement experienced by rural migrants. During these years Hank Williams, the quintessential honky-tonker, largely contributed to the music's growing thematic focus on realistic portrayals of domestic struggles, including previously taboo subjects such as infidelity or alcoholism.[9]

Because domestic life has traditionally been considered the female realm in American society, this focus on domestic issues afforded working-class women a unique opportunity during the early 1950s. While larger society offered virtually no outlet through which to express discontent over increasingly rigid gender codes—codes that had slackened immensely during the Rosie the Riveter war years—country music provided an arena for male-female dialogue. This discourse thrived particularly in the form of duets and answer songs, in which women sang responses to male songs (e.g., Margie Bowes's release of "Understand Your Gal" after Johnny Cash's success with "Understand Your Man").

Kitty Wells, the "Queen of Country Music," would come to represent a major ideological focus around which women who listened to honky-tonk oriented their "side" in what was to become a veritable battle of the sexes. Her 1952 song, "It Wasn't God Who Made Honky-Tonk Angels," the classic answer song, reached #1 in the *Billboard* country music charts and maintained its position for six weeks. Responding to Hank Thompson's hit, "The Wild Side of Life," in which he scorns his ex-wife for leaving him and not "mak[ing] a wife," Kitty quips, "Too many times married men think they're still single / Which has caused many a good girl to go wrong." Thereafter Kitty produced a string of songs offering the message that women would fulfill their domestic duties if men acted as responsible partners. She succeeded in initiating a dialogue addressing postwar gender discontent and introducing what the country music audience perceived as the woman's side of the story. Loretta Lynn says of "It Wasn't God Who Made Honky-Tonk Angels," "I thought, 'Gee, here the women are starting to sing!' I think with that song she touched in me what I was living and what I was going through and I knew there was a lot of women that lived like me. I thought, 'Here's a woman telling our point of view of everyday life.' "[10]

Women were quick to identify with Kitty, and she subsequently charted in *Billboard* with twenty-six hits between 1953 and 1961. In addition, country music magazines named her best female performer from 1952 to 1965. Kitty's success directly correlated to her rapport with the women of the honky-tonk audience. As Minnie Pearl, country comedian, remembered, when women heard Kitty, "they went out and bought the records."[11] Women, then, composed a recognizable contingency in country music consumerism, and Kitty Wells represented a collective, female voice, creating a standard by which the audience and media would judge other female performers.

Although Kitty was widely popular and her message of female resentment toward male irresponsibility remained grounded within a traditional female role (that of wife and mother), the media and the audience considered her music to be somewhat radical. NBC, which broadcast the Grand Ole Opry, censored "Honky-Tonk Angels" due to its "suggestive" nature, even at the height of its popularity.[12] Such controversy did not taint her commercial success, though, and producers suddenly noticed women's potential marketability. Producers began to record more material from female artists, which in turn may have spurred radio programmers to target their material more toward female audiences.[13] The country music audience's interest in an open male-female discussion was turning a profit for record labels.

Against this backdrop entered Charline Arthur, who began her recording career in 1953 with Chet Atkins. Atkins apparently recognized the profit potential of music offered from the woman's side in the male-female dialogue and expected Charline's contribution to receive popular approval in sales. In fact, he may have insisted that Charline stick with her assertive identity despite initially low album sales. In a 1985 interview, she stated that "[Atkins] and I would get up in arms. . . . He always had songs that he wanted me to record that I didn't want to record, and I had ones I'd written that he wouldn't let me record."[14] Most of the songs Charline herself composed were actually the most mainstream material that she recorded, including love songs such as "Dreaming of You," "I Was Wrong," or "Too Long, Too Many Times." One might infer that Charline, whose RCA contract seemed to indicate success and stardom in the not-too-distant future, wished to moderate her image in order to find broader appeal, while Atkins may have insisted that Charline's feistiness *was* her appeal. Although rockabilly was at this point in its formative stages, Atkins may have perceived Charline as a part of this development and hoped that she would appeal to the country audience or younger listeners who eventually formed the rockabilly audience. Record producers certainly did not contrive Charline's individualistic, assertive persona; before joining RCA, she had been known for her aggressiveness and strong personality because of her performances, in which she was often the only woman among male performers. At the same time, though, it is important to recognize that Charline wanted commercial success. As Bufwack and Oermann note, toward the end of Charline's life, she "would sit and watch The Nashville Network and weep at the sight of her former Music City friends and coworkers."[15] Charline wanted to be a star; she wanted people to love her and her music.

While Charline sought stardom, her image, both before and during her years at RCA, differed substantially from the contemporary image of female honky-tonk success. She most conspicuously distanced herself from other female performers through a bold sexual aggressiveness, typified by her use of sexual innuendo. Not only did this open female sexuality challenge acceptable lyrical content, but it also tested the stylistic boundaries of the country tradition. As several historians argue, the importance of the lyrics in country music has typically surpassed other aspects of the music; the instrumentation is generally simple, while the songwriters and performers focus on candid lyrical expression. The late John Hartford aptly dubbed country songs "three minute word movies."[16] Country, especially honky-tonk, traditionally relied upon realistic portrayals of life, with believable characters confronting everyday struggles in everyday settings. While the music strives for candor, though, it is also generally expressive. The realism successfully impresses upon the listener the emotional depths experienced by the performer.

Because commercial honky-tonk lyrics tended to be straightforward and unambiguous, and female performers did not generally address female sexuality from a personal perspective, Charline's use of innuendo clearly confused the country music media.[17] This quandary is especially vivid in regard to Charline's "Kiss the Baby Goodnight" (1955). In it she sings, "Hold me til I'm thrilled to death / Kiss me til I gasp for breath / I won't settle for anything less / So kiss the baby goodnight." This verse blatantly demonstrates the narrator's sexual assertiveness. The chorus, on the other hand, proceeds, "When I was a little girl / My mom would tuck me in / Though I've grown up quite a lot, I've never lost the yearn." Without listening to the rest of the music, these lines could be interpreted as lacking sexual content, but within context it is overtly sexual, and her vocal expression further emphasizes the intended sexual overtones. In 1955 the Grand Ole Opry invited her to perform the song, but the program also partially censored it by compelling her, according to Charline, to "leave out some of the racy parts."[18] The Opry strategically removed the blatant allusions to sex, but allowed the more subtle innuendo to remain. A review in *Country and Western Jamboree*, a country fan magazine, reveals a similar approach to censoring her songs. The review grants her four stars (the highest rating is five), and curtly states that Charline "wants to be kissed goodnight—just like a little girl."[19] By referring only to these two lines

of the chorus, the writer functionally disregards the song's sexual component, and essence.

A focus upon physicality to the exclusion of emotional attraction further separated Charline from her contemporaries. For example, in "He Fiddled While I
Burned" (1953), in which she sings, "And while my two thumbs twiddled / He
played with his fiddle / Oh what a fool, he fiddled while I burned," she not so
subtly expresses intense sexual desire. She does not, however, express emotional attachment to the man; the song only reveals a physical basis for the relationship. Likewise, she sings in "Honey Bun" (1955), "Your kiss is what I want."
Although she also tells the person to whom she speaks, "Your love is what I
want," she then easily dismisses him with the line, "If I can't have it, then take
it away." While Kitty Wells was singing, "I can get someone to kiss me / I can
get someone to care / But when I need someone to love me / You're not easy
to forget," the characters in Charline's songs were often carousing. They were
looking for a good time with whomever happened their way.[20]

In "Just Look, Don't Touch, He's Mine" (1955), Charline discloses another
component of her assertiveness: fierceness. Portraying herself in a typical
honky-tonk bar setting, one generally open only to men and disreputable
women, she cautions a woman to stay away from her man and then
brusquely states (does not sing), "I'm not the kind to worry, but I am the kind
to fight / And I get to be a buzz saw if the situation's tight / . . . Stay away
from him 'cause I don't like the county jail." Charline distances herself quite
dramatically from Kitty Wells's submissiveness; she lacks any and all pretensions of a domesticated lady, to the point that she would fight another
woman and would endure (already *has* endured) prison. Whereas the typical
"honky-tonk angel" existed in honky-tonk settings as an anonymous prop for
the male character, Charline's characters maneuver as distinct personalities
within this sphere, even performing a role generally reserved for men, as in
the territoriality she expresses in "Just Look."

Instrumentation complemented Charline's lyrical assertions. "The Good
and the Bad" (1954), which she coauthored, shows her at her best, conveying
creativity and wit through her voice and playful accompaniment. In this song
she contrasts two aspects of the psyche: the angel, who represents social
conscience and advises the narrator to adhere to social etiquette, and the mischievous vamp, who represents raw desires. The third voice symbolizes the

narrator's persona: an amalgam of the voices. Charline uses her own spoken voice accompanied by a lone steel guitar to represent this character as mutual ground for the vamp and angel alike.

The personalities in "The Good and the Bad" find themselves faced with a moral dilemma when the narrator sees a boy "across the street" and she "want[s] to kiss him." In response to the urge, the angel, personifying social propriety with her ethereal voice states, "I knew that wasn't quite ladylike." Throughout the song the angel speaks in free verse, which creates a suspension of the music's rhythm. The fiddle, relying upon slides that create a comical effect during the melody, also hesitates when the angel begins to speak. Imitating the angel's inhibitions, it begins a melodic line, which it then cannot seem to complete. The vamp, on the other hand, is gutsy, growling, and demanding. Ragtime piano and strong rhythmic emphasis accentuate her sensuality and forcefulness. She retorts: "Go get your man / Love him while you can / Tell the world that you don't want to be sad." Ultimately the vamp overrides the angel, who concedes, "I think I'll just go on over there and tell that boy exactly how I feel / I think that would be the right thing to do." The vamp is victorious and sings the concluding line, "Well that's the good with the bad."

Charline visually transmitted this assertive persona through stage animation, and she showed the same boldness in her attire. Animated stage performers, women included, claimed a richer heritage in country music than in other entertainment industries. The Grand Ole Opry, for instance, initially rejected Kitty Wells because, as her husband Johnnie Wright put it, "They said that they didn't think Kitty had the personality to sing on the Grand Ole Opry. They said she didn't move around and jump and dance, you know, like a lot of the girls did."[21] This liveliness, though, normally appeared within the context of religion (e.g., Martha Carson) or comedy (e.g., Minnie Pearl). Charline was unique because music appeared to be the catalyst when she lost control on stage. In 1985 she stated, "I was the first to break out of the Kitty Wells stereotype and boogie woogie. . . . I was shakin' that thing on stage long before Elvis even thought about it."[22] Photographs and oral accounts indicate that she was very animated, leaping from amplifiers, for example.[23] In a photograph used in *Welcome to the Club* she slides across the stage on her side while her four male backup musicians look on with amusement. She presented an independent act at a time when most female performers traveled with male escorts (e.g., Kitty Wells and Rose Maddox) or in groups (e.g., the Carter Family and the Davis Sisters), though Jean Shepard is a notable exception.[24] Charline performed as "Charline Arthur." She attempted to identify herself as a country performer rather than one of the "girl country singers."[25]

Dress codes during the 1950s were particularly gender specific, and attire was therefore an obvious means by which Charline rejected a traditionally feminine image. Consider, for instance, the divergence between Charline's and Kitty's self-identifications, as illustrated by two photographs. On the cover of her 1954 album *After Dark* (Decca Records), Kitty personifies propriety.[26] As if she were delivering an aria, she stands perfectly poised, clasping a handkerchief with both hands, her mouth open in song. Her gingham dress, however, staunchly announces her country roots. Its wide sash and puffed sleeves also emphasize her hour-glass figure, and the abundance of lace underscores her femininity. Although the photo does not include her feet, Kitty almost invariably wore high heels.[27] She looks doll-like and fragile, and the prominence of her wedding band attests to her identity as a wife and a mother.

In contrast to Kitty's self-conscious poise, in the photograph on the back cover of *Welcome to the Club*, Charline stands in a relaxed manner with her arms by her side and her feet spread about shoulders' width apart. The cowgirl motif of the dark-colored western fringe dominates her blouse, and, along with the dark-colored elaborate embroidery, contrasts starkly with her suit's pale blue. In comparison to Kitty's muted color scheme, the dark and light of Charline's suit is bold. Rather than highlight her curvature, as Kitty does, she de-emphasizes it. Her blouse has a simple button-up collar, and she wears a knotted necktie. Her blouse tucks into her loose-fitting pants, and she dons a large belt. While Kitty emanates a sort of bashfulness as she gazes upward and away from the viewer, Charline stares directly ahead. Her positioning above the viewer's eye level suggests an easy straightforwardness and independent nature. In contrast with the implied domestic stability of Kitty's wedding band, the car in the background connotes that Charline is going somewhere, and the image of the road in country music carries undertones of restlessness and independence normally associated with men. A final detail is the cigarette that contrasts with Kitty's handkerchief. Such iconography, widely associated with Johnny Cash and countless other male performers, almost exclusively described masculine personas in early-1950s mainstream American culture.[28]

In this photo the cigarette, the car, Charline's masculine wardrobe, and her direct gaze combine to present an identity of assertiveness that was typically appropriated only by male country musicians during the 1950s.

This image became especially problematic for Charline in relation to the country fan magazines, an important venue in which artists could "package" themselves, or market their personalities to the honky-tonk audience. In magazine articles and photographs, Charline's entertaining stage presence and musical ability could play only a limited role. It is impossible to account definitively for country fan magazine readership in the early 1950s, but *Country Song Roundup*, the longest running fan magazine, indicates that women largely composed its readership. The advertisements almost solely targeted women, for instance. Aside from ads for products designed to enhance the female appearance (to increase bust size, to eliminate acne, to lose weight, etc.), others advertised money-making opportunities for women, such as dress-making and selling items like greeting cards, while still others advertised schools of nursing. Some described books that claimed to train women in proper interaction with the opposite sex, and many ads displayed women's clothing. Another clue linking women to the magazines was their prominence in fan clubs. In one 1955 *Country Song Roundup* report on "Your Favorite Stars," eleven of twelve writers were women, and they updated the readers on recent activities of popular musicians.[29] *Country and Western Jamboree* points to a similar tendency. In a 1955 issue, women wrote four of five letters to the editor, responding to articles in recent issues.[30] In another issue, women wrote fifteen of sixteen letters in the "Fan Club Corner."[31]

In addition to indicating whom fan magazines were targeting, advertisements illustrate the extent to which the era's cultural images underscored the importance of feminine appearance. During the early 1950s *CSR* devoted at least half its contents to ads for products intended to help attract a prospective husband. "Husband" is the key word in this scenario because, for the women depicted, the ultimate goal was marriage. (Some Charles Atlas ads appeared, encouraging men to build musculature, but a disproportionately large number targeted women.) Though the concept of "allure" presented in these ads paralleled mainstream American ideology, the sheer quantity of advertisements centered on attracting men cannot help but startle the present-day reader.[32] In one 1950 ad for "The Bunomo Ritual," a man, Tom, is centered between photos of two women, both of whom are wearing blindfolds. One woman, Mary, is flat-chested, while the other, Alice, is buxom. The caption reads, "Do men choose Mary or Alice?" Tom, of course, chooses buxom Alice, and the ad continues:

> Tom's choice was not surprising. For it is the woman with a beautiful, alluring bust contour who most often wins the admiration, popularity and affection every woman desires. . . . Yes, there are many lovely "Marys" whose wit, charm and friendliness cannot compete with the natural law of man's attraction to beauty fulfilled completely.[33]

Mirroring similar sentiments, the magazine reporters discussed female performers foremost in physical and domestic terms. Musical capabilities were secondary. In 1957 *Country Song Roundup* issued its official "Year Book," complete with descriptions and biographies of the most popular country musicians at the time. The first sentence of Jean Shepard's biography described her as "vivacious" and "blonde."[34] Kitty Wells was introduced as "a lovely picture of fine American womanhood. She stands a tall 5 feet 8 inches and weighs 137, has jet black hair and brown eyes."[35] DJs and fans alike thought Kitty was the decade's best female performer, but the writers felt compelled to obscure her musical identity with her identity as a wife and a mother. The commercial success of this identity is evident; Kitty portrayed herself (and then was portrayed) as a homemaker, and she made money this way. Similarly, her fans chose to identify with her as a homemaker. The interacting forces behind the identity's success were inseparable. Cultural images, such as magazine ads, dwelt upon appearance, which reinforced such notions among readers, who in turn bought more records from performers like Kitty, whose producers in turn encouraged a similar identity for other performers, and so on and so on.

Photographs and write-ups of Charline in *Country Song Roundup* detail her musical accomplishments. Because she did not conform in appearance or character, she appeared lost. While photos depicted female musicians such as Goldie Hill and Kitty Wells smiling, and often engaged in domestic activities like cooking, Charline's candid shots repeatedly showed her in a business-like manner. One such photo captured her earnestly looking at and listening to a reporter. She is so enthralled in the conversation that she appears to be scowling.[36] Another photo caught Charline during a coffee break.[37] She stares intently, possibly purposely, away from the camera, and, as in the other photo, she seems almost to frown. While the other female artists radiated warmth and a carefree demeanor, Charline appeared serious and focused. The writers did not attempt to personalize her either. They described female performers variously as "lovely," "beauteous," "cute," and even "talented," but no such adjectives were used to describe Charline; writers and photographers maintained their distance from her.

The significance attached to audience reception of a country performer's personality should not be underestimated. Due to honky-tonk's avowed focus on realism, the audience expected performers to be believable and straightforward. Such a rapport between the audience and the performer is still important in country music, so much so that historian Jimmie Rogers has entitled this relationship a "sincerity contract."[38] The magazines' distancing Charline would certainly have harmed her career.

In addition to Charline's inability to establish a "sincerity contract," women may have disregarded her for other practical reasons. One is that her music did not address domestic struggles. Kitty Wells spoke to women's everyday concerns, and women's response to her therefore represents an initial, and early, rising of consciousness. While Charline offered women an undaunted female role model, this image denied the realities faced by women at this time, for example, the consequences women could suffer for being sexually active outside of marriage in the 1950s, including pregnancy without access to financial resources. As Kitty Wells and Charline Arthur illustrate, the domestic ideal disillusioned women who listened to country music, but they were not looking for a fundamental reconsideration of gender.

At some point Charline realized that her image did not correspond to what the honky-tonk audience wanted. After her recording career with RCA ended she altered her approach and recorded largely subdued, mainstream music. Her last RCA recording session, for example, included the songs "Later On" and "What About Tomorrow," both of which she wrote. In "What About Tomorrow," she sings

What about tomorrow, will you still feel the same as today?
What about tomorrow, will I still hear you say
That you love me forever, or will you have another love affair?
What about tomorrow? Darling, will you still care?

Her earlier boldness is gone. The music is rhythmically fast, but lyrical. Her 1968 recordings of "My Heart Sings" and "That Was a Long Time Ago" are similar. Reflecting the Nashville Sound, both lean toward pop. A string orchestra accompanies the lyrics, which again describe a generic relationship. She sings lyrically, without exuberance, and she maintains careful enunciation rather than a country accent.

The altered approach of these later recordings, as well as the more pop-oriented songs that she wrote during her early career, may evidence an accommodation that Charline felt necessary in order to attract broader interest. During an interview in 1985, she said that her first musical inspiration had been Ernest Tubb, and when, as a youngster, she saw him perform, she thought, "I wanted to sing like him. . . . He inspired me more than anyone."[39] As this statement suggests, Charline first and foremost adored the music. The independence that male musicians claimed through country music attracted her and led her to be, by virtue of her sex, a "trend-setter . . . an original."[40] Charline was always an "original," and half a century later, with 20/20 hindsight, she is appreciated for her innovations, both musically and culturally, which contributed to the course of country and rock development.

I Don't Think Hank
Done It That Way

Elvis, Country Music, and the Reconstruction
of Southern Masculinity

MICHAEL BERTRAND

Describing his first impression of Elvis Presley in performance, country singer Bob Luman vividly captured the image of a generational fissure set to rock the southern cultural landscape. His account centered on a mid-1950s touring country music jamboree headlined by the venerable Hank Snow. As adults watched and listened to the traditional artists who made up the majority of the playbill, teenagers sat nervously in anticipation, waiting to see for themselves the new hillbilly singer whose records sounded so exciting, so alive, so . . . non-country. Finally, and abruptly, a handsome "cat" dressed in red pants, green coat, and pink shirt and socks sprang onto the stage, a sneer gracing his face as he stood behind the microphone, searching for his adolescent audience. Then suddenly the nineteen-year-old "Hillbilly Cat" banged on the leather-covered acoustic guitar that hung from his broad shoulders, nonchalantly breaking two strings before diving into a recent rhythm and blues hit, pelvis at full throttle. Various girls in the audience began screaming, fainting, or dashing toward the stage. Pandemonium shook the auditorium. Young Luman felt chills run up his neck, and as he recalled years later, "That's the last time I tried to sing like Webb Pierce or Lefty Frizzell."[1]

Luman and adoring teenagers, of course, were not the only ones who quivered at the sight and sound of Elvis Presley. In a highly energetic sermon, the Reverend Jimmy Snow revealed that foes were just as fervent. With arms flailing and voice breaking, Snow, a former country entertainer who had recently traveled with his father Hank and Presley in package tours, warned his congregation of the evil Elvis.

> I know how it feels when you sing it. I know what it does to you. I know the evil feeling that you feel when you sing it. I know the lost position that you get into. And the beat. . . . Well, you talk to the average teenager of today, and you ask them what it is about rock 'n' roll music that they like, and the first thing they'll say is "the beat, the beat, the beat."

Lathered into a frenzy, the born-again preacher linked the music to race and sex, thus exposing a larger regional anxiety concerning the recent federal order to desegregate southern institutions. "Before he came on the scene," Snow railed, "country was country, pop was pop and rhythm-and-blues was rhythm-and-blues. Elvis [recklessly] ran them all together."[2]

And what a cataclysmic collision it caused. According to the popular music canon, the merger between country music and rhythm and blues (along with gospel and mainstream pop) produced rock 'n' roll. Yet this much-acclaimed synthesis may be one that is taken for granted much more than it is understood. That the fusion contributed rhythm and energy to the repertoires and performances of white country artists, for instance, is both audibly and visibly obvious. Often overlooked, however, is the substantial convergence that occurred outside of the musical realm. For in drawing extensively upon and overlapping different social categories, rock 'n' roll muddled many of the boundaries that its society worked so hard to keep intact. Accordingly, contemporaries granted it a significance not often credited to a popular culture "fad." As Atlantic Records executive Herb Abramson declared in 1956, "No future history concerned with the life and times of the twentieth century can leave out rock 'n' roll. It's that important."[3]

Nowhere was it as important as in the South. While the specific circumstances surrounding rock 'n' roll's birth and birthplace will no doubt be endlessly debated, there is little dispute over its southern character. Given the geographical and cultural origins of its early practitioners, it is safe to say that the former Confederacy left an indelible mark on the music. The timing and nature of its inception likewise acknowledged another important regional connection. A popular biracial working-class phenomenon, it emerged at the same time and in the same space as the civil rights movement. Ironically, young listeners in Dixie often referred to rock 'n' roll as rockabilly, a label that implied integration by alluding to the consolidation of "white" hillbilly music and "black" rhythm and blues. *Billboard* writer Bill Simon implicitly linked this group, including an adolescent Elvis, and the black freedom struggle when he wrote that the "rhythm and blues influence has manifested itself with the country and western public and those who once craved an exclusive diet of hillbilly platters; they certainly don't practice segregation in their platter preferences."[4]

In its heyday, between 1954 and 1963, rockabilly shook the country music establishment. Its popularity compelled the industry to react and adapt to a new and profitable commercial environment. Nashville record executives and producers subsequently encouraged and often insisted that older and veteran country performers hop on the rockabilly bandwagon—no matter how reluctant they may have been—and perform highly charged material associated more with New Orleans shouter Roy Brown than with Smoky Mountain boy Roy Acuff. The music's greatest impact, however, occurred among the younger set, specifically the generation of southern whites who, upon reaching adolescence in the late 1940s and early 1950s, fell under the sway of rhythm and blues. They were members of an audience who unexpectedly built a bridge between black and white working-class music. These adolescents introduced Acuff to Brown and discovered that older traditions could be modified and updated. Suddenly country music had a fresh face, one that appeared to be younger, less inhibited, and more open to innovation. As one *Billboard* writer noted, rockabilly's "new approach and modern styling has greatly boosted [its] stock" among "younger country music fans."[5]

Those who successfully incorporated r&b into their renditions of country music included women as well as men; such artists as Carl Perkins, Wanda Jackson, Jerry Lee Lewis, Barbara Pittman, Buddy Holly, Jean Chapel, Gene Vincent, Brenda Lee, Conway Twitty, Janis Martin, Johnny Cash, and Jo-Ann Campbell comprised an ever-expanding rockabilly roster. Through musical tastes and performance style, all blatantly tested the racial boundaries of their era. Yet in violating societal taboos related to race, they also disturbed conventional views regarding gender. As Mary Bufwack and Robert Oermann have suggested, "rockabilly threatened the social order when men adopted slithering wiggles and emotional sobbing, previously female-identified behavior; likewise, women challenged the status quo when they took on sassy manners and musical aggression." The rockabillies indeed demonstrated, to paraphrase historian George Lipsitz, that no one lives his life completely or solely in racial (or class or gendered or generational) terms. Any experience with race is "automatically inflected" by other social classifications, such as gender, class, generation, history, and regional identity. To understand the story of rockabilly is to reconcile these various sectors.[6]

To integrate such categories, however, threatens to disrupt existing boundaries and interpretations. Indeed, as the transgressive activities of the rockabillies forced the country music industry to enlarge its traditional purview, so too, should a reevaluation of the regional phenomenon push scholars to expand conventional explanations regarding the relationship between popular culture and those who utilize its products. For rockabilly, which fused the music and mannerisms of the black and white working class, provides an invaluable glimpse into the process by which individuals and groups employed popular culture to define themselves and the world around them. The specific adoption of black male urban style by white teenagers, for instance, arguably had as much to do with establishing an identity and dignity in a new and unsettling urban context as it did with finding an exciting alternative to the seemingly bland and homogenous popular music of the postwar era. Like honky-tonk, a genre that addressed the physical and cultural dislocations of an older generation, the southern version of rock 'n' roll represented a vehicle through which Dixie's younger displaced migrants could also adjust to an uncommon urban and modern environment. That many of the rockabillies looked upon black masculinity as a valuable "tool" to be used in their adjustment therefore raises issues that go beyond standard appraisals that focus solely on racial appropriation as a form of commercial exploitation. Examining rockabilly as a multifaceted manifestation of larger and conflicting postwar social forces promises to ask and perhaps even answer questions that will advance historical scholarship.

Bob Luman and Jimmy Snow, of course, each realized that various and contradictory social categories provocatively intersected in Presley, a white working-class teenager from Tupelo, Mississippi, who sounded black and possessed both feminine and masculine appeal. Yet despite the seismic reverberations Elvis and his musical and cultural promiscuity set off in the early years of the atomic age, historians have rarely been as moved as either Luman or Snow. Instead, they have customarily assigned Presley and rocka-billy footnote status in the growth of a national consumer culture that fol-lowed the Second World War, marginalizing the entire affair into quaint trivia. Even chroniclers of the South have adhered to an interpretation stressing mainstream homogeneity and slick packaging over regional diversity and sub-stance. Ultimately, this view maintains that the phenomenon represented little more than a superficial and tasteless diversion that briefly defied the monotony of the Eisenhower years. And if one accepts the postmortem exam-ination conducted by the historical profession, cultural guardians and institu-tional forces successfully isolated and contained the contagion, thereby preventing Elvis and rockabilly from causing any serious damage or leaving any permanent scars or impressions. As one esteemed historian of the twen-tieth century definitively concluded in a blurb, the singer was simply a "con-sumer culture hero" who sang "tunes that were instantly forgettable."[7]

Such a dismissal is emblematic of a mass culture perspective that reflects more the subjectivity of the historian than it does an objective depiction of the historical event. Yet in addition to highlighting the obvious political nature of "history," this viewpoint is also rudimentary; it assumes that through manipu-lation an omnipotent culture industry readily transforms dynamic individuals into a homogenous mob of passive consumers. By ignoring or obscuring a variety of inherent tensions and contradictions, it oversimplifies (and helps mystify) the popular culture process. For instance, there is little doubt that pop-ular culture, or more precisely, commercial culture, is subservient to corporate prerogatives and market forces and that its "agenda" is purely mercenary. This is a fact no one familiar with scholarship on the subject can deny. The author-ity of the corporate few, however, is not absolute. The domain in which they operate is chronically unsettled and fragmented, and is one where ingenuity is typically limited to appropriation. Culture industries may stimulate latent desires in order to mass produce, promote, and distribute product, yet they do not necessarily create that which is eventually sold. They must extract and exploit "raw" materials from elsewhere. This leaves ample room for active and genuine consumer participation, for the "masses" provide both "natural resources" and markets. Conversely, it is not always clear as to what audiences are "receiving" when they consume popular entertainment. Customer reception and application do not inexorably correspond to producer intention. Consequently, popular culture remains in everyday life, if not in academia, an often intricate, enigmatic, and persistently open-ended phenomenon.

Thus while the culture industries may have unveiled him to the larger world, they did not create or manufacture the culturally schizophrenic "Hillbilly Cat." Of course, this is not to suggest that Presley did not utilize popular culture to invent himself; to the contrary, he may provide a case study as to how consumers typically manipulate what they consume into a shape that meets their own needs. Still, despite his seemingly unorthodox appearance, demeanor, and singing style, he was an individual whose identity was connected to a particular place, time, and musical genre: the post–World War II American South and country music. While his success eventually transcended these original parameters, Presley's professional pursuits arguably had their greatest impact within the land of his birth. By referencing African American genres, he also acknowledged and reinscribed an ongoing country music narrative to which performers as diverse as Jimmie Rodgers, Bob Wills, Bill Monroe, Rose Maddox, Moon Mullican, and Hank Williams had already contributed.[8]

On the surface, equating Presley with country music may appear misguided. Some could reasonably argue that his relationship to country music seemed at best peripheral. After all, Elvis spent more time on Hollywood sound stages and in Las Vegas showrooms than he did at the Grand Ole Opry. True, he began his career as a hybrid hillbilly with the independent Sun Records label and spent the first eighteen months of his entertainment career touring the country music circuit of the South and Southwest. His country credentials also included a lifelong tendency to record in Nashville, using session musicians and background vocalists indispensable to artists such as Eddy Arnold, Patsy Cline, and Jim Reeves. During the latter years of his final comeback, he also became a fixture on country music popularity charts, ironically fulfilling mid-1950s predictions of his being the most promising artist in the hillbilly field. Yet as early as the autumn of 1955, RCA (the major recording company to which Sam Phillips of Sun Records sold Elvis's contract) made a calculated decision to exploit Presley's ability to reach various audiences, with no one region, style, or market predominating over any other.[9]

Contemporaries, however, recognized that Presley, despite the valiant efforts of public relations handlers, did not embody "the down-to-earth quality of the boy next door" essential to corporate strategy. Selling him would not be easy. Indigenous to a region that was historically impoverished and seemingly backward, benighted, and overtly racist, the black-sounding sharecropper's son from Mississippi *did not* inspire sitcom images of soda shops, manicured lawns, and *Ozzie and Harriet*. Rather, he resembled, as the national media proclaimed in drawing upon familiar and stereotypical images of both the South and country music, "a jug of corn liquor at a champagne party."[10]

As a southern white truckdriver who enjoyed a rags-to-riches ascent on the strength of a black gospel and rhythm and blues-inspired performing style, Elvis engendered controversies that have yet to subside. His explosive emergence indeed catapulted the unseemly issues of race and class onto a national stage, thus crashing the cold war celebration of melting pot unanimity and consensus. Yet what Presley's story can reveal is missed if he is simply and conventionally dismissed as an unthinking "Horatio Alger in drawl" or a misappropriating musical miscegenate. To crown him as "royalty" or disparage him as a "cultural thief" likewise achieves little. On the other hand, an approach that examines how he exemplified his generation and region might reveal a great deal.[11]

For instance, long before he titillated impressionable young lasses in poodle skirts while literally driving nervous parents, clerics, and television network censors into an arthritic tizzy, Presley behaved like many of the other 800 or so working-class white male students who attended L. C. Humes High School in Memphis. He loved working on and driving cars and motorcycles, playing rough-and-tumble sports such as football, going to the movies, and listening to the radio. Many of these adolescent activities would never be abandoned, even as Elvis grew into middle age. In addition, he was, by all accounts, an untrained and amateur musician who made choices in the recording studio as if he were a patron in a record store. He developed a varied repertoire based on what he and his fellow teens heard on the radio or on the jukebox. Unable to write his own songs, he parlayed a fan's eclectic and undisciplined approach to music into an enormously successful entertainment career. A voracious consumer of popular culture who longed to be the hero of the comic book while styled in the garb and guise of a Brando-like iconoclast, Elvis firmly believed that he owed his success to a Christian God who had mysteriously and inexplicably plucked him out of the crowd. Consequently, despite attaining vast wealth and fame, he remained, in many ways, a member of the audience he entertained, epitomizing the aspirations, frustrations, tastes, and especially the contradictions of a southern working class in transition. Arguably, the singer's greatest significance may have been his blurring of the racial boundaries that had for so long constricted his world, making him a telescopic figure for those seeking to comprehend the regional dynamics between race, class, and popular culture in the postwar era.[12]

Yet to understand fully the relationship between Presley's working-class background, racial transgressions, and investment in popular culture requires that one examine the singer from a perspective that also includes gender. Presley was, after all, an individual and performer who intentionally used his body to communicate, and not just in the manner popularly associated with his hip-swivelling stage routine. A teenaged Elvis's immersion in African American culture after he and his working-class family moved to Memphis from a small Mississippi town, for instance, was at least partly an attempt to manipulate his "body" and create an identity that would mitigate a migrant's invisibility. His appropriation of black music and comportment, combined with a zealous emulation of Hollywood actors, certainly contributed to a distinctive masculinity that Presley displayed through hair style, sideburns, clothing, speech, demeanor, and, of course, an explicit hedonistic and sexual stage presentation. In taking on such an exaggerated persona, Presley was arguably trying to establish that he was "somebody." Recalling the lyrics of two popular rhythm and blues songs from the early 1950s by Muddy Waters and Bo Diddley, respectively, Presley and those of his generation who followed a similar path proclaimed to the world, "I'm a Man!"

In emphasizing the importance of "manly" behavior and attitudes, Presley definitely heeded the southern working-class tradition of utilizing bodily expression to prove one's worth. Not confined to either side of the color line, this patriarchal ethos (independence, honor, dominance, and violence) typically manifested itself in the form of a physical presence that exuded self-assertiveness, aggressiveness, and competitiveness. Wilbur J. Cash provided the classic description of such behavior: "To stand on his head in a bar, to toss down a pint of raw whiskey at a gulp, to fiddle and dance all night, to bite off the nose or gouge out the eye of a favorite enemy, to fight harder and love harder than the next man, to be known eventually far and wide as a hell of a fellow—such would be his focus." And as one African American mother indicated, the "hell of a fellow" who engaged in violent behavior, sexual aggression, hedonistic activity, and excessive alcohol consumption was not limited by race: "Now my son, he has lots of entertainment. He goes to all dem dances on Saturday nights. I ain't feeling so favorable to that.... But he's got to look out for hisself now. He's a man like everybody else, I 'spects." W. E. B. DuBois indeed referred to such "loud and vulgar" manly affairs as "the transgression of the poor" represented by "disorder of all sorts, theft and burglary, fighting, breaking the gambling and liquor laws and especially fighting with and killing each other."[13]

Presley's wielding of visceral qualities that stressed an outward display of masculinity was apparently not unusual in the rural working-class South. It was expected. To do otherwise would have seemed odd and out of place. By turning to African American males in constructing their identities, however, Elvis and his contemporaries significantly modified the legacy they had inherited. In contrast to forebears who strenuously denied black contributions to their own deportment, Presley and others like him consciously and conspicuously emulated African American male urban style. Ironically, the larger ramifications and results of this dramatic reversal and how they may have contributed to or reflected the South's larger transformations in the post–World War II era have rarely been assessed or even acknowledged.

Yet it is a metamorphosis that deserves consideration. As historian Carl Degler has contended, whites have so adamantly denied the African American influence on their culture that the denial itself serves as a major theme of southern history. That many of the rockabillies rejected or at least ignored a tendency that had literally become a regional birthright is significant. Arguments that claim that they were simply obeying the dictates of mass culture do not fully reflect the intricacies of the moment. Contemporaries, for instance, noted that southern whites like Presley began listening to and venerating rhythm and blues performers long before it became fashionable elsewhere. As *Jet* magazine noted in 1954, "When white teenagers in the South go into a record store and ask for a 'cat' record, they mean one featuring Negro musicians." Significantly, the activities of these white "cat music-minded teenagers," like the music itself, long remained underground and below the entertainment industry's radar. In other words, they were ahead of the national rock 'n' roll curve. This raises an intriguing question. Why would southern working-class whites, steeped in a segregationist doctrine that considered African Americans to be debased, suddenly, by their own volition, turn to that minority culture to redefine themselves?[14]

The explanation that many historians and pop writers have provided is that whites like Presley, trapped within a bland, materialist, and conformist postwar American cultural straitjacket, sought an outlet through the mystery, excitement, thrills, and danger they associated with African Americans. These "white Negroes" or hillbilly hipsters assumed "black" characteristics as a means to find release from the confinement of a regimented and repressed mainstream culture that furnished little inner satisfaction. Temporarily morphing into imaginary black men allowed them to live dangerously and on the edge, to escape the boredom and homogeneity associated with a rapidly evolving corporate and mass society. It was this urge to rattle the placid fifties to which Greil Marcus referred when he suggested that "Rockabilly was the only style of early rock 'n' roll that proved white boys could do it all—that they could be as strange, as exciting, as scary, and as free as the black men who were suddenly walking America's airwaves as if they owned them."[15]

Marcus's premise is intriguing and does establish an important starting point for any investigation concerning Presley's explorations into black masculinity. It certainly raises questions as to what Presley and his contemporaries saw or imagined when they viewed African American males. Yet such a paradigm seems to discount that black and white southerners had been in contact for several centuries and that their shared regional experiences (however separate) may have lent a distinctive cast to rockabilly's racial appropriations. In his exploration of Southern culture, Wilbur J. Cash noted, "Negro entered into white man as profoundly as white men entered into Negro— subtly influencing every gesture, every word, every emotion and idea, every attitude." Surely Cash's conviction that there was an organic connection between black and white in Dixie suggested an atypical relationship. This is not to imply, of course, that stereotypical representations of black sexuality did not inform the racial perspectives of southern whites. The culture of segregation, with its various veils, masks, and myths guaranteed nothing less than misdirection, exaggeration, and outright fabrication. Furthermore, there is little question that rock 'n' roll, rockabilly, and rhythm and blues often presented African Americans as eccentric, exotic, and stereotyped Others. These representations undoubtedly appealed to and stirred the racial imaginations of southern white adolescents. It would be difficult to deny that popular rhythm and blues songs such as "Sixty-Minute Man," "Good Lovin'," "Honey Love," "Work With Me Annie," and "Big Ten Inch" did not reiterate traditional notions of black difference, particularly in regards to sexual behavior.[16]

Indeed, race and sex intertwined have long consumed white southerners to the point of obsession, a fixation that has historically produced tragic and violent consequences. African Americans have traditionally embodied a disgusting yet fascinating hypersexuality in the Caucasian imagination. This dialectic has had the effect of distorting and dehumanizing human beings. Did this objectification of black bodies fuel southern rockabillies in their quest for public virility? It certainly kindled an earlier entertainment form that many often compare to rock 'n' roll, blackface minstrelsy. Performing in greasepaint and burnt cork allowed whites (artists and audiences) to act out their own exotic, erotic, or primitive fantasies while rarely referencing real people. As Nathan Huggins noted, "the white man who put on the black face modeled himself after a subjective black man—a black man of lust and passion and natural freedom." When Presley and his contemporaries adopted their versions of a "black" persona, were they engaging in a similar endeavor? In its crossing of the color line, did rockabilly simply update a spurious blackface tradition?[17]

Ironically, the postwar rhythm and blues artists to whom Presley's generation regularly had access often presented an image that accentuated sexuality. *Tan* magazine, for instance, noted that B. B. King, a contemporary of Presley who had also migrated to Memphis from Mississippi, had replaced his rural mannerisms with qualities characterized as stylish and manly. "The boys along Beale [Street]," *Tan* intoned, "recognize B.B. as one of the sharpest cats on the stroll." Strolling, of course, signified an aesthetic personified through attire and body language, as Jackie Wilson revealed when he declared, "You've got to be cool in your duds." It also intimated something more basic. Explaining his enduring popularity as a well-dressed and suave rhythm and blues shouter, Wynonie Harris made a point that both audiences and artists well understood: "It's all because I deal in sex." In expressing themselves in this manner, r&b vocalists and musicians arguably contributed to and embellished an already elaborate mythology concerning the sexual conduct of African Americans. Significantly, these performances were not contrived for naive whites, whose relatively small numbers made them incidental to the rhythm and blues arena, but were instead directed almost exclusively at a minority audience. What role, then, did this particular emphasis on masculinity serve in the larger working-class black community?[18]

Perhaps the answer lies in Ralph Ellison's "Riddle of the Zoot." In 1943, the future author of *Invisible Man* advised the African American elite to heed the voices of the black working class, even though those voices might be expressed and couched in symbols and rituals that seemed strange, unfamiliar, and antithetical to middle-class mores. For to recognize the larger significance of music, dance styles, and apparel, Ellison proposed, would provide an innovative and effective framework in which to understand how "ordinary" people both resisted and accommodated themselves to the existing social order. As he surmised, "Much in Negro life remains a mystery; perhaps the zoot suit conceals profound political meanings; perhaps the Lindy-Hop conceals clues to great political power—if only Negro leaders would solve the riddle."[19]

The riddle of the zoot, if not the outfit itself—the ensemble emerged in the World War II era—had its origins in the turn-of-the-century South. Beginning in the 1880s and 1890s, and continuing in a cyclical fashion for several decades, depressed economic conditions drove countless numbers of African Americans from the land, where they toiled and lived as sharecroppers, and into the city, where they hoped to find work. For black women, the search often proved fruitful, as urban middle-class white women desired domestics to labor in their homes. For black men, however, the results were not so auspicious. Unable to find permanent employment in the racially segregated industrial and commercial sectors of the city, African American males tended to move from one demeaning job to another. More often than not idled by lack of opportunity, they generally found themselves pushed to the fringes of their community, both literally and figuratively. It was not uncommon, for instance, to find in urban areas groups of unemployed or underemployed black men habitually congregated on street corners and in pool halls and jukejoints. Many typically relied on pool hustling, petty crime, and simultaneous relationships with several different employed women, usually domestic servants, for their livelihood. It was a harsh existence that arose in response to their social, racial, and economic marginalization. Out of psychological necessity, as historian Joel Williamson has ascertained, these estranged individuals produced a set of values that justified and romanticized their way of life.[20]

It was a set of values that exalted a street-corner, countercultural, and male adulating society. The "victims" of racial and economic oppression transformed themselves into "heroes" who haughtily inverted the reasons for their less than utopian existence. If one could find no available employment (in an environment where there was little work to be had), he rationalized that he was too smart to work. If he could attain no marital stability (in an economic, racial, and gendered climate that emasculated men), it was because he was too highly sexed to be satisfied with one woman. If he fathered numerous children with several different women (in an impersonal world that denied his very being), he could boast of his generative power. Williamson identified these black male protagonists as "hipster-tricksters," deftly placing them within an oppositional or subversive tradition that harkened back to slavery and that continued to evolve later within the blues. While unlikely to enhance their status with whites or African Americans of the middle class who would have considered such behavior dubious at best, hipster-tricksters nevertheless utilized a value system that provided a feeling of personal satisfaction, fulfillment, and triumph. And as Charles Kreil has suggested, the working-class community from which they emerged considered them not to be social deviants, but rather cultural heroes to be admired and emulated. They had, after all, defied several obstacles meant to deprive them of their individuality, pride, and dignity.[21]

In seeking to understand the "hipster-trickster," historian Robin D. G. Kelley has argued that it is imperative to place the figure within both a sociohistorical and aesthetic context. He maintains that the "hipster-trickster" represented a masculine formation that served several purposes. It facilitated "constructing an identity, communicating with others, and achieving pleasure." While definitely a "coping strategy" utilized daily against racism, poverty, and oppression, this example of ritualized black masculinity also embodied something more. Specifically, it provided a means for men to create an alternate space or identity so that they could rest, play, and recuperate under conditions that they controlled. Doing so allowed them to take back and do what they wished with their own bodies. In this regard, for example, clothing was extremely important in enhancing one's attractiveness to the opposite sex, which in turn heightened one's self-esteem. Having fun, making fun, and playing with words and images were also part of this equation, as they had been for generations of African Americans seeking to ameliorate historically insufferable conditions. Surely Lovin' Dan of "Sixty-Minute Man" (and perhaps more importantly of "Can't Do Sixty No More") fame did not likely correspond to an actual individual; yet in representing an imaginary upside-down world where the oppressed outwitted, outperformed, or supplanted the powerful, he did recall the traditions of playfulness, storytelling, and irreverence central to black vernacular culture. Ironically, his purported libidinous antics may have also suggested the absurdity of prevailing racial and sexual stereotypes.[22]

Overall, as Kelley has asserted, the activities, accessories, attire, and apocryphal anecdotes that accentuated the appearance of black male potency provided young African American working-class men with a sense of empowerment and gratification that is difficult to measure or ignore. Often adorned with bravado, humor, or nonchalance, or a complex combination of all three, the black expression of masculinity indeed embodied a style and language that conveyed pride, poise, and pleasure to all within the community.

As fans of rhythm and blues, young working-class white adults like Elvis gained entry, albeit a limited one, into this community. Once inside, their own estranged social position surely affected how they perceived and acted upon the imagery of black masculinity that they encountered. As the sons of tenant farmers, sharecroppers, truck and tractor drivers, factory workers, miners, and sundry blue-collar laborers whom southern society had derisively reconfigured into "white-trash," "crackers," "rednecks," and "hillbillies," these white r&b enthusiasts knew what it meant to be marginalized and stripped of dignity. Indeed, they lived in a hierarchical society that caustically emphasized both white supremacy *and* white inferiority. As Hortense Powdermaker observed, "crackers," "rednecks," and other dependent men represented "the most despised class in the South, shunned and scorned by both whites and Negroes." One historian of the region declared that the general perception has almost always been that such whites exemplified the "last dregs of our sick society, the ultimate bottom of the barrel." Thus,

Elvis Presley's affinity for African American culture went beyond his love of music. In emulating the attire, hairstyles, and demeanor of black rhythm and blues artists, Elvis arguably sought to enhance his own masculinity. Bobby "Blue" Bland and "Little Junior" Parker, pictured here, utilized a style and deportment that helped them to attain dignity and respect within a culture of segregation. Ironically, they also became the role models for a young and impressionable Elvis.

while recent scholars have suggested that "whiteness" represents a form of property protected and esteemed in the public arena, this group demonstrated that its value widely fluctuated according to differing times, places, and social conditions. For many whites in the Jim Crow South, any objective appraisal would certainly have declared their "property" condemned.[23]

Possessing little power, integrity, or "property" that others in the larger community were obliged to recognize or respect—William Alexander Percy, for instance, admonished that "they were the sort of people that attend revivals and fight and fornicate in the bushes afterward"—the South's white masses, like their black counterparts, were also accustomed to having to create alternate spaces where pride and pleasure could be attained. As a people who, despite laborious efforts and exertions, traditionally enjoyed few gratifications associated with material success or political privilege, such recuperative intervals and postures furnished a significant source of personal satisfaction. Unable to win, or even join the game, according to existing middle-class conventions, they instead followed their own rules. In short, they focused upon assets other than work, accumulation, and self-discipline to enhance their self-worth. To achieve self-fulfillment as well as self-respect within their own community, they concentrated more on *"being* than *becoming."* And "being," Louis Rubin explained, meant focusing "on one's existence as a recognizable individual in a social fabric designed above all to provide for individual identity."[24]

From the perspective of the elite, this emphasis on "being" was synonymous with the inability of working whites to control their sensual and instinctual urges and only confirmed their inferiority. In characterizing the poor southern white male in search of emotional and physical gratification as "one of the most complete hedonists ever recorded," Cash indeed touched upon a quality that reiterated for many the ultimate debasement of the southern masses, black and white. They were a people whose lifestyles flouted middle-class notions and whom others recognized by their "improvidence, moral degeneracy, lack of ambition, and indifference to profitable labor." In a status-oriented society that valued order and class-based notions of civility, in other words, they were out of control. For the region's proletariat, however, being "out of control" represented a liberating space that literary scholar Mikhail Bakhtin would have characterized as carnivalesque—a Saturday-night romp typified by "a suspension of all hierarchical rank, privileges, norms, and prohibitions," a time where "life is subject only to its laws." In other words, it was where the powerless subverted authority and freedom reigned, at least within its particular space. Sociologist Charles Johnson stressed that such endeavors were "characteristic of all peasant merrymaking, a reaction to, and escape from, the other extreme of their life-cycle." And in a patriarchal culture where men stressed competition as a means to prove their worth—indeed, women were often viewed as objects to be possessed or prizes to be won—such "Saturday-night" venues and incarnations provided the opportunity for men to phrase or couch their search for dignity, pleasure, and escape in sexist terms. For the southern community expected men to sow their wild oats—or as Florence King noted, "what passes for [male] sanity is dependent upon heterosexual performance." As I. A. Newby understated, "This was a society of male prerogative and double standards."[25]

Bill Malone has argued that the preservation of honor compelled southern white men to excel at both physical feats and oral displays of masculinity such as boasting, bragging, and exaggerating. Given this regional heritage of male privilege and rivalry, it can be argued that Presley's immersion in black music and style represented a novel and distinctive reading of southern tradition. It was an attempt to assert his individuality by patterning his behavior and demeanor on that of strong male role models available to him, specifically rhythm and blues performers. Rather than a modern-day blackface excursion into romanticized darkness, *a la* Huggins or Marcus, Elvis was adopting a masculine persona associated with actual working-class African American males. And he was appropriating this form of *machismo* for the same reason that black men utilized it, mainly to demonstrate his manhood within a society in which his dignity and self-respect as a gendered being had traditionally been under constant assault.[26]

Presley's adaptation of a particular African American male persona, of course, would not produce an exact facsimile. Nevertheless, his excursions across the color line highlighted the distinctly biracial nature of Southern culture. What many often assume to be a "black style," for instance, may more accurately be assessed as a product of working-class regional culture. For instance, the characteristics that Eric Lott has attributed exclusively to African American males, mainly the qualities of "cool, virility, humility, abandon, or *gaite de couer*," could be assigned in similar forms and at various times to southern white men on the bottom of the socioeconomic and status pyramid. Charles Joyner has even surmised that traits emphasizing this form of masculinity could have originated in Great Britain, developed further in a southern Anglo-American milieu, and then found their way into the African American community. As he proposed, thus muddying existing interpretations even further, the masculine attributes which some scholars assume that white males appropriated from African Americans may have been "in fact characteristics learned by the slaves from Celtic whites."[27]

Consequently, rockabilly represented the culmination of a centuries-long dialogue between two underclass groups the southern elite lumped together as lazy, dependent, and biologically inferior. The upper-class inclination to minimize racial differences among working-class natives conceded that while law and custom may have kept blacks and whites legally and physically apart, they could not keep them culturally separate. Due to a corresponding low position on the socioeconomic and status structure, a similar elite abhorrence of each, and an analogous reliance on a preindustrial or folk lifestyle, working-class southerners of both races were predisposed to the merging of black and white along cultural lines.[28]

To be sure, the merger was not necessarily a welcome one, especially among marginalized working whites whose social and economic impotence openly flouted the logic of white supremacy. After all, as Hortense Powdermaker noted, many whites painfully recognized that blacks "are making progress, and for the most part, they [themselves] are not." To have failed so miserably in a racial system that privileged whiteness indeed left an indelible mark. As Gunnar Myrdal discovered, "This class of whites knows that upper-class whites are disposed to regard them as 'just as bad as niggers.' " Not surprisingly, working-class white southerners were openly antagonistic toward any suggestion that their culture represented a biracial mélange. Surely no group worked harder to escape or prevent interaction with their African American counterparts. Surely no group believed more passionately in the resolve, as stated by historian U. B. Phillips, that the "South shall be and remain a white man's country."[29]

Such a resolve suggested a cultural impossibility. Yet individuals maintained the illusion by adhering to an informal set of codes known as southern etiquette. Granted an urgency by the perpetual threat of violence, etiquette demanded that southerners engage in outward behavior that sustained white supremacy and black inferiority. Both black and white took to the social stage, acting out roles that were assigned to them. For African American males, this meant public displays of passivity, submission, and deference. For whites, the masquerade involved the concealment of intimate or human feelings for their black counterparts. It was an extremely inhibiting system, one that stressed pretense. Whites believed only what they saw;

African Americans revealed only what whites expected. Over time, standard-ized routine became so ingrained that its practice was simply taken for granted. Yet its effect was remarkably powerful. Southern etiquette worked at separating the races more effectively than any legislation ever could have accomplished. Blacks and whites may have lived side by side for centuries, yet as southern native William Alexander Percy tragically noted, "the sober fact is we understand one another not at all."[30]

Nevertheless, etiquette allowed southern whites to dwell not on what they were, which was often socially, politically, and economically disfranchised, but to focus on what they were not. And what they were not were African Americans. They thereby conjured a mythical world where African Americans were perceived as completely alien and different from themselves. The gov-ernment-endorsed doctrine of separate and *unequal* created a system of institutional discrimination that only reiterated their differences. Accordingly, whites convinced themselves that their black neighbors were savage, uncivi-lized, and inhuman. An imperfect logic became a rationale that evolved into a burdensome tradition. This inheritance helped sustain a cultural environ-ment where myth and reality were indistinguishable. The result, as Ralph Ellison noted in 1947, was that the southern community was a place where blacks received "uninterested-in-you-as-a-human-being" stares, "the kind that swept over a black man as though he were a horse or an insect."[31]

When examining Presley's explorations into black masculinity, it is impor-tant to keep southern racial reality in mind. After all, this was a region where whites, in order to deprive African American men of their dignity and individ-uality, habitually refused to call them "sir" or "mister" and invariably referred to them instead as "boys." Indeed, negative and disrespectful attitudes toward the black southern male were historically ingrained deep in the psyche of the white southerner. Such perspectives had existed for generations. Fur-nished with this knowledge, the historian must then address rockabilly's larger implications. While many assume that it represented little more than a meaning-less teenage consumer and musical craze, such a view disengages the pheno-menon from its southern racial, class, and gender roots. It ignores southern racial etiquette.[32]

As a musical form, of course, rockabilly was not unusual in its merging of black and white. Southern vernacular music claimed a mixed West African and British ancestry that historically defied strict racial classification. The durable interracial nature and appeal of such genres as the blues, jazz, country, and black and white gospel truly provided rockabilly with a substantial musical pedigree. Yet such earlier forms generally existed within confines that southern etiquette prescribed. Musicians and audiences understood and adhered to the rules and roles that custom dictated. This was especially true in what many traditionally referred to as the hillbilly field.[33]

In country music prior to the 1950s, cultural and racial practices decreed that the black influence inherent within many white male performers remain strictly implicit. This despite the fact that the rural and isolated South of the first half of the twentieth century often necessitated that black and white natives share a common performance repertoire. It was not unusual, for instance, for rural black and white musicians to render music customarily identified with one race or the other. The music's racial origins, however, were rarely emphasized. Even when the African American influence within early country music appeared quite evident, allusions to it consistently remained cryptic. While several country artists professed that exposure to African American musicians during their formative years had definitely been an important component in their own makeup, the environment in which they performed as mature artists prohibited a direct or open association with their black contemporaries.[34]

This is not to suggest, however, that the racial dividing line within country music was always observed. In the 1920s and early 1930s, several individuals, such as Henry Whitter, Frank Hutchinson, Dick Justice, Jimmie Tarleton, the Allen Brothers, and the Delmore Brothers performed in styles that often crossed traditionally observed racial parameters. Others, like Jimmie Davis, Cliff Carlisle, and a young Gene Autry, engaged in blues material that emphasized a risque sexual symbolism also associated with African American males. Similarly, after World War II, hillbilly boogie artists such as Arthur "Guitar Boogie" Smith, the Maddox Brothers and Rose, Moon Mullican, Red Foley, and Tennessee Ernie Ford successfully incorporated the latest blues techniques and trends into their existing music and stylings. Yet no matter how much such country musicians may have borrowed from their African American counterparts, their music, style, appearance, and demeanor remained orthodox in relation to their genre and culture.[35]

The blackface minstrelsy tradition that persisted within the southern and country entertainment field through the early years of the post–World War II era arguably helped protect this color line. Many white country artists dabbled in blackface or black-based humor and they, like their audiences, were very cognizant of the racial boundaries they could or could not cross. Although some, like Jimmie Rodgers, may have exhibited a certain degree of intuitive attachment to black culture through repertoire or style, many others executed black material or routines within a satirical context that negated any possible perception that imitation represented the sincerest form of flattery. While there did exist a tradition of "nigger-picking" and "nigger-singing" in white country music, the performance of "nigger blues" for many whites simply meant "going through an accepted act." Again, southern etiquette precluded any serious or nonstereotypical interracial transactions to occur between black and white. It denied that the two groups actually shared a culture. To correlate their experiences with those of their black counterparts would have seemed absurd, if not offensive, for southern white natives accustomed to viewing African Americans only as caricatured and loathsome Others.[36]

What distinguished many rockabilly artists and audiences from their hillbilly predecessors, therefore, was a willingness to identify completely with the rhythm and blues singers they emulated. They were not pretending to be, making fun of, or ridiculing black artists. Neither were they middle-class "slummers" momentarily escaping into an exciting and thrilling world that granted them a freedom, spontaneity, and emotional catharsis traditionally repressed within a bourgeois culture of which they were not a part. They were members of a southern working class that had not internalized conventional middle-class values or decorum. Their distinctive behavior (particularly sensuality), dialects, tastes, and dispositions separated them from the rather constrictive character of the bourgeois mainstream. This very alienation made them culturally closer to their black counterparts than conventional or blackface interpretations indicate. While this does not necessarily explain Elvis's attachment to African American style—after all, countless numbers of previous country performers had analogous life experiences and they did not gravitate to rhythm and blues—it does place Presley's racial appropriations within a more precise context. In short, Presley emerged from a "hillbilly" culture that was neither bland nor uninventive.

Why, then, *did* Presley and others like him gravitate toward rhythm and blues? The answer lies only partly with the music itself, since rockabilly did not erupt out of a social vacuum. It emerged from the still-shifting gravel of a "bulldozer revolution" that, beginning in the early 1940s, had induced regional instability and readjustment. An isolated rural world of tradition, poverty, and racial segregation hesitantly yielded to one of industrialization, urbanization, and integration. Migrants, especially those who were older, often confronted the new realities with reluctance and trepidation. They also braved the reformation armed with their music. For many, that music was honky-tonk, a genre that attempted to create a sense of community and continuity for rural migrants seeking work and a better life in the city. While by no means an absolute characterization, the music appealed to many people who had failed; their move to urban areas ultimately signaled their inability to succeed where many would have preferred to stay.[37]

Electrically amplified to be heard over the din of crowded venues, honky-tonk addressed the painful predicaments and problems of everyday life in a way that resonated with its alienated listeners. The music reflected themes that centered on the difficulties of social readjustment: isolation, frustration, loneliness, unfamiliarity, domestic tension, marital infidelity, drinking, and the honky-tonk itself. Countless numbers of displaced men, suddenly made insecure in their status and identity, gathered together in barrooms to reassert their manhood. They shared a sense of fellowship that converged around their recollections of the past, tribulations of the present, and visions of the future. Their feelings were confirmed and given voice as they listened to jukeboxes blaring songs that stressed within their lyrics and imagery both the past and the present. In creating a bridge between tradition and modernity, honky-tonk helped acclimate untold numbers of former inhabitants of the countryside to the rhythms and demands of urban life. For many, however, it also revealed that backward-looking fathers, uncles, and older brothers were not necessarily the best role models for dealing with a new and exciting urban cultural landscape.[38]

Like their parents and older siblings, the younger sons, daughters, brothers, and sisters who migrated to the city also struggled with transition. Not as deeply rooted in a rural past, they generally came of age in a modern setting that forced them to develop a different world outlook. Significantly, unlike that of many of their parents, their first brush with modernity signaled promise, not failure; the future, not the past. This was particularly true in regards to the issue of race. In contrast to previous natives whose attitudes were defined and conditioned by southern etiquette, postwar adolescents had varied racial perspectives presented to them at a relatively early age. Younger people consequently were exposed to a novel terrain that included "black appeal" radio programming which emphasized the affirmative nature of African American life, an urban street-corner culture that stressed black male dignity and independence, and an aggressive rhythm and blues that neutralized feelings of isolation and immateriality. Gaining such exceptional access to racial realities that challenged traditional segregationist ideology and etiquette encouraged many southern white teenagers to reassess previous convictions. Though never perfect or comprehensive in their course or scope, the ensuing negotiations divulged that the racial attitudes of younger working-class white southerners during the postwar period were neither monolithic nor uncomplicated. They were under construction.[39]

Uprooted working-class southern white adolescents arguably turned to black culture because African American males had already demonstrated an ability to make a successful transition from a rural to an urban environment. Black males had established their individuality and identity within the unfamiliar confines of the city by accentuating their masculinity. In emulating black style through dress, speech, demeanor, and the manner of presenting themselves, many of the rockabilly generation were attempting to connect to their African American counterparts. In their search for a means to accentuate *their* masculinity, they had indeed discovered that they and African Americans shared common ground. Consequently, the lines distinguishing black from white suddenly became less obvious, thereby creating room for negotiation. It was a space that allowed many to go beyond convention, to traverse the racial divide. Black-oriented radio played a major role in this aspect; it was a nonvisual medium that allowed many whites to relate to the voices and consequent stories, anecdotes, and experiences they heard. Accordingly, it was the unprecedented degree of its attachment to black music and culture that separated the rockabilly generation from its more orthodox country forerunners.

Far removed from the anguished sounds and worldviews of cynical honky-tonk heroes Webb Pierce and Lefty Frizzell, Presley's r&b-spiced hillbilly renderings indeed met the needs of this younger, more optimistic audience. The music was exciting, and when artists and audiences raised in the country music tradition shouted on and reveled in songs such as "Good Rockin' Tonight," "Put Your Cat Clothes On," "Rave On," and "Whole Lotta Shakin' Goin' On," no one confused the resulting pandemonium with what had become recognized as the "cry in your beer" character of honky-tonk. Such a departure from contemporary convention, however, upset the music's traditional followers. The honky-tonk shadow was a long one. Critics bemoaned Presley's inclusion in the country field as an alien invasion, ultimately objecting that he was "not real country." As one fan complained, "I hate to think that such wonderful fellas as Red Foley, Ernest Tubb, and Marvin Rainwater are being lumped together into the same category as Presley." Another emphatically suggested the singer be allowed to ply his trade in another field: "Elvis Presley (the tin god of teenagers) has no business in country music. Let him take his hiccoughing style and howl elsewhere. He has degraded country music long enough!"[40]

Indeed, as one disk jockey told his listeners, "Rhythm and blues does not belong and has no business in the country music field. It never has in the past; it does not now in the present, and will not in the future." Many referred to the merging of country with rhythm and blues as "mongrel music." A writer to a music trade magazine explained that she did not think rhythm and blues was country music. "In my opinion, its not any kind of music. I love country music too much to want to see it polluted for even a little while." And as another letter writer complained, "This junk called rhythm and blues is not good listening. It doesn't make sense, and it has no message. Nothing but a heavy beat and a meaningless jumble of words and very little melody." One observer stated simply: "I don't think that [the] r&b and bop boys should invade the country and western field because they murder our country music!"[41]

That rockabilly's emergence coincided with the Supreme Court's *Brown v. Board of Education* decision desegregating public schools cannot be discounted when addressing such criticism. Demonstrating that culture and society do not act independently of one another, the music's racial ambivalence obviously agitated an already volatile environment. Much of the opposition it generated amongst traditional country music fans, therefore, embodied a complex set of emotions. It is interesting, however, that rockabilly represented only a limited union of country music and rhythm and blues. African American artists themselves did not accompany black music into the commercial hillbilly field or popularity charts. As one music insider explained, "After all, this was the Deep South in the mid-1950s, and I didn't think the region's country music fans were quite ready for a black performer." Countless numbers apparently were not prepared for rhythm and blues-singing white performers, either. "Most of our regular patrons were traditional country music fans, a big percentage of them in their thirties, forties, fifties, and even older. This music was so different from anything these people had ever heard before they didn't know how to react." Several industry executives displayed no such ambivalence; they were very direct in their assessment. They wanted Presley expelled from country music because "he sings nigger music."[42]

The blatant synthesis of country and rhythm and blues shocked the multitudes because it did not appear to be "natural." Its white practitioners seemed to be flaunting tradition, not embracing it. Their overt sexuality particularly proved disconcerting. When Bill Malone, a fan and future historian of rural roots music, first encountered Presley's act in a 1955 Hank Snow jamboree, for instance, he was repulsed and dismayed. There to see the popular and conventional Snow, Malone instead watched in horror as hordes of teenagers ardently displayed their devotion for what appeared to be an unconventional pelvis-grinding exhibitionist. According to the then University of Texas student, "the future of country music was dim." Later, Malone would alter his opinion, claiming that Presley and the other rockabillies "were actually fusing the crucial elements of southern music—country, blues, gospel—in creating their own vital styles." Veteran *Billboard* columnist Paul Ackerman realized at the time what Malone later came to comprehend. Southern country artists like Presley, he observed, understood rhythm and blues—"much more so, it may be said, than many [national] pop artists and writers who aspire to R&B." As Ackerman astutely argued, the rhythm and blues and country music categories, though socially and commercially segregated, "have never been far apart."[43]

Although Ackerman was referring to music, his assessment subtly addressed the complex and often contradictory relationship between race, class, and gender in the South. If Elvis and rockabilly indeed ushered in a regional "revolution," it was one that ultimately revealed the illegitimacy of southern racial etiquette. As Eldridge Cleaver once insisted, Presley, by openly acknowledging and associating with African Americans, "dared to do in the light of day what America had been doing in the sneak-thief anonymity of night—[he] consorted on a human level with blacks." And by doing so, by breaking down an artificial barrier, Presley and the music he espoused gave southern whites the opportunity to do away with pretense—although obviously not all would do so—and develop a sense of humanity that southern racial etiquette had always prevented. In short, it allowed people to be themselves, to develop relationships unencumbered by restrictive custom. It relieved them from the South's heaviest and most tragic burden.[44]

By adopting elements of African American style, Elvis also confounded regional definitions of white manhood. Historically, to be a black male in the segregated South, where a wrong move invariably carried the potential of violent reprisal, ordinarily involved maintaining a persona that expressed itself covertly or in ways that did not openly threaten the racial order. The qualities of "cool," "abandon," or "humility," however, while seemingly safe means of racial subversion, could be characterized by the dominant culture as signs of weakness or submission, and therefore associated with femininity. The same held true for physical adornments. Loud or garish apparel, pompadours, and ornate jewelry, although used to confer individuality, otherwise had little utilitarian value and were generally considered effeminate. Yet as Charles Kreil has suggested, African American men utilized such attributes to enhance their sex appeal, a move that likewise heightened their masculinity: "Prettiness (wavy hair, manicured nails, frilly shirts, flashy jackets) plus strength, tender but tough—this is the style that many Negro women find irresistible." In creating his persona, Presley found it irresistible as well, and for the same reasons as his black counterparts. Accordingly, his "biracial" public identity was one that embraced bravado *and* sensitivity. It conveyed both "male" and "female" qualities as they were perceived by his society.[45]

As Presley sang and gyrated in Bob Luman's hometown, he exhibited a sense of freedom of which many teenagers would partake. By crossing racial boundaries and violating taboos in regard to his musical tastes, he indicated that he would not submit to authority or be shackled to the past. Even more, his physical appearance and mischievous dancing on stage insinuated that he, and no one else, had control over his own body. He would express himself in whatever manner he chose. His audiences, many of them young women, responded accordingly, showing that they too, possessed the power to determine how they would act. Thus, as Bob Luman's description at the beginning of this essay suggests, Presley's muddling of the rules regarding race also obfuscated the lines that governed gender in Dixie. Or was it his muddling of the rules regarding gender that obfuscated the lines governing race?

In scholarship, as in life, the singer obviously remains an enigma. He was not political in any sense and surely did not intend to change his society, yet his emergence certainly raises questions concerning the relationship between popular culture and social change. Placing Elvis and his sexually charged persona and musical style into a larger historical context that recognizes the interrelationship between race and gender (as well as class, generation, regional identity, and popular culture) indeed affords a glimpse of the tensions and conflicts that dwelled below the postwar southern societal surface. Granting Presley serious regard in this manner has the potential to complicate an era and region that we have often assumed to be uncomplicated.

"I Wanna Play House"

Configurations of Masculinity in the Nashville Sound Era

DIANE PECKNOLD

The Nashville Sound, producer Billy Sherrill once quipped, was made for "the housewife washing dishes at ten a.m. in Topeka, Kansas." Music critic John Morthland suggested a similar audience for the smooth countrypolitan style in the 1960s when he observed that, "like country people, country music was moving to the suburbs," in the process becoming "primarily listening music, even easy listening music." If honky-tonk had been the lament of men displaced by war and economic upheaval, and rockabilly the sexual braggadocio of their adolescent sons, then the Nashville Sound, with its angelic backing vocals and orchestral strings, was the soggy reverie of the postwar suburban wife. "Pandering to that imaginary housewife's sense of propriety," journalist Patrick Carr has argued, eviscerated country and quashed innovation in the 1960s. "The honky-tonk blues, the hillbilly fever, the rockabilly fire—all core ingredients of the country musician's most powerful creative reality—couldn't be allowed to show in public," presumably because female listeners could not appreciate them. Drifting oil-field cowboys were replaced by effete crooners in dinner jackets. Country music's masculine edge, the consensus seems to indicate, was driven underground to winter over until the emergence of the Bakersfield sound and the Outlaw movement.[1]

A number of commentators have observed that performances of masculinity constitute an important part of country's "core" identity, particularly in rusticated styles like honky-tonk, the Bakersfield sound, and the Outlaw movement. But just as honky-tonk's appeal drew on its ironic performance of the stereotypical poor white Southern male, and the Outlaws on their half-serious burlesque of the rugged artistic individualist as frontier gunslinger, so the mature, commercialized aesthetic of the Nashville Sound represented its own brand of masculinity. This vision, in keeping with postwar social norms, cast masculinity in a distinctly domestic light, as a combination of father-hood, breadwinning, and, for white-collar workers, corporate success.[2]

This particular ideal of manhood became important in Nashville in the late 1950s and early 1960s not only because it was prevalent everywhere in the nation, but also because it meshed with changes in the way country music was produced. Music Row emerged during those years as a fully formed commer-cial music center, complete with sophisticated recording facilities, licensing agencies, and local representation of major record labels. This elaboration of the corporate structure was accompanied by the rise of a new generation of executives whose personal histories were steeped in mainstream corporate culture. As it achieved full integration with the larger popular music industry, those in the country music field worked to fashion a new professional image for themselves, to counter the prevailing consensus that theirs was music made "by hillbillies for hillbillies." Much of that effort fell to the Country Music Association (CMA), which assumed the task of marketing country music to entertainment, advertising, and broadcasting executives. Through sales pre-sentations, consulting projects, and other public relations activities, the CMA challenged the traditional cultural hierarchies and stereotypes that had long denigrated the country field. Gender discourse became a key symbolic lan-guage for communicating the industry's claims to professionalism and respect. Country music's representatives wanted to reach broadcasters and advertisers where they lived—literally—by capitalizing on what they imagined to be the intimate life of the white-collar male: his relationship with his wife, his status anxieties, his personal investment in the ideology of the self-made company man. The experience of the middle-class breadwinner both moti-vated and underpinned the industry's efforts to revise its professional image.[3]

But even as the CMA and other elements of the industry deployed middle-class gender norms to make the country music business palatable to media executives, the genre's commercial power remained rooted in the image of the blue-collar man. The Nashville country industry staked its claim to indepen-dence from the popular music establishment by proclaiming its unique ability to deliver the nation's average working men as "the largest unduplicated audience in the world." Despite complaints that country music was selling out to middle-class pretensions, the commercialized image of the Nashville Sound was intended for working-class audiences, and it reinforced the era's prevailing faith that the fruits of American democracy were best represented by the universal consumerism it made possible. While other popular culture media, particularly film, represented the working-class male as sexually aggressive, violent, and authoritarian, country music celebrated the success of the blue-collar patriarch, especially his dignity as a skilled worker and his achievement in providing his family with the consumer commodities that defined the good life.[4]

This analysis challenges the standard historical assessment of the Nashville Sound era, which equates the softening of the genre's sound with a feminization of its target audience. Instead, it suggests that the industry pursued a bifurcated strategy that sold middle-class masculinity and a blue-collar male audience to media executives, while marketing country music to its traditional working-class audience. This approach also shows that the redirection of country's image in these years can be described in part as a response to men's experiences of corporate culture and their expectations about family life. Finally, it extends work by scholars who have identified home and family as core themes in country music by demonstrating that these values have structured the genre's production as well as its imagery and defined male as well as female experience.[5]

The Man in the Grey Flannel Nudie Suit

In 1958, Jack Stapp, former program manager at WSM, home of the Grand Ole Opry, made a recruiting speech on behalf of country music's newly formed professional organization, the Country Music Association. Addressing several hundred artists, DJs, and businessmen who had gathered for WSM's annual DJ convention, Stapp urged those in his audience to invest in the future of their profession by joining the CMA. But rather than positioning his male listeners as artists or executives, he appealed to them first as fathers and husbands. "Country music has helped to house you and your family, it has medicated your children, it has furnished you with the automobile you are driving," he told them. "This is your livelihood. This business is furnishing you with the funds to raise a family and make you secure." The CMA, he promised, would help "accomplish our real goal: the goal of making more money for you, your family, and raising the prestige of our industry."[6]

Stapp's appeal that day was very much in earnest. The CMA was a fledgling organization with uncertain prospects, and membership dues were sorely needed. While later public relations pronouncements often served mainly as paeans to the grand tradition of country music, this first recruiting speech offered an unvarnished assessment of the serious problems that faced the country music industry as the new decade approached. "We all know that there has been hushed-up and toned-down talk about country music," Stapp said, confiding what his audience already knew about the genre's recent sales slump. "It's unpleasant, but let's be true to ourselves and admit that one year ago at this convention the question was raised . . . 'How long will there be a country music disc-jockey?' "[7]

In this context of unease, Stapp's evocation of the private lives of his listeners seems particularly significant. By appealing to his mostly male audience in their roles as fathers and breadwinners, he hoped to use the ideology of 1950s masculine domesticity to spur them to action. The postwar emphasis on marriage, family, and distinct gender roles for men and women was neither simply a continuation of older mores nor a natural result of the scarcity of war followed by the prosperity of peace. Instead, as historian Elaine Tyler May has shown, it represented a response to specific features of American society during the cold war. Large corporations increasingly eclipsed small, self-owned businesses as the mainstay of the employment market, and the home offered men an opportunity to balance the anonymity and conformity of organization life with an expressive personal life. A secure home and children also symbolized a connection with the future in the face of possible nuclear annihilation. And with ethnic and community ties attenuated by geographic and social mobility, the nuclear family became for many Americans their central connection to the past and its traditions. The family was idealized as a central site for emotional fulfillment, personal autonomy, and even the maintenance of a healthy democracy.[8]

The weighty expectations attached to the ideal of the prosperous nuclear family necessarily created anxieties for those charged with satisfying them. Many men found themselves trying to live out an "impossible synthesis of sober responsible breadwinner, imperviously stoic master of his fate, and swashbuckling hero." The role of breadwinner became synonymous with manhood; earning power and success within the corporate structure were increasingly the measure of masculinity. In one survey conducted during the 1950s, fathers rated breadwinning as the second most important aspect of their roles as parents, just slightly below "guide and teacher." Fathers described themselves as "the guy who pays the bill" or "a good meal ticket." A respondent to another survey acknowledged that his professional ambitions grew out of his home life; "a family which I very much admire and enjoy doing my best to provide for," he said, had made him "more eager to succeed in business and financially." Other observers were more pointed in their assignation of gendered duties, particularly where income was concerned. One sociologist declared that, "Women must bear and rear children; husbands must support them." His colleague expanded the maxim beyond fatherhood to define manhood itself: "The American male, by definition, *must* provide for his family. He is *responsible* for his support of his wife and children. His primary area of performance is the occupational role."[9]

The CMA's appeal to the private lives of male country music professionals was thus well calculated. In light of the ideology of postwar domesticity, their self-images as professionals and their definitions of success were probably inextricably connected to their ability to provide for their families. This was certainly the way RCA producer Chet Atkins portrayed his career in his autobiography, *Country Gentleman*. Atkins's narrative ties together his professional ambitions and domestic responsibilities in much the same way as Jack Stapp's speech. For Atkins, music was a path to social mobility even in his youth. "I *picked* my way out of East Tennessee," he once told an interviewer, explaining how the isolation and poverty of his childhood had motivated him to refine his guitar skills. But as an adult, his musical talent and ambitions were also frequently obstacles to providing for his family.[10]

Atkins's account of his life returned again and again to the insecurity that beset him when his career made it impossible to fulfill his role as husband and father. He recalled his frustration at being unable to ask his future wife, Leona, to marry him because of his meager income and unsteady job prospects. His confidence was further challenged when Leona had to pick up a singing job at a local radio station to make ends meet. "It didn't do too much for my morale," he later said of the situation, making reference to his sense of responsibility as a breadwinner. "There were times when I felt so proud of Leona, and other times when I felt as though I wasn't doing my job of supporting her."

Chet Atkins, with his wife Leona and daughter Merle, on the front step of their Nashville home. Atkins's ability to provide for his family was a continual worry throughout his early career, and the house symbolized his personal success as a breadwinner and his professional success in joining the new white-collar corporate hierarchy of Music Row.

Chet—Merle—Leona

Throughout the narrative, each professional setback was amplified and symbolized by its impact on his young family. Even after he was well established at RCA as Steve Sholes's protégée and the producer of "Heartbreak Hotel," Atkins still fretted over his ability to provide. He finally began work on the spacious house he thought his wife and daughter deserved only when he could pay for it in cash because, he said, "I was still afraid I would get fired and wouldn't be able to pay for it." For Atkins, the house represented not only his ability to succeed without compromising his artistic integrity, but also the tension between creative freedom and his sense of domestic duty. "I could have built that house a few years earlier if I had been content with just being a sideman," he wrote, "but I preferred to be a leader." When asked by an interviewer in the 1980s how he felt about the role he played in commercializing the Nashville Sound, he summed up his motivation in the most prosaic of terms. "We were just trying to make a living. . . . I was just trying to keep my job."[11]

Chet Atkins's experience of the country music business typified the problems many men faced as they tried to live up to the prevailing gender norms of postwar America while working at the margins of the music industry in a field that offered little financial security. Atkins was somewhat unique, however, in that his career encompassed two very different eras in the organization of the industry. As a young man, he traveled from radio station to radio station, one of hundreds of musicians and DJs who constituted a far-flung collection of barn dances and hillbilly shows connected mainly by informal personal relationships. When Atkins arrived at the Grand Ole Opry in 1950, he became part of a dramatic shift in country music's culture of production, from a loose fraternity of artists to a corporate hierarchy centered in Nashville. The new order allowed for more effective articulation with the rest of the pop business, but just as importantly, it helped bring a measure of stability to the lives of those who earned their living by making country music.

The elaboration of the business infrastructure of country music, and the gender politics that accompanied it, were nowhere better symbolized than in the origins and evolution of the annual WSM DJ convention, the event that served as the forum for organizing the CMA. As the convention became the event that defined the field for outsiders, it came to embody the industry's aspirations to white-collar professionalism and the domestic security that status implied.

The origins of the DJ convention, as early organizer Biff Collie later remembered, lay in a very informal, all-male social gathering. In the late 1940s, *Billboard* had begun a special column on country music disk jockeys, which helped to solidify the DJs' conception of their own field and their role in the industry. It also provided a venue for just getting to know one another. "The guys who read that column found common ground and became acquainted with each others' names, then began corresponding," Collie told an interviewer. This series of personal correspondences resulted in a 1950 meeting of a handful of DJs who, in Collie's words, "met there for the first time and got drunk and visited and whatever else we did." Collie's contemporary Joe Allison remembered a similar air of informality and male bonding. "We already felt like brothers," he said of the networking that produced the meeting, "Nobody had any thoughts of doing anything other than socializing and getting drunk." The atmosphere of homosocial camaraderie was short-lived, however. At the group's third annual meeting, WSM management invited them all to a party at the Andrew Jackson Hotel to celebrate the Opry's 27th birthday. The following year, the station turned the party into a full-blown convention.[12]

The DJ convention immediately became an important factor in the way the music and radio industries understood the country field, and thus one of the central ways leaders in the field could influence the way outsiders viewed them. *Billboard* launched an annual feature section to report on the convention and the latest developments in country music, and a number of other trade papers offered expanded coverage of the events in Nashville. Through public relations announcements and reportage on the convention, those sympathetic to the growing industry in Nashville studiously sought to counter "the picture many people . . . many New York offices, many important producers, have of the country music artist . . . as an uncouth, unintelligent, no talent, no appeal individual." *Billboard* editor Paul Ackerman warned that the music industry was almost compelled to take country music seriously in light of the DJ convention. "It will be virtually impossible for advertisers and their agencies to overlook the promotional implications of . . . country music," he wrote. "To consider it a local manifestation when some 400 disc jockeys pay their way to attend the festival is obvious blindness." Joe Allison connected the professional activities of those hundreds of DJs with their personal aspirations, suggesting to his readers that the men who earned their living by country music were just like those in any other profession. "Almost to man, the country disk jockey is a man respected in his community and his profession," Allison argued, and his goals were dictated by the era's definitions of middle-class masculinity: to find success in "a respected community as a home owner, taxpayer, and prosperous citizen."[13]

Even after it had become an official event, though, the convention retained vestiges of its initial informal, and decidedly masculine, atmosphere. Chet Atkins remembered the convention's early years as being "like the American Legion and Shriners' conventions and a fraternity beer party all rolled into one." As late as the early 1960s, the convention was so famous for its drinking and carousing that the Executive Director of the CMA, Jo Walker, learned that her assistant could not stay overnight at the convention hotel like other CMA staff because the young woman's husband would not allow it.[14]

By the late 1960s identifying the proper tone and image for the DJ convention had become something of a conundrum for the CMA and WSM. The meeting was attended by both fans and professionals, and its down-home, good-ole-boy atmosphere helped to distinguish Nashville's business culture from the rest of the music industry. On the other hand, the heavy drinking and overtones of licentiousness that contributed to that atmosphere evoked a bit too vividly the charges of drunkenness and promiscuity attached to the traditional hillbilly stereotype. In the end, the CMA's desire to highlight the similarities between those in the country field and executives in any other area of business proved decisive. In their effort to convince executives in the broadcasting and music industries that they were dealing "not just [with] professionals, but top professionals," the CMA and WSM launched a concerted effort to discourage fans, most of them women, from attending the convention. Adopting a definition of professionalism that, tellingly, relied on the concept of the breadwinner, the convention's organizers ultimately limited registration to those who were gainfully employed in the country business. Female fans particularly complained that their contributions to the industry were being unfairly devalued because they were unpaid volunteers. They also resented being blamed for the poor conduct, especially the sexual misbehavior, of the professionals. "I have been told 'they' say there are too many fans attending the convention," one woman wrote in a fan-produced newsletter. "I have never drank [or] hank-pankied around . . . while attending the convention," she complained. "I wish I could say the same for some business people, DJ's and artists!"[15]

Projecting a thoroughly professional and respectable identity for the men in the industry depended in part on the exclusion of nonprofessional women, but the CMA also profited from the presence of polished, capable female professionals to domesticate and refine the field's image. Drawing on the traditional representation of women as agents of cultural uplift, the association was eager to show both its dignity and its modernity by highlighting the role women—such as executives Jo Walker and Frances Preston, songwriters Cindy Walker and Felice Bryant, and artists Anita Kerr and Sarah Colley Canon (better known as Minnie Pearl)—played in the country business. In truth, the early representation of women in the business was as much a marker of country's relative lack of profitability as it was a reflection of cultural uplift. CMA Executive Director Jo Walker was originally hired as an assistant to the organization's first executive director, former WSM station manager Harry Stone, but the CMA soon found itself unable to pay both salaries and, as Walker later put it, "mine was a lot less, and besides I could type."[16]

As was the case with female artists, women in the industry were almost always presented publicly in both their professional and domestic incarnations, and an emphasis on femininity helped to lend a more genteel air to Music Row. A profile of Jo Walker in the Nashville trade paper *Music City News*, for example, called her the "den mother of country music" and described her as having "the willowy air of a fashion model, the cold calculating skills of an IBM machine, the southern charm of a plantation belle, and the shrewd cunning of a UN diplomat." The reporter went on to reassure readers that, "Her family takes her job well. They don't feel they have lost mother—they feel they have gained a celebrity." Another article remarked that, while Walker was sometimes mistaken for a man because of her name, "That mistake never happens twice. She is both feminine and attractive, yet has all the drive and know-how needed to carry out her often difficult functions. . . . She directs in a very executive yet charming way." As they so often had onstage, professional women in the office suites of Music Row served as metaphorical mothers, attesting to the good manners and morals of the men in the business and demonstrating that even provincial Nashville could subscribe to the progressive values of the 1960s.[17]

Over the course of the 1960s, the unifying business culture of the country industry in Nashville was transformed from a fraternity of DJs into a corporate family composed of all segments of the industry and represented by the CMA. In 1964, Joe Allison produced a recruiting speech in the form of a scripted conversation between CMA President Tex Ritter and Board of Directors member Roy Acuff. By way of explaining the organization's success, Tex told Roy, "We're more like a family, and we have very unique problems and we've solved our problems, but as a corporation." The malapropism unwittingly highlighted the way Nashville's new business culture relied on the intertwined discourses of domesticity and corporate professionalism, united in the concept of the breadwinner. People in the pop field, the CMA boasted, were "beginning to wonder what we do and how we do it." The answer, in the most personal terms, was that the CMA promised members like Chet Atkins access to the contemporary ideal of white-collar masculinity: a wage that supported the breadwinning role within the family and a vision of a professionalized industry that offered its practitioners a respected place in a corporate hierarchy.[18]

White-Collar Blues

The Country Music Association embodied a new professional identity for the country field based on the personal desires of the men who dominated the industry. But the association's most important practical mission in its early years was to increase the amount of airplay country music received on the nation's radio stations. Since the mid-1950s, the country field had seen its relative share of radio time steadily decrease; by 1961, full-time country stations accounted for less than 2% of radio broadcasting. The CMA's first mission, then, was to communicate more effectively with the sponsors who bought radio advertising time, and it undertook this task with a particular vision of the white-collar soul in mind. Centered on a series of live luncheon presentations to groups of advertising executives and industry leaders, the CMA's broadcasting campaign deftly used gender imagery to reassure these men that they would not be degraded, publicly or privately, by working with country music.

Capitol Records executive Ken Nelson, who was charged with organizing the radio campaign, drew on his own experience in imagining the positions of the men he wanted to reach. The guiding hands behind the CMA—men like Nelson, publisher Wesley Rose, and broadcaster Connie B. Gay—had long personal histories with the country music business, but they were also shaped by the corporate values of mid-century America. All of them had experience in large organizations and were well acquainted with the pressures of corporate life. Ken Nelson had climbed the corporate ladder at Capitol, where he started out by handling local sessions for the label in Chicago, was promoted and transferred to Hollywood to oversee the transcription department, and was later elevated to head of the label's country and western division. Before his father asked him to run the business operations of Acuff-Rose Publications, Wesley Rose had worked for a number of years as an accountant for Standard Oil. Connie B. Gay had worked for the Department of Agriculture for nearly ten years before he decided to parlay his experience as an announcer and producer of farm radio shows into a broadcasting empire of his own in Washington. He astutely cultivated influential political connections all his life and was a master of the symbolism "of affluence and power," as business weekly *Broadcasting* told its readers in 1959. The CMA's choice of Harry Stone as its first executive director, though ultimately an ill-fated one, was made explicitly because he "knew how to work on a high echelon of corporate level."[19]

Ken Nelson approached former DJ Joe Allison to write the scripts for the association's lunch presentations to broadcast and advertising groups. Allison, too, had gathered from his experience as a radio consultant some insight into the personal anxieties that many white-collar men suffered at the thought of being professionally associated with music as déclassé as country and western. He remembered particularly vividly one incident that occurred at radio station KRAK, where he was invited to manage the transition from a middle-of-the-road pop format to country. When he arrived, Allison learned that the station manager had bought each of his advertising salesmen a cowboy hat and a walking stick and proposed that they should approach potential sponsors in the silly get-up. When Allison announced that the costume should go, he could sense the relief among the salesmen. The incident made him acutely aware of the personal humiliation many men experienced in corporate life and informed nearly everything he did in consulting and freelance work for the CMA. "If you're not careful you can take these regular businessmen and make caricatures out of them," he later said of his consistent emphasis on creating a dignified image for country music.[20]

The personal experience of the CMA leadership provided them with a keen understanding of the anxieties of the average white-collar male, but they could also rely on a growing body of popular sociological wisdom promoted in bestsellers like William Whyte's *The Organization Man*, David Riesman's *The Lonely Crowd*, and Vance Packard's *The Status Seekers*. Such works argued that one reason for the exaggerated importance of men's roles as breadwinners and fathers was the trend toward large bureaucratic organizations. Older definitions of masculinity, they suggested, had been based on the notion of the self-made man, the independent entrepreneur who owned his own business, took his own risks, and answered to no one. Many men, like Chet Atkins, found it difficult to reconcile their desire for autonomy with the reality that more and more of the nation's jobs were in large, bureaucratic organizations where rugged individualism went largely unrewarded. Journalist Vance Packard told Americans that the national orgy of competitive domestic consumerism reflected an effort to compensate for the loss of prestige and identity once established through men's working lives. Work in "the organization" could be humiliating for those who failed to move up the corporate ladder, a failure of will that translated into emasculation at home. Packard particularly noted what he viewed as the pernicious effects of status-conscious wives who "need some way to indicate their husbands' importance when chatting with the girls."[21]

The connection between men's status at work and within the family combined with traditional stereotypes about women's role as cultural guardians to create among CMA organizers a powerful, if probably fanciful, image of the role censorious wives played in their husbands' anxieties about country music. Recalling that advertising and broadcast executives frequently tried to influence playlists in favor of more pop-oriented styles, Joe Allison remarked, "They were all that way. Almost to a man. They were trying to find something that their wife could talk about at the country club and not be ashamed of it." Even Jo Walker, whose personal experience must surely have made her more sensitive to the politics of gender stereotyping than some other industry leaders, relied on this negative stereotype to explain why CBS cancelled the popular country variety show *Hee Haw*. "I was told that several of the CBS executives' wives said . . . 'We're just becoming known as the hillbilly station,' " she told an interviewer. "And so then they just dropped *Hee Haw*." Allison countered such anticipated criticism by reminding broadcasters, advertisers, and time salesmen of what the genre's economic success might mean to them at home. He later told an interviewer that whenever he addressed a group of executives, "I would always add, 'If your wives don't think it's dignified for you to be involved in, tell her how much money you're making,' I said, 'that'll take care of everything.' "[22]

Allison's approach to his scripts for the sales luncheons incorporated his belief that men's professional status anxieties were merely reflections of women's insecurities and ambitions. To satirize the cultural snobbery of advertisers who looked down their noses at the country audience in his sales show scripts, Allison uncharacteristically employed a female character rather than a man. Sales show host Tex Ritter told audiences that the barriers country airtime salesmen faced could be "classified as a study in snobbery" and brought the contention to life by conjuring up a female time buyer whose exaggerated sense of her own sophistication prevented her from considering advertising on a country station. "The 'Grapes of Wrath' image was hard to shake from this young lady who had started with the agency at the reception desk and worked her way up to the position of *buyer*," he told the executives. This portrayal anticipated the pressures Allison thought white-collar executives would encounter at home, and dismissed it as prejudice born of insecurity. But it also metaphorically emasculated the buyer who would not take a chance on country music;

and it allowed Allison to poke fun at the hollowness of the organizational peck-ing order and lampoon middle-class ambitions without seriously threatening the self-images of the executives whose masculinity was measured in part by their success in climbing the corporate ladder.[23]

Even as he tried to minimize what he perceived to be the effects of such personal pressures, though, Allison worked hard to assure those in atten-dance that country artists and businessmen subscribed to the same values of middle-class domesticity he assumed governed his audience. The stars of country music, the sales scripts reminded broadcasting and advertising exec-utives, "manage to keep in fairly close contact with their families, confer with their brokers, tally their oil stock dividends, buy and sell real estate, send out the laundry and regulate their highly successful lives in general."[24]

The CMA's effort at domesticating the image of the country industry, and that campaign's roots in the personal experience of the industry's executives, reached its fullest form when the organization offered its sales presentation to the executives next door at the Nashville Chamber of Commerce. Here the association sought not only to convince local entrepreneurs that country music was an increasingly important part of Nashville's economy, but also that country artists and executives were the kind of neighbors you would hope to find in any middle-class community. The pitch was not just a reflection of entrepreneurialism, though it was offered in the hope that some of those attending might contribute to the construction fund for Nashville's major new tourist attraction, the Country Music Hall of Fame and Museum. It also arti-culated once again the more personal aspirations of Music Row's profession-als to fit in with the local Nashville elite. In spite of the wealth that many of them had accumulated, the stars and executives of the country industry were generally ostracized by Nashville society. As one local resident explained, "You've got these people in town who wear tuxedos and go to the symphony, and they just don't care for the country-music crowd." While all of the CMA presentations included material reminding audiences of the mainstream demographic characteristics and family orientation of country professionals and their listeners, the Nashville show dwelt more notably on the very ordinary lives of the stars and executives responsible for the music.[25]

The message was delivered with ingenious subtlety in a narrative that traced through Nashville's economy the money generated by a hit song written by "that paragon of community integrity and his altogether charming and lovely wife," Boudleaux and Felice Bryant. Joe Allison opened this segment of the script with an image of Felice and Boudleaux hard at work in their suburban retreat, "their private recording studio . . . in the basement of their luxurious home . . . on the banks of Old Hickory Lake." Using a catalog of household expenses as a kind of literary conceit, Allison offered Nashville's business elite a window onto the private lives of those in the country industry. "The money dispersed by this musical piece," host Tex Ritter told the audience, "is enjoyed by a florist on Felice Bryant's birthday, and by a carpet cleaner when the Bryant children spill the ink, drop a sandwich, or some new secret formula goes awry from within the mysteries of their new chemistry set." The same trail of money led into the everyday lives of other prominent members of Nashville's country business. "Wesley Rose, the publisher of this tune, uses part of the money . . . on the night his company bowling team meets," Ritter recounted, and "Leona Atkins, Chet's wife, has to have a few dimes on Saturday afternoon when she plays 'first up, closest, and first in' with the other girls during their golf match at the country club." Their neighbors on Music Row, the CMA implied to Nashville's business community, were no different than themselves—parents, husbands, and wives who were active in their communities and joined the country club just like other members of the white-collar middle class.[26]

As elsewhere in its radio campaign, the CMA's portrayal of the conventional lives of country music's entrepreneurs fused the desires of its members with the fears and prejudices they ascribed to white-collar culture. By tapping into discourses about masculinity and the corporate ladder, about the role women were perceived to play as cultural guardians, and about the connection between men's personal and professional anxieties, the CMA used the symbolism of gender to break down the cultural hierarchies that denigrated country music.

Blue-Collar Radio

The CMA was certainly interested in selling white-collar executives on the notion of working with country music, but its strategy for doing so had little to do with the music itself. The association was not particularly concerned with whether advertisers or broadcasters liked country music, only with whether those constituencies thought the genre could be profitable for them. The real commodity the CMA offered was not music, but the country music audience, and the only way the organization could increase access to radio airplay was to convince advertisers of the economic value of that audience as a potential market. Just as it had mobilized gender discourse to challenge entrenched cultural hierarchies and improve the status of industry professionals, so the CMA played on another set of gendered imagery to confront persistent stereotypes about poverty-stricken ignorant hillbillies and brutish working-class bullies. Through its model for radio programming and highly publicized survey results, the organization presented advertisers with the hillbilly's alter-ego—the modern country gentleman, the backwoods boy who made good in the big city—and promoted him as the "middle-income majority" who composed the great mass of the buying public.

As Appalachian studies scholar J. W. Williamson has argued, the image of the hillbilly has long been a mirror for hopes and fears about American masculinity, whether as the embodiment of frontier freedom and self-sufficiency or as the personification of darker impulses to lust and violence. In the 1960s, as the great rush of southern migration to northern and western urban centers finally drew to a close, this tradition fused with popular and academic cultural beliefs in the authoritarian personality of the working-class male to create a particularly powerful stereotype of primitive, aggressive masculinity. In Elia Kazan's 1957 film *A Face in the Crowd*, for instance, Andy Griffith portrayed a lecherous hillbilly singer plucked from the anonymous ranks of the rural poor and elevated to the position of media demagogue. His roguish behavior might have been laughable in another context, but in this telling his seductive and predatory nature make him a threat to civilized society. Ethnic working-class characters like Marlon Brando's Stanley Kowalski in *A Streetcar Named Desire* evoked a similar threat by virtue of their excessive virility and violent impulses. As they joined the working class, then, male southern migrants became the objects of these two mutually reinforcing discourses. Regional and class images meshed completely in stories like *No Down Payment*, a 1957 suburban potboiler in which a southerner and returning World War II veteran named Troy Boone finds his social mobility blocked not only by his regional identity

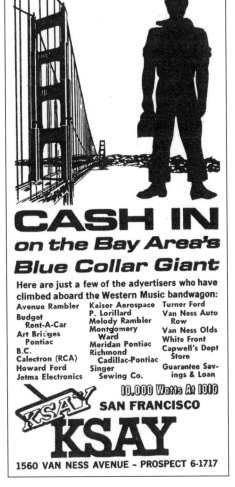

Ads like this one, from the broadcasting trade magazine *Sponsor*, highlighted the masculine blue-collar image the Country Music Association cultivated for its audience, but obscured the importance of female fans.

and lack of education but also by the violence, anger, and eroticism that are an uncontrollable part of his nature. Boone is eventually killed by his own wife, the perpetual victim of his rage, after he attempts to rape a neighbor.[27]

The presence of such images in the late 1950s and early 1960s was all the more notable because so few countervailing models were available. Until the late 1950s, television had offered a different understanding of working-class masculinity, one centered on tightly knit urban ethnic communities and dedicated, if sometimes ineffectual, family men. Near decade's end, though, such portrayals gave way to more upscale images of suburban family life focused on the middle class. By the 1960s, country music was, as historian James Gregory has noted, almost "alone among the major expressive media" in its emphasis on depicting and reaching a working-class audience. But where the working-class television series of the 1950s frequently confronted the tensions between the consumer expectations of working-class families and the inability of laboring fathers to provide the standard of living to which they aspired, the CMA's promotional story continually emphasized the material success of the blue-collar male, especially as that success was defined by his ability to provide for his family.[28]

Typical of this approach were the uses the CMA made of a special survey it commissioned from the day's most prominent radio ratings service. The surprising composite sketch the survey produced was widely remarked by the broadcasting press:

> He lives in San Francisco or New Haven or Cleveland; he's 45 and most likely owns a brand new Chevrolet; he also owns his own home and has a wife and two children to make some noise in it; he spends his day operating a machine that requires an experienced hand. . . . Who is he? According to a special *Pulse* survey, he's the typical country music listener.[29]

The country listener the CMA encouraged advertisers to imagine was an updated version of the western gentleman, the still-rugged flipside of the pathological working-class male, the hillbilly domesticated for consumer society. Here was a man who had taken risks, acquired the skills necessary to make something of himself from humble beginnings, and found success in the "blue-collar aristocracy." This gentlemanly image drew on a cultural history as entrenched as that of the hillbilly; the chivalrous cowboy had first been invoked by the country industry in its bid for respectability during the 1930s. In the context of the 1960s and the cold war, however, the poetics of the natural gentleman on the mountain or western frontier also echoed the thoroughly modern story the CMA wanted to tell about its audience. Like the settled frontiersman, the working-class head-of-household the CMA described as the typical country listener was the quintessential expression of the

American Way. Both images promised that any man could achieve a real measure of autonomy thanks to the widely available land and abundant consumer goods created by American faith in democracy and capitalism.[30]

This was an image that the country audience seems also to have embraced. The same kinds of fanzines that promoted feminine domesticity, as Peter LaChapelle has argued, also represented idealized manhood as a synthesis of working-class machismo and middle-class masculine domesticity. A feature on Eddy Arnold in *Country Song Roundup* showed the crooner baling hay in jeans and t-shirt on the family farm and included the remark from his wife that the couple tried to "instill in [the children] the idea that their father has a job just like the fathers of their friends, that he is really no different from anyone else." Arnold's reward for his hard work was a respectable home and a peaceful family life. Photos in this section of the feature showcased a typical suburban family life, from a group photo taken "on their spacious outdoor patio" to a portrait of Eddy relaxing "in the library of his ranch-style home in Brentwood." "The Arnolds like the idea of just being together," the article concluded, "But that's nothing unusual. Every American family feels the same way."[31]

A nearly identical article on Ferlin Husky a year later showed him working on the farm with his children and pointed out that their new home was just across the fence from Hank Snow, in an area that was "shaping up as a sort of gathering place for country music folks who have enough love of the soil to desire an out-of-town location." This particular version of the suburban dream not only encouraged empathetic responses from thousands of rural-to-urban migrants in a similar position, but also echoed the CMA's sales pitch to white-collar executives by presenting a domestic haven that paralleled and balanced working lives on Music Row. "Morning on the Husky farm finds Ferlin spending a few moments with [his family] before going out for the day's work" on the farm (or in the studio). "Ferlin finds family and farm life fun," the article concluded with an alliterative flourish.[32]

Through a handful of consultants who helped many major-market stations reformat to country, the CMA deliberately steered radio broadcasters away from the hillbilly and toward the western or country gentleman. When WJJD, Chicago's first country format radio station, advertised itself as "the home of the Western Gentlemen," station management meant the phrase to refer not only to its DJ staff, which collectively went by that moniker, but also to its male audience. Another jingle in the WJJD promotional package evoked the same imagery by declaring, in a style reminiscent of the *Rawhide* television show theme, "For a listenin' man, it's the JD brand."[33]

The CMA's marketing and demographics data also obscured the individual choices of the female country music fan and cast her primarily as a domestic consumer acting on behalf of her husband and family. "The majority of country music listeners are the every-day working people of any city," one article on country broadcasting announced, "the man who works for the dollar and the woman who spends that dollar." Surveys showed that women accounted for as much as 40% of the country audience, and that about half of these women commanded their own salaries. Nonetheless, the country industry emphasized its adult male listenership because this was considered a particularly important demographic and because major national sponsors like car manufacturers and airlines assumed that big-ticket items would be under male control. One article revealed this logic, and the way women were subsumed by the family when it wrote,

> The results of many C&W station audience surveys show that the blue-collar worker or industrial worker . . . is the chief country and western fan. He's a good target; the average industrial worker's income is up over 500% in two decades . . . plus a working wife and/or children creating a multi-salaried income of over $7,000. He's the man who accounts for more than half of the big-ticket sales, including such items as high-fi sets and air conditioners.[34]

Indeed, this particular portrait was unusual in recognizing the economic contributions of married working women to their families. In spite of the universal recognition that radio listening, after the advent of the transistor and dashboard model, was becoming more and more individualized, the CMA focused its survey and promotional attention on the notion of the "country and western household," a term that allowed the organization to tout healthy household incomes without undercutting the stature of the male breadwinner by mentioning working wives.[35]

It was probably no accident that the CMA described a model of working-class masculine domesticity that reflected broadcasters' own white-collar image. Part of the association's guiding philosophy was that, in spite of their important taste differences, the fundamental values of rural and urban, middle and working class, northerner and southerner, were not so different at mid-century as they had once been. But this was neither an effort at deception nor an attempt to reconfigure its core audience. Notwithstanding popular concerns that Nashville was softening country music to make it palatable to the middle-brow snobs who had always snickered at the sound of a steel guitar, country artists, producers, and radio programmers continued to target the audience they had courted since the 1940s: rural dwellers and rural-to-urban migrants who labored for a living. The blue-collar patriarch represented the CMA's understanding of the very real transitions this audience had undergone since the end of World War II.

In 1951, Eddy Arnold scored a #1 hit with his recording of "I Wanna Play House with You." The song captured the vision of masculine domesticity that would order the development of the country music business for the coming decade and beyond. "I'll pay the bills if you'll provide the thrills," Arnold crooned to his sweetheart. "I'll build a bungalow that oughta go to show, I wanna play house with you." As it had since the 1920s, country music in the Nashville Sound period expressed the longing for home and search for identity experienced by those displaced in the rush to industrial modernism. But in the postwar era, that sense of longing was as much a hope for the future as a lament for the past. Ideals of masculinity remained as central to the music and its production as they had been during the honky-tonk years, as important a set of tropes as they would become in the Outlaw revolution. But in the late 1950s and the 1960s, those visions were infused with a new sense of optimism, confidence, and self-possession. They provided a gendered language with which to describe the emergence of a business and an audience whose commercial clout symbolized the appeal of consumer democracy in the cold war.

Patsy Cline's Crossovers

Celebrity, Reputation, and Feminine Identity

JOLI JENSEN

Patsy Cline is far more famous now than she ever was in life. But who is this posthumously celebrated Patsy Cline? What is her connection to the Patsy Cline who recorded songs from 1957 until her sudden death in 1963, fell into obscurity, and then sparked a revival in the 1980s that turned Patsy Cline into a "country music legend"? Patsy Cline has had two careers—one when she was alive and trying to make hit records, and another after she became a posthumous star. The posthumous Patsy bears only a partial resemblance to the live Patsy, who we can now know only through interviews and pictures. We can explore how femininity is constructed in country music, and in popular culture in general, by what has happened to Patsy Cline's image over time.

Before and after her death, Patsy Cline's image has been created and shaped in response to her gender. I begin this essay by describing the iconic posthumous Patsy as depicted in the 1991 collection of her recordings released by MCA Records. I then explore my earlier discovery and search for a biographical Patsy, in relation to the wider Patsy Cline revival. I show how the posthumous Patsy has been able to speak to various audiences across time. Throughout this account, I raise questions about how we interpretively construct the woman we want Patsy Cline to be, in relation to her own contradictory attempts to construct herself into what she wanted to become, in relation to what the music industry of the 1950s and early 1960s could allow. What did it mean to be a "girl singer" in the late 1950s and early 1960s? What does it

This essay draws on portions of "Posthumous Patsy Clines: Constructions of Identity in Hillbilly Heaven," to be published in *Afterlife as Afterimage: Posthumous Celebrity in Popular Music*, ed. Steve Jones and Joli Jensen (New York: Peter Lang, Inc., forthcoming).

mean now? By exploring how Patsy Cline was shaped by, and shaped, being a female country music singer, we illuminate some of what was at stake in country music's definition of femininity then, and what remains at stake now.

Gently Tinted Patsy Clines

In 1991 MCA released a definitive, well-documented boxed set of Patsy Cline's recordings, in chronological order. My version of the *Patsy Cline Collection* has four cassette tapes, side by side, and each tape has a different, but similarly tinted and enhanced, head shot of Patsy Cline. Each picture of Patsy has been adjusted for size, airbrushed, and colorized. Each tape has a different, but coordinating, color as a background except around her hair—in each picture, Patsy has the hint of a halo. In the first three pictures she is smiling at something off camera, in the last, she looks directly at the lens.

Each cassette draws its title from one of her songs of the period. In the picture on the first cassette, titled *Honky Tonk Merry Go Round*, the earliest Patsy is dressed in a tailored shirt and jacket, with chin-length hair, looking like a '50s career girl. The second picture, on the cassette *Moving Along*, has her in a dark lace evening gown, wearing (apparently) the same earrings as in the first picture. In the third, on the cassette *Heartaches*, she is wearing a patterned shirtwaist dress, looking like a well-groomed early '60s housewife, and in the fourth, on the cassette *Sweet Dreams*, she is draped over a pillow, in pink and black lace, looking directly at the camera. In the last picture, the scars from her 1961 auto accident have been completely airbrushed out.

The cover picture of the boxed set has yet another version of Patsy Cline, similarly tinted and enhanced, with her chin on her hands. At first glance she seems to be wearing white shoulder-length gloves and a cocktail dress, but a closer look shows instead that she is wearing fringed white buckskin gloves. What looks like a stole on her shoulders is fringe, and she is wearing dangling cowboy boot earrings and a neck scarf. So what seems at first glance to be an uptown evening gown is actually stylized western wear.

This visual trick enacts the contradiction that characterizes Patsy Cline's life and recording career—the tensions between uptown and downhome, pop and country music, a sophisticated sound and a rural sensibility. Patsy Cline's

In this cover photo for the 1991 MCA box set, the *Patsy Cline Collection*, Patsy's gloves and cowgirl fringe are glamorized, feminized versions of western wear, suggesting the beginning of the tensions between uptown and downhome that characterized her career and her posthumous images.

complicated, contradictory collection of images is a response to the complexity of gender in country music in general, but also to her temperament and voice, in relation to the particular tensions of the country music industry during the '50s and early '60s. What was the country music industry to do with a girl singer who dressed in flashy western fringe, refused to be demure or wear gingham, and fought the pop sound that was ultimately to make her famous? And what are we to make of the variety of dated versions of Patsy that we find on her old album covers—the cowgirl fringe, the co-ed striped sweater, the helmet-haired housewife, the gold lamé–booted hipster, the cocktail-dressed torch singer? All of these images are in the documentation and discography that accompany the set. But the cover pictures of the MCA collection offer us, decades after Patsy Cline's death, a colorized and unified vision of a woman of many congruent parts, a semicoherent combination of cowgirl, career girl, housewife, and chanteuse. That is the Patsy Cline who became "a legend."

For the fan who only knows the most famous Patsy Cline songs ("I Fall to Pieces," "Crazy," and "Sweet Dreams"), the MCA collection shows us how many false starts were made in the search for the Patsy Cline sound. But at the same time, the collection organizes, softens, and makes sense of Patsy Cline's visual image. Her clothing may be dated, and semiotically contradictory, but for the cover pictures, her look has been updated and sanctified, thanks to colorization and haloing. We still have her incredible voice, now remastered but not significantly altered. But the person who sings the songs, the Patsy Cline who has become posthumously famous, and who we know now only through her posthumous imagery, is an updated, sanctified Patsy, airbrushed, softened, and gently tinted to our specifications.

Discoveries and Rediscoveries

In the fall of 1978, I discovered Patsy Cline through listening to a battered LP I'd checked out from the public library in Champaign-Urbana, Illinois. It was a "Greatest Hits" album, and it didn't even have a cover. Hard as it is to believe now, in the 1970s, almost no one I knew had heard of Patsy Cline. The library had no books or articles about her, and the country music encyclopedias had only a brief paragraph about her life and death. I couldn't even find out what she looked like. I became obsessed with finding out more about her, so the next summer I went to Nashville to do research on her life.[1] There I was met with cordial bemusement by both country music historians and industry participants. Why was some graduate student interested in this obscure pop-crossover singer after all these years? Patsy Cline wasn't famous—heck, she wasn't even country.

Most of my friends and colleagues thought I was nuts to spend all my savings going to Nashville to do biographical research on a long-dead country music has-been.[2] But I was on a quest—eager to salvage this no-doubt wonderful woman from the anonymity into which she had inexplicably fallen. I had only the sound of her voice on that vinyl record, the knowledge of her tragic early death, and the recognition that she was being ignored. That was enough for me to feel a deep connection to her, and to begin to imagine "my" Patsy. I longed to give her sound a context, a life, an explanation. I yearned to understand what made her so extraordinary. It felt, at the time, like a calling.

I was mystified by her absence from country music scholarship. What explained it? Was it because she was a woman? I was quick to assume this, and I saw my efforts to explore Patsy's contribution to country music as comparable to the efforts (then current in English departments) to put women back into literary history. But during my first summer of research in Nashville it became clear that there was more to her obscurity than simply being a woman—it was the kind of woman she was, and the kind of music that made her famous, that had contributed to her absence from the country music canon. In the 1970s, Patsy Cline's role in the development of country music was ambivalently understood, and her personal style was problematic, given what country music was deemed to stand for.

It is hard for contemporary fans to understand how and why Patsy Cline was not defined, in the late 1970s, as "really" country. But from the 1960s to the 1970s she was a marginal figure because she had "crossed over" into the pop charts in the early 1960s, during the then-maligned Nashville Sound period. When country music was believed to be at grave risk, thanks to the "onslaught" of rock 'n' roll, Patsy was one of a number of country music performers (Eddy Arnold, Jim Reeves, and Marty Robbins were others) whose work sold in pop music markets. To fans of the period, and even into the 1970s and 1980s, that kind of crossover was ruining what made country music authentic.

The staff of the Country Music Hall of Fame Library was supportive of my research, and I remain deeply grateful to their expertise and guidance, but it was clear that Patsy Cline did not then count for much in the history of country music, as they understood it. Both scholars and fans, at the time, believed that the early 1960s was a time when country music was "almost ruined." Patsy figured in this as someone who had helped the music "sell out."

But the pop/country charts weren't the only borders she was crossing. Patsy Cline was clearly not a "girl singer" like Kitty Wells, one of the few other country music options of the time. She had, as people told me, "grown up hard," was sexually frank, swore, drank, and held her own in male company. So Patsy both was and wasn't country, not only in her music, but in her persona. In the public country music world of the 1950s, girl singer meant modest or demure. Kitty Wells's answer song, "It Wasn't God Who Made Honky-Tonk Angels" was one of the first mentions of an alternative form of "country girl" who spent time in bars and hung out with the boys. Honky-tonk angel was far closer to Patsy Cline's experience and live performance style than girl singer, but throughout her biographical career, efforts were made to promote her as a pert, fresh, country girl. She was billed as "Miss Patsy Cline" in her early career, but from 1957 on her publicity photos offered a range of images, from salacious cowgirl to gingham-dressed girl next door to sultry chanteuse.

To get a sense of Patsy's life and career, I spent the summer of 1979 leafing through hundreds of old newspapers and fan magazines in search of references, tracking down performers, managers, and songwriters. I found the 1956 *Washington Post* story calling her "the Hillbilly with Oomph," and a 1958 article in the fan magazine *Trail* pointing out that her sparkly earrings were nonetheless "in excellent taste," and gushing about her "very lovely complexion . . . just come back from a morning walk in the cool spring air." I pondered the disjuncture between a picture of a voluptuous, languid Patsy draped over a metal folding chair, heavily made up and perhaps drunk, entertaining at "a Nashville DJ bash" and its caption, "Here's pert Patsy, entertaining stars and fans." Each picture, each story I heard from those who knew her, was adding a new and unexpected piece to a puzzle I assumed I could somehow put together—a portrait of the real Patsy Cline.

So Patsy Cline's music had disappeared from the airwaves, except on a few oldies shows or in cover versions on albums. Her albums had to be special ordered, and only a few were easily available. Record collector and cataloger Don Roy offered to tape her songs for me, chronologically, so that I could track her vocal development. The article I wrote from those interviews and tapes became the first scholarly account of Patsy Cline's career; his work became the first Patsy Cline discography.[3]

By the early 1980s the Patsy Cline revival had begun. My personal discovery was only a year or so ahead of the wave of popularity that began after Loretta Lynn's biographical movie *Coal Miner's Daughter*, released in 1980. After that came the Patsy Cline movie biography, *Sweet Dreams*, starring Jessica Lange. Ellis Nassour revised his 1981 interview-based biography as *Honky-Tonk Angel: The Intimate Story of Patsy Cline*.[4] Canadian singer k. d. lang playfully claimed to be the reincarnation of Patsy, and suddenly there were reissues of her records, tribute albums, and remade duets with Jim Reeves (also dead), and within a few years "my" Patsy had become "the late, great Patsy Cline." Her life has been condensed into a few key phrases—"hard life, tumultuous marriage, incredible voice, changed country music, tragically killed in 1963, finally found fame that had so long eluded her." She even had her own U.S. postage stamp.

Her records have been reissued, including early live performances, with thorough analyses of each session. Concurrently, her biggest hits have become classics, and the Nashville Sound she represented has come to be seen as a lost age of more authentic country music.[5] Now there are carefully researched biographies, popular plays, numerous articles, casual references, and—the final imprimatur of fame—Patsy Cline impersonators.[6] So who is the Patsy Cline who has become so posthumously famous? How does she connect to the one who struggled to achieve success in the country music world of the '50s and early '60s?

Why Patsy? Which Patsy?

Media renditions of Patsy Cline's life drew on aspects of the biographical Patsy and have played a significant part in her renown. Loretta Lynn's book, *Coal Miner's Daughter*, sold well enough to become a movie, and Beverly D'Angelo's portrayal of Patsy in it was very engaging. D'Angelo's Patsy was sassy, brash, tender, down-home but wise and compassionate. She was the perfect mentor and guide for Sissy Spacek's Loretta Lynn—a generous, glamorous, independent woman who, as Lynn wrote, had a heart of gold. The movie also introduced people to some of Patsy's most famous songs. The Ellis Nassour biography was widely distributed and offered a disjointed, gossipy account of a rowdy, sexually active "fighter" who became a star.

The movie *Sweet Dreams* offered a classic tale of triumph and tragedy, with Jessica Lange portraying Patsy as fighting for honor and integrity in a troubled, violent marriage.

Lange's Patsy was characterized, by *New York Times* reviewer Janet Maslin, as having "rollicking, warm-blooded vitality," portraying a "passionate, larger than life personality."[7] Maslin thought that Lange "makes herself into a perfect physical extension of the vibrant, changeable, enormously expressive woman who can be heard on these recordings." Pauline Kael, in the *New Yorker*, described Lange's portrayal of "an American backcountry version of Anna Magnani," a "hot, woman-of-the-people heroine with a great melodic gift." Kael pointed out that this was a "feminist picture not because of any political attitudes but because its strong-willed heroine is a husky, physically happy woman who wants pleasure out of life . . . what the movie makes you feel is her lust for living . . . there's no call for the heroine to be punished, and no suggestions that she shouldn't want *more*."[8]

Meanwhile, k. d. lang was in her "torch and twang" persona, publicized as believing she was Patsy Cline reincarnated, and performing extraordinary versions of undistinguished Cline songs like "Three Cigarettes in an Ashtray." Female country music performers began frequently citing Patsy as "opening the door to women" in the country music business, and their somewhat awkward embrace of k. d. lang connected 1960s Nashville Sound performers to contemporary alternative music fans and artists.

So was the tsunami of interest in Patsy Cline during the 1980s and 1990s *caused* by media attention? Addressing questions of why particular performers, styles, or genres become popular can involve at least four different kinds of explanation. We can address popularity from a production perspective, a consumption perspective, an aesthetic perspective, and a semiotic perspective. The production perspective on Patsy Cline focuses on the media coverage that circulated her fame; the consumption perspective explores the ways that audiences responded to her; the aesthetic perspective explains her popularity through the qualities and characteristics of Patsy Cline's performances. While I address all of these here, I ultimately rely on a semiotic perspective to explain the Patsy Cline revival—exploring how she was symbolically presented and interpreted, in her time and ours. The semiotic perspective seems to me to be the best way to address Patsy Cline's feminine identity, then and now.

We can explain at least part of the Patsy Cline revival by noting that there was a media-based "creation" of Patsy Cline, that she was portrayed and memorialized in movies, books, and records in ways that explain her popular appeal. It could be argued that "the media" purposely shaped her persona in ways that ensured her popularity. As one commentator notes, the movies "glamorised the struggle that was much of her life. In these movies Patsy was revealed as a woman who was forced to fight for her craft. She fought against agents who exploited her, she fought the misogynist Nashville establishment, and most of all, she fought her husband, Charlie Dick."9

Part of the production phenomenon argument is an argument about Zeitgeist—the spirit of the times. The times were ripe for these particular media renditions of Patsy for several reasons. Previously ignored female writers, artists, and performers were being rediscovered in a number of fields— here was another example of a woman who had to "fight her way to the top" in a male-dominated business. And she offered an image of a passionate, down-home woman, tough but tender, sassy, beautiful, and full of life.

But from a consumption perspective, people were also "ready" for Patsy Cline's voice, life, and persona. I can use myself as an example. I was already primed to fall for Patsy's voice by exposure to female soft-rock, semicountry singers like Emmylou Harris and Linda Ronstadt. The sound Patsy had did not seem to me at the time to be "too country" (by which I and others meant nasal or whiny) and yet it had enough steel guitar to satisfy my new-found love of the honky-tonk style.

Patsy Cline's voice was astonishing in its range and power, but her life drew me, too. I imagined her, with very little evidence, to be a woman who had the courage and independence to make it in a man's world on her own terms. I sensed, from her songs and then from the stories I began to collect, that she combined a brash and self-assured veneer with inner kindness and vulnerability. I also assumed she was a victim of scholarly discrimination—as a woman and as a country music performer she was being pushed aside. Her death at the peak of her career added piquancy to this victim image and helped me believe I had a duty to restore her to her rightful place in the world.

As an audience member, I was predisposed by a number of factors to become a Patsy Cline fan—developments in music, trends in popular feminisms, social narratives of tragedy and triumph, the idea of repairing damage, and a dream of posthumous restoration combined to ensure her appeal for me. These are consumption factors, making me and other audience members likely to respond to and embrace a figure who sounds right, and acts in ways that catalyze and enact stories that engage us. My desire to write the biography that would retrieve Patsy Cline for renewed fame can be seen as my personal version of posthumous fandom. As a graduate student and aspiring writer, I wanted to be the one to do research and write her biography. But listening to records, reading biographies, visiting grave sites, and hanging out on websites are comparable forms of fandom—through our affections we protect and defend a figure fate has taken from us and fame has given us back again.[10]

Commentaries from the 1990s offer evidence of just these kinds of consumption processes. Patsy's voice is described as "contemporary" in that "if you didn't know that Patsy Cline was dead, you would take her for one of today's recording stars."[11] In another instance, "Patsy Cline sounds like a product of the past to be sure, but the past of only a few moments ago."[12]

This semimodern sound implies that Patsy does not sound "too country." Unlike Kitty Wells, whose voice is always described as "nasal" or "twangy," Patsy Cline's voice is called "smooth" and "rich." This vocal distinction, combined with arrangements that relied on strings and vocal groups, rather than steel guitar and fiddle, marks the difference between "too country" and "contemporary."

As another writer noted, in her early years, "many doubted that Cline's powerful, bluesy voice was right for the twangy, hillbilly sound associated with Nashville."[13] Bill McCoy, who knew Patsy in her teen years, describes her first recordings as more "real country," but notes that it was her later arrangements that made her famous. McCoy says, "Her first stuff was more with the steel guitar, but the last stuff, the big hits, were strings."[14] McCoy then criticizes current country music as "too citified," thus placing Patsy back with "real" country music, even as he notes the distinction between her earlier and later recordings.

Unlike her "not dated" and "not country" voice, her life story has a mythic quality that is connected to country music and the past. One writer summarizes her life: "She was born poor in Virginia and her father walked out when she was 16, reducing her to singing on street corners for her family's supper.

She worked behind a drugstore counter, sang at night and made a true country-music marriage to the aptly named Charlie Dick, who loved her but also drank, sponged, cheated on her and beat her up from time to time."[15] As another put it, "The girl from the wrong side of the tracks in Winchester worked hard and played hard; her reputation as a forward, at times promiscuous woman, stayed with her for life."[16] But the overall story is that this hard, "country" life didn't get her down. In fact, the Patsy Cline persona offers a vivacious woman who was ahead of her time: "Patsy Cline was spunky, audacious and boldly sexy by the standards of the day."[17]

"Ahead of her time" has complex meaning in relation to Patsy. Those in the Nashville community can use it to describe the style of her singing, but they also used it, in interviews with me, as a coded way to say that she was sexually confident, or forward, or demanding, or brash, or aggressive. But in general, being ahead of your time is desirable—biographer Ellis Nassour says she was "not only twenty years ahead of the pack musically—the female singer responsible for changing the course of country music—but also twenty years ahead as a feminist."[18] Tragically, of course, this "ahead-of-her-timeness" is always shadowed by the inescapable fact of death "before her time." The fight to rise from poverty to stardom is juxtaposed by the tragedy of a life cut short. Such a death is not only memorable and moving, but offers a form of persona protection. As Paul Kingsbury notes, "We will always remember her as a feisty woman on the way up, with everything to live for, not as someone who had her day, who is embarrassingly unwilling to get offstage."[19]

These accounts suggest that Patsy's fame involves an audience that is responsive to things she apparently represents—a voice that isn't country but a life that is, a feistiness and sexiness that wasn't country then, but can be now, a prescient force for music and feminism, and a death that stopped her too soon, but allows her to "live again" through our responses to her.

Explaining fame by arguing for some combination of media attention and audience need ignores what connects media and audiences—the content itself. The dominant popular explanation for why Patsy Cline has become posthumously famous is that she was so great that she *had* to be rediscovered. This aesthetic perspective sees Patsy Cline as an extraordinarily gifted singer. As an artist, her work can sustain critical scrutiny; it continues to offer intense emotional experience across time, space, and social groups.

Such an argument assumes that there is a connection between the essential qualities of a cultural form and its later success—it "stands the test of time."[20] Belief in a canon of works that radiate their greatness across time, space, race, gender, and class has been soundly critiqued in recent academic discussions. But it characterizes a number of aesthetic explanations for Patsy's revival—her "greatness" has rightly made her into the star she is today.

Comments about Patsy Cline's "timeless sound" are evidence of the aesthetic perspective. "There's nothing dated about her approach or presentation. If you look at pop acts from the fifties and early sixties they fitted a sound of that moment whereas Patsy's was an indefinable sound."[21] Patsy's "indefinable" sound implies that she has transcended the barriers that confine lesser figures. Thus Patsy is distinguished, often, from Kitty Wells, who is seen as being confined to the past and the genre that Patsy has escaped. One article refers to Patsy's "boundary blurring signature sound." It describes her first hit, "Walkin' After Midnight," in glowing terms, arguing that it "combines the emotional transparency of country, the robust tonality of Tin Pan Alley pop and a hint of gritty r&b into a sound that was Cline's alone."[22]

Having a "signature sound" implies that you, the artist, have something unique and inimitable. Music writer Nick Kimberley argues that it is the "teardrop" that gives country music its authenticity, and suggests that Patsy's artistic triumph is her mastery of "the teardrop."

> The teardrop can take many forms. It can be a break in the voice, close to a sob; it can be a willingness to sing a note flat or through clenched teeth; it can be all manner of melismatic embellishments. Such mannerisms can sound sentimental and crass, but a singer like Patsy Cline, whose voice encompassed almost every teardrop possibility, makes them superb emotional vehicles.

Kimberley describes various examples of "a voice luxuriating in its craft" and complains that some of her recordings are "sullied" by vocal group intrusions. He concludes by saying, "There is a gossamer thread between sentiment and sentimentality. Patsy Cline walked that thread with the precision of an artist."[23]

From an aesthetic perspective, unique artists create great works, ones that deserve careful, detailed appreciation. Kimberley's analysis of "I Fall to

Pieces" demonstrates how close aesthetic critique can be used to illuminate a single song:

> The male vocal group is there, but well back in the mix balanced by the authentically Country [sic] steel guitar. The first phrase, the song's title, provides a neat resume of Cline mannerisms: the slight hesitancy in finding the note on "fall," a delicate portamento on "pieces," the note then extended over the beat on the final syllable, the whole line delivered with an almost imperceptible gruffness. Each vocal trope is understated, barely hinting at the emotional turmoil the words describe.... Cline scoops up to notes, drifts downwards, and, most tellingly, feigns a moment of difficulty in getting the note at all. Each repetition of the title is handled slightly differently, not with the outrageous abandon that a jazz singer might relish, but with a careful attention to tiny variations.[24]

Because the aesthetic perspective presumes that renown is based on the qualities of the work, not the life, there is an insistence, in the aesthetic analyses, on this separation: "It wasn't the plane crash that made Cline important, though; it was the music, and this [boxed CD] set makes sense of her complete body of work for the first time."[25]

Polysemic Patsy Cline

So far, explanations of Patsy's posthumous fame have involved imagining certain forces that determine popularity—from a production perspective that force is the media; from a consumption perspective it is the audience; from an aesthetic perspective it is the work itself. But in a semiotic perspective, popularity is not caused or determined, but rather "made possible" by the symbolic complex of the cultural form. I believe that the semiotic perspective is the best way for us to address Patsy Cline's feminine identity. It allows us to explore how she has been symbolically constructed to allow for multiple meanings—in semiotic terms, she is polysemic. In a semiotic perspective, the posthumous Patsy Cline becomes a collaborative construction of all three levels of explanation—the media, the audience, and her body of work. She is a bricolage—an assemblage of accrued meanings that can be variously read, at various times, by various people. Her fame is enabled by the multiplicity of readings her symbolic complexity allows.

From this perspective, Patsy Cline is not just an artist or a person, but a subject position, someone whose life and work can be made to mean a variety of things for a variety of people. The posthumous Patsy Cline is socially constructed to have enough power to appeal widely, without enough specificity to exclude or repel. Popular commentary on Patsy's iconic status, as well as fan and scholarly interest, seeks to cut through these symbolic accretions, to retrieve the "real" Patsy. Only a few commentators directly address the possibility that the currently popular Patsy, like any celebrity icon, must always be a fabrication.

For many, the "real" Patsy Cline has not been captured by the movies and books that have been written about her. The ability to discern the "real" Patsy involves having known her, or knowing those who have known her, or knowing more than those "other" fans. Bill McCoy, one of her early supporters in Winchester, says that the movie *Sweet Dreams* "was a bit uptown. That's Hollywood style." The "real" Patsy would never have stood for such abuse from her husband, Charlie Dick: "Like I've heard alot of people say, if he'd have treated her like that, she'd have took a two-by-four and busted him over the head."[26]

Ellis Nassour criticizes the movie as an insider: "It is a good movie if you know nothing about Patsy Cline."[27] Charlie Dick, Patsy's second husband, dismisses the Nassour biography as well as the movie, and describes Patsy as "just an ordinary girl. She loved home life, you know, cookin', cleanin', lookin' after her family. Sure we argued, we were fightin' all the time, we had a passionate relationship. But we didn't do knock-down, drag-out fightin'. Not once."[28] The Nashville community of performers who knew Patsy also responded with some dismay to the movie versions of Patsy's life. They criticize them as Hollywoodized and suggest that they do not accurately portray her complex personality.

But who is the real Patsy Cline? My interviews in 1979 gave me a picture of a contradictory woman who hadn't yet been "figured out" by those who knew her. They told me bits and pieces of their encounters with a rough, rowdy woman with an amazing voice and great ambition. The people I interviewed were cautious, hesitant, and spoke to me in a semicode about her sexuality, "toughness," marriage, troubles, reputation. In later visits, in 1980, their stories were much more polished, simplistic and impermeable. The Nassour biography was dismissed as full of gossip, the movie as too uptown, but the revival was defined as a tribute to her tremendous talents. The "real" Patsy, even when based in the accounts of her friends and family, is still a symbolic construction, designed for specific purposes.

So what about elements of the polysemic Patsy Cline that have become "hers" after death? Memory is always a self-interested reconstruction, and the country music world is constantly writing stories about itself, stories that obscure as well as idealize elements. Patsy Cline's persona required revision during her lifetime, and the woman she has become after death is far different from who she might have become had she developed and matured in the 1960s, 1970s, and 1980s.

Roseanne Cash has written one of the most insightful accounts of this tendency in Nashville to obscure and idealize, and of its frustrations for her, personally. She is herself country music "royalty," the daughter of Johnny Cash, who later married June Carter, of the Carter Family. Her essay on Patsy Cline appeared in a 1996 *New York Times Magazine*, among others by well-known women about "Heroine Worship." In the issue, the 1990s are dubbed the age of the female icon, and Patsy is included with Elizabeth Taylor, Eleanor Roosevelt, Oprah Winfrey, Martha Graham, Indira Ghandi, Coco Chanel, Doris Day, Aretha Franklin, and Jackie Onassis, among others.

Cash's account describes how "those with real memories of her have been somewhat revisionist in their collective retelling." She suggests that this is because "she was so damned great . . . that perhaps they felt a need to polish and repair her wild and willful personality in order to complement the magnitude of her talent, particularly since she was a woman in an era that did not suffer female accountability gladly." The Cashes had Patsy over to the house shortly before she died. When pressed about the disjuncture between the voice and body and Patsy's "roughness," June Carter backs off; when Roseanne asks if her stepmother was disappointed when she met Patsy, her mother answers, "Well I wouldn't want that to be said—she was ahead of her time, that's all."[29]

Again, "ahead of her time" can stand in for the contradictory legacy of voice, sexuality, and aggressiveness that was so difficult to label and contain.

From the semiotic perspective, we see how Patsy becomes what the particular reader needs or wants her to be. As Sandall notes, "Posterity has seldom inherited such a promising bundle."[30] Her contradictions, in combination with her life and her gifts, readily support a variety of readings.

Patsy has been particularly popular among gays and lesbians. Andy Medhurst, a Sussex University professor who writes about gay icons, calls Patsy, "The nearest thing to a diva country music has." According to White, Medhurst explains her appeal for the gay and lesbian community in terms of her image as someone who "overcame abuse by a brutish uncaring husband who tried his best to stifle her career." White goes on to suggest that Cline has "all the requisite elements" to be a "gay favourite," including "tragic early death, a portfolio of dark and poignant songs, and an allegedly miserable personal life."[31]

A more nuanced interpretation is offered by Caz Gorham, who organized an all-Patsy night that "drew 900 lesbians to a nightclub in South London." Patsy's appeal involves a combination of her "strong image as a woman" and her musical persona. "Her music has a sense of unrequited passion, you know, heartache, which is meaningful to those who are unable, because of outside pressures, to express feelings openly. But there is also a tongue-in-cheek element. Those clothes, that style. I don't think you can buy into it without a sense of irony."[32]

The irony that Gorham describes is complex. It is not postmodern cynicism, but a more playful recombination of elements—Patsy is constructed to be idolized and ironized. The gay diva Patsy is a "knowing" Patsy, a way to play with the ways that Patsy is both real and constructed. Such a "postmodern" Patsy is even better able to inspire or orient the fan. As the *New York Times Magazine* collection on heroines suggests, icons help us invent and sustain identities.

It is this inspirational Patsy that Roseanne Cash describes; the Patsy she imagines is much like the Patsy I first sought in 1979. She is/was, as Cash writes, "A woman who is truly and spontaneously alive, who is rooted in her body like a redwood in the earth, who is in command of a startling sexuality that infuses everything and who is the vehicle for a preternaturally affecting voice that both reveals and obscures her essence."[33]

Cash realizes that her voice "both reveals and obscures," but goes on to describe how Patsy is

> a profound source of inspiration to those of us without immediate memories of her, those of us whose voices weren't so full-bodied and fully formed from the beginning and whose values were not so exquisitely self-determined. . . . In my private quandaries, musical and otherwise, it gives me a lot of satisfaction to connect her teeming personality to the gifts she possessed. She lived a life utterly her own, messy and self-defined, and it all fed and merged with that voice.[34]

This iconic Patsy Cline—mine and Roseanne Cash's—has been alchemized from the disturbing particulars of her life. She has become mythic—her marriage, her troubles, her struggles have all become a story of triumph over tragedy, in life and now, again, in death. The "messy, self-defined life" is disheveled in ways that will inspire, not trouble or repel us. This is best illustrated in the evocative comments of Mary Harron, as she analyzes the appeal that Patsy Cline has for her. Harron argues first that "A singer constructs a persona simply by the songs she chooses." She uses the most famous Patsy Cline songs to describe the Patsy persona: "Patsy's true mode is existential loneliness: an isolation so complete that it comes as a surprise to hear she had a husband and children."[35] This, Harron argues, sets her apart from singers like Tammy Wynette and Loretta Lynn, where "personal history seeps into their music until it seems the function of personal tragedy is to provide more songs."[36]

What is noteworthy, what makes her special to Harron, is that

> Patsy Cline doesn't give you that kind of detail. There's no Tennessee mountain home, no trailer park, no runny-nosed kids or dishes in the sink. I always picture her in two settings. One is walking along that midnight highway. The other comes from what may be her best song, "She's Got You," where she sits alone in her living-room, late at night, with a few objects in front of her: a photograph, a ring, a record spinning on the turntable.[37]

The semiotic Patsy, then, has been constructed in ways that suppress or eliminate the particular life, the specific husband, children, sinks, and trailer parks. Instead, she offers a "promising bundle" of signifiers that can be detached from their origins in an actual life, while gaining significance from the hints of that life—abuse, misery, loneliness—and beliefs about triumph over it.

The Consequences of Transformation

Does it matter how Patsy is interpreted? Does it make any difference if the "real" Patsy is different from the constructions of her? A key aspect of posthumous fame is the inability of the figure to counter the personas that are ascribed to his or her image—death prevents authorial revisions. But others still insistently take up the battle, offering corrective claims to show the "real" figure behind the image, as the image evolves and transforms.

This desire to retrieve the real from its symbolic packaging is a continuing feature of modern life. Is there anything about the "real" Patsy that might be worth saving? Why do people, with Patsy and others, endlessly return to the idea of a "real" or "essential" celebrity? Why don't they just revel in what some literary and social critics take to be a postmodern carnival of symbolic constructedness?

Concern with saving the "real" in a celebrity parallels Patsy's role in the development of a form of country music that was not originally deemed "real country" but that now has become, retrospectively, "real." Concern with the real also connects to 1950s anxieties about the homogenization of culture, the ways that the particularity of folk and high arts were being watered down for wider dissemination. This dilution of a cultural form's particularity, its pungency, was described as commercialization—the cultural form had been corrupted in order to make money.[38]

The country music sound that is associated with Patsy, and with the Nashville Sound, was dismissed, in the late 1970s, as a dilution, a homogenization, a commercialization of country music. Those on Music Row were accused of having "sold out" country music. This is a longstanding concern in country music circles. Whenever country music becomes more popular and lucrative, it is invariably accused of having "lost its soul."[39]

Yet today, when country's "lost soul" is bemoaned, it is in relation to a Nashville Sound that has become "authentic" in retrospect. Patsy Cline (among others) is now revered as being not only ahead of her time, but as being "really" country. She and her music represent a form of genuineness that contemporary performers honor. In fact, this Patsy is seen as also having triumphed over the attempts to subdue or commercialize her; she has escaped the "discipline" that current critics like Sandall see as having softened and weakened country music in the past thirty years.[40]

Thus the "real" Patsy is yet another construction, one that can be made to represent a heritage, a tradition, a mode of being that is being lost in today's even more commercialized, homogenized country music world. Her outspokenness, roughness, sexual aggressiveness, and lack of polish and sophistication (so troublesome during her lifetime) have become elements of authenticity that make her "really country." No matter the pictures of her in evening gowns, tailored suits, cocktail dresses, gold lamé pants, and evening gowns; no matter the swooping violins, Anita Kerr Singers, and pop modulations. Patsy Cline's country authenticity is in her biography and projected into her voice, so that her experiences can make even her most pop-orchestrated songs seem and feel "really country."

Social Class Crossovers

What is interesting in this reimagination of Patsy is that the battle that defined her recording career, and helps to explain her choices and performance style, has been reworked to form her iconic image. In life she was aggressively, if self-consciously, lower class; she loved rowdy, twangy country music and had to be convinced, over and over, to do the kinds of smoother music that won her fame. She, like many country music fans of the time, equated the use of violins and background vocals with pop music, and pop music with "them": upper-class, wealthy people who disdained country fans and music—and her. To "cross over" into the pop charts was also to sell out one's friends, family, and heritage. It was to abandon class position, to assimilate, to try to "pass."

These social class issues underlie the concern over the crossover music that shaped Patsy Cline's recording career, and are, of course, what most debates about country music's "soul" are about. But it is unusually difficult to talk about continuing class tensions in American life—we use terms like "down-home" to counter terms like "trailer trash," and turn derogatory terms like "redneck" into badges of honor. When Patsy's look and sound were made more "sophisti-cated," they were also being made less "country," and this was a transforma-tion charged with social class tensions that are still very difficult to discuss.

They are also difficult to reconstruct across time, space, and social class. It is clear that Winchester, Virginia, was not ready to celebrate Patsy Cline until the 1990s, and even now it is a somewhat awkward embrace. Why? Because coun-try music is still deemed "low class," or because Patsy Cline herself was from the "wrong side of the tracks," or because people still revile her involvement, at age sixteen, with her mentor and married bandleader, Bill Peer?

It is also clear that Patsy herself was both drawn to, and repelled by, the smoothness and sophistication represented by sequined gowns and pop music. She sounded like pop singer Kay Starr, whom she deeply admired, and began to perform in the cocktail dresses and evening gowns that pop singers like Kay Starr and Connie Francis wore. But Patsy performed, even into the 1960s, a mix of rousing uptempo tunes like "Come On In," and "Won't You Come Home, Bill Bailey," along with pop standards. She spent most of her brief performance career doing live shows for country audiences, and her preferred performance style was one designed to knock out a live country audience.

Let me illustrate the difficulty of understanding and decoding the social class issues that Patsy embodied. When I was in Nashville interviewing various people who knew and recorded with Patsy, I heard from Ray Walker, of the Jordannaires, that Patsy sometimes showed up at the recording studio with her hair in curlers. Why was that important? By telling me about the curlers, Walker was trying to explain to me how different Patsy was, in life, from her voice. He was also trying to explain to me, a graduate student twenty years later, how and why she fought with Owen Bradley over singing in a smooth, pop way. He wanted me to understand her class background and related temperament, and why she fought against the uptown sound that would make her famous.

I have pondered this image ever since—the publicity pictures of Patsy with her fringed cowgirl outfits, full makeup, heavy red lipstick, and (later) sparkly earrings and sequined clothes, and how they contrast with the remembered

Patsy clowns with a visiting Florida DJ during the annual WSM convention. Her sparkling earrings, lacy dress, and dark eyebrows present a brash and pop (rather than demure and country) Patsy Cline. The scars from her 1961 auto accident, airbrushed out of many posthumous depictions, are clearly visible.

image of a frustrated, unhappy woman showing up at Owen Bradley's studio for an expensive, important recording session with no makeup and her hair in rollers. What could it mean? Was she showing her contempt for the contract she was under? For Bradley's attempts to take her uptown? For the gendered demands for beauty and poise and "pertness" from the country music industry? Or were the hair rollers a realistic recognition that what counts is "what's in the tracks," not what she looks like? Was it a rebellious assertion that women at work don't need to look beautiful? Or was it evidence of her lower-class sensibilities—a kind of social class identification?

I can't know. It is hard enough to retrieve the meaning of hair-roller-wearing in public in general—in the late 1950s and early 1960s, I remember lots of women in southern Indiana going out in full makeup, well-dressed casual clothes, and hair rollers under chiffon scarves. It could be an act of practicality, custom, rebellion, contempt, class honor, and/or personal style. As I understood the interview, Ray Walker was trying to help me understand how rough Patsy Cline was, and how scared. He was trying, from a man's point of view, to be understanding of Patsy's character, but was (it seemed to me) still baffled by, and disappointed in, Patsy's showing up to work in rollers. So what did it mean?

In the Margaret Jones biography of Patsy, a musician who played with her recalls that she'd drive around Winchester in a red and white convertible with her hair in curlers, under a bandana, stopping to yell "Hi Hoss," just, in his words, "rougher than hell."[41] For him, the rollers and the greeting were both evidence of a "give-'em-hell" attitude to the snobbish people of Winchester. So it may mean that she didn't ever let go of the style that worked for her in Winchester, even as those around her (like Owen Bradley and the Jordannaires) tried to reassure her that she could at least let herself *sound* soft, and vulnerable, and sophisticated. She could stay as "rough" and "country" as she wanted inside, but to have hit records, she needed to project a smooth, uptown sound and self.

Decontextualized Patsy

The tension between rough and smooth, and the battle for social legitimacy it represents, has virtually disappeared, now that the Nashville Sound has been redefined as an age of authenticity. The heritage of the Nashville Sound is still with us, except now it is used to criticize today's hat acts. The new form is "country-tinged" music, without the hayseed image. Like the decontextualized Patsy, shorn of any actual connection to snotty noses and kitchen sinks, newer versions of country music are seen as having been progressively detached from their earlier authenticating elements. They have been reconfigured as "good" and "honest" music that uses real emotion, rather than as twangy, nasal, hillbilly music.

Similarly, the Patsy we get has been decontextualized. The Patsy I found in the late 1970s was a Patsy defined by the country/pop tension in her music, and one who was clearly lower class. That made it easier for me, as a middle-class academic, to focus on analyzing her music rather than writing about her life. My personal discomfort shows why Patsy "works better" when she is lightly attached to biographical or sociological markers.

My initial trip to Nashville was a quest to find out who Patsy Cline "really" was. I sought clues, angles, insights that would tell me who the woman was whose singing knocked me out. My initial Patsy was a tantalizing, talented, powerful, intelligent woman who was, it seemed, speaking to me from beyond the grave, waiting for me to find her. She was Roseanne Cash's Patsy—an icon that could inspire me.

My early interviews with those who worked with her gave me a series of stories that tried, awkwardly, to construct a rowdy Saint Patsy—rough but with a heart of gold, always generous and giving. Later interviews, as I showed that I knew a fair amount about her personal life but wasn't trying to smear her, involved cautious analyses of her contradictions, hot temper, and personal difficulties. The more I found out, the more I sympathized with, but was confused by, her temperament and motives. I sought, as all biographers do, a narrative that would make sense of disparate glimpses. Was there a story line? What was it?

Three incidents steered me away from writing her biography. They showed me that the Patsy I had created for myself was significantly different from the Patsy I was finding, in ways that meant I couldn't really understand her life, although I could probably analyze her musical career and role in the industry. The first incident was a birthday card she'd given Owen Bradley—he'd saved it over the years, and pulled it from his desk drawer during my interview with him. It was the kind of card you get in a truck stop, tacky-cute. "My" Patsy would not have sent it.

The second was my visit to her hometown of Winchester, where, at that time, she was barely acknowledged. The town showed clear class divisions in ways that mystified me. The newspaper had no file on her and no intention of putting one together. The Chamber of Commerce had collected no material on her and seemed insistent on keeping it that way. The people I found who knew her told stories about ostracism that were distressing but also entirely alien—what kinds of class conflicts were these, and how was I ever to get inside of them? "My" Patsy was immune to all this stuff, could laugh it off and move on, but clearly, class snobbery in Winchester was a key to her character.

And finally, I met her husband, Charlie Dick, and could not possibly imagine "my" Patsy having anything to do with him. During my first summer of research he was courteous to me and told me his collection of Patsy Cline stories, but I knew, after talking to him, that if she loved this man, then I could not ever understand her well enough to write a good biography.

The semiotic Patsy I had constructed, from the voice and the outlines of her life story, was one that I needed for myself—a powerful, independent, intelligent, gifted Patsy—the "redwood" Patsy that Roseanne Cash describes and that the movies sort of reference. The Patsy I wanted to find would never send a tacky card, be crude enough to be ostracized, or marry Charlie Dick.

The Consequences of Repositioning

In Patsy Cline's current iconography, the particular issues of class and commerce that defined her life have dropped into the background, while the more general issues of temperament, personality, and "overcoming barriers" have been airbrushed and colorized, like the photographs in the MCA collection. Class and commerce figure in her story as things she was able to transcend—her "greatness" becomes her ability to "be herself" in a world imagined as trying to trap or inhibit her.

This is how celebrities manage to speak to "everyone." Things that might limit or drive away parts of the audience are incorporated and refined, made into something that isn't crude or repellant. Tammy Wynette, Loretta Lynn, Kitty Wells have the concrete specificity, the trailer and runny-nosed kids, the twang or the whine. They are, therefore, defined as "dated" or "too country" in comparison with Patsy.

But Patsy also had those "country" traits—they were her life, too, and she fought hard to keep them in her music. But she was convinced, by those who recorded with her in Nashville, that her key to success was a softer, smoother, more pop sound. Owen Bradley and the Jordannaires and the other musicians were right. Her temperament was honky-tonk, but her voice was best suited to crossover pop, and it is with the crossover that she found her audience and laid the foundations for her posthumous fame.

This means that the particularities of her class origins were erased from her music, and they continue to be diluted in her iconic image. Particular elements—the abusive husband, the rough language—remain, but as examples of spunk and feistiness, not trailer-trashhood. Much like the steel guitar that still appears in songs to signify "country," selected elements of Patsy's life lend a touch of authenticity, but just a touch—not enough to cause anyone to turn away. Patsy Cline is now firmly ensconced in Hillbilly Heaven, that place that a series of country songs invented for their late, great stars. Her embattled relationship to that ambiguous term hillbilly—the reason that country music isn't pop or rock 'n' roll, but also the reason it is ridiculed—has almost disappeared from view. The particular biographical, gender, and musical issues that defined her have become—for reasons I've considered here—as hazy and sentimental as the colorized portraits of her in the MCA collection.

Dancing Together

The Rhythms of Gender in the Country Dance Hall

JOCELYN R. NEAL

The pathway from Nashville, Tennessee, to the Atlantic coast spans nearly seven hundred miles, a stretch of land that houses many of country music's oldest and richest traditions. The country music that emerged from that area has blended with other sources and styles, evolved, and morphed into the current commercial genre, and this commercial country music is readily accessible through radio stations, recordings, and live performances across the nation, undifferentiated by regional traditions. That very sameness in available commercial country music has led to criticisms of blandness and homogeneity that have plagued the genre in recent years. However, in spite of the national access to a central brand of commercial country, a remarkable streak of individuality remains in the region's many night clubs and dance halls where fans listen to country music. Within this stretch of Tennessee and North Carolina, the country dance venues in each city house unique traditions and dance practices that merge with the music to form distinct communal identities, and it is the gendered roles adopted by each venue's fans that most strongly define and amplify those identities.

This study explores the country dance halls situated in night clubs along Interstate 40 from Wilmington, North Carolina, to Nashville, Tennessee.[1] The dance halls considered here all share certain characteristics, including merging the urban environment of the night club with the code of rural authenticity that is embedded in country music and its fandom. From these venues emerges a blend of behaviors and practices that are inextricably tied to the histories of social dance, country music, and socialized entertainment, but that are enacted through carefully determined gendered roles within the fan populations. How the women and men interact on the dance floor and in the

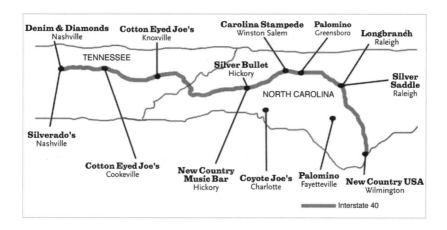

surrounding spaces, literally how they dance with each other, varies from club to club, and subverts the larger shared tradition of country music through strongly differentiated local practices.

The anthropological principle that significance resides in the whole is frequently invoked in the study of social dance, arguing that consideration of either music or dance needs also to consider the relationship between the two.[2] Country dance does not and cannot exist in the absence of music, at the very least inferred in the minds of the dancers; reciprocally, country as a genre carries deep roots as a music made for dancing. Within the boundaries of commercial country music, songs written about dancing, employing dance-step lyrics, and drawing on dance situations for their narrative context abound; these songs, in turn, are often the impetus for evolution in dance practices. These sorts of mutual influences occur most apparently within the domain of lyrics, but they also exist in the more subtle uses of tempo, rhythms, and intertextual references to other "dance" songs. Within this intertwined relationship, the fans' responses to the music through dance become part of the music's external and internal identity.

The roles that fans and artists project in country music culture have been the raw material for ironic commentary, comedy, biting social criticism, and conservative political agendas for over half a century, both within the musical tradition itself and within surrounding scholarship and journalism.[3] Within the song texts, the characters or caricatures of the honky-tonk angel tempting the well-intentioned husband to cheat on his good-hearted woman are so per-vasive that songwriters use them as foils for other equally well-established characters. Within the fan culture, a general code of chivalry, sometimes self-described as "southern manners," is often projected by the men, while the women often navigate between the idealized, faithful partner immortalized in many songs, and active participation in the fan culture, which allows and even requires attendance at honky-tonks.

Specifically within the dance halls discussed here, fans have not only cre-ated unique communal identities centered around each club, but have adopted, altered, and sometimes circumvented the heavily gendered charac-teristics of traditional roles. What emerges from these dance practices is a col-lection of behaviors that complicate the characterization of country music within American culture, most notably by their diversity from one community to the next and by their flexibility as they evolve over time. By extension, that diversity colors the meaning and interpretation of social codes within country music itself.

This study first offers a basic overview of the practices in these dance halls, then focuses more specifically on the mainstream media industry's efforts toward organization and homogenization that have occurred in the past decade. Finally, a more detailed examination of three individual styles of dance—line dancing, choreographed partner dancing, and lead/follow partner dancing—provides a detailed portrait of the individual dance hall communi-ties, their unique regional identities, and the diversity of roles that fans create and embody through their dancing and within country music's culture.

Music and Dance Symbiosis

The depth of the relationship between country music and its fans' dance tra-ditions deserves further elaboration. The dance hall requires that music be supplied for dancing, but the music is equally dependent for its very exis-tence on the shared cultural understanding of country dance traditions. In its prototypical lyrics, country music uses dance as a setting, as an event in the plot, and as an established frame of reference for metaphysical and emo-tional metaphors. Often these settings, actions, and metaphors are implicitly present as a background for the topics and emotions expressed in the songs, and country music as a genre simply assumes the listener understands what those references mean.

Dancing has become one of the many culturally shared experiences that country music uses to construct interdependent and reflexive meaning.[4] The discourse of country music includes the habits, emotions, and physical actions of dancing, but often fails to articulate the details of those multifarious practices. Instead, the music tends to rely on the assumption that fans intuitively understand what it is like to dance—in spite of the fact that the actual experiences of country dancing are so varied and diverse that there is possibly no consistency among those fans. To some, it references line dancing with sorority sisters from college; to some, it references the precursor in a dive bar to a one-night stand; to some, it references a family tradition passed on from grandfather to granddaughter. Therein lies the wealth and diversity of the shared music/dance experience: the genre assumes a common experience, but the fans bring unique and individual understandings to that notion.

The phrase "then we danced . . . ," sometimes tells a tale that extends the relationship far beyond the dance floor. Where the literal invocation of the dance hall environment and practices ends, country music has long relied on dance as a metaphor for sexual encounters.[5] These particular depictions of dance rely on certain stereotypes and a narrow range of dance practices: the heterosexual dancing couple, in physical contact, compelled by the music to move together rhythmically. Beyond those metaphoric references to sexual encounters, there are many instances where dance is used in country music to depict down-home traditional entertainment, country authenticity, and the unifying act of joining together with friends.[6] Furthermore, country music has frequently used the metaphor of dance for its greater philosophical considerations, most notably in Garth Brooks's "The Dance," the Dixie Chicks' "Some Days You Gotta Dance," and Lee Ann Womack's "I Hope You Dance."[7] What all of these uses have in common is the basic dependence on the audience's understanding and acceptance of country dancing as a shared, universal experience within country culture. That those songs, and commercial country music in general, are shared almost universally by fans across the nation is quite clear; that their dance practices are as well is highly questionable.

Homogenization?

Near Raleigh, North Carolina, there are three locations on the FM radio dial that easily pick up country stations: 94.7, 96.9, and 101.1. The latter two are broadcast frequencies for a single station (WKIX); all three are owned by the same corporation, Curtis Media Group, controlled by Don Curtis, and share the responsibilities of program director through a central planning office. The general manager of WQDR 94.7 has pointed out that all three play the same power rotation of the top songs on the industry's country charts, and while WKIX slides quite a few songs from past years into its playlist, the musical diet is straight hot country out of Nashville with marketing considerations driving every aspect of the radio business.[8] Yet ironically, the presence of Curtis Media Group stations in that region is a small mark of regional independence; across the nation, increasingly large media conglomerates are consolidating ownership of most radio stations into the hands of fewer and fewer corporations, with Clear Channel Communications leading the way.[9] The occasional populist accusation that country music has become a generic, cookie-cutter sound produced by a single mainstream industry is reinforced by this situation, where radio options for the listening public are increasingly centrally controlled.[10] In a business where artistic success is sometimes measured in album sales, advertising revenue, and chart placement, the interconnections within the industry sometimes result in more streamlined, and therefore narrower, options for fans to access their music. Because one of the commercial goals for an artist is that his or her song reach the largest possible audience, the same popular songs are heard by the listening public clear across the nation, and a certain homogenization of musical identity occurs.

Just as the country music industry has sought increasing commercial success through national distribution and standardization of its product, country dance practices have undergone several easily documented efforts toward central standardization. The range of dance practices that appear in the country night clubs addressed here include lead/follow partner dances such as Two-Step, Swing, and Waltz; various choreographed partner dances that have predetermined footwork patterns; line dancing; and, occasionally, freestyle dancing borrowed from the rock tradition. Although attempts to standardize

Men and women individually crowd the floor of the Longbranch Saloon as they line dance.

dance practices have affected each of these different dances, the most concerted efforts have been directed toward line dancing.[11]

The most prevalent forms of contemporary line dancing find their immediate
roots in the disco era. The 1977 movie *Saturday Night Fever*, the 1982 release of
Michael Jackson's video for "Thriller," and the immense popularity of Van
McCoy's song and dance "Hustle" all speak to the burgeoning adoption of line
dancing by the American public in the early 1980s.[12] The commercial appeal of
line dancing led country music to forge a strong alliance with the practice by the
mid-1980s. Choreographers could be hired to create dances for individual
songs; the marketing package for those songs could include both the dance
steps and a video that incorporated that dance. Across the nation, local dance
instructors could generate significant business from collecting and teaching
these line dances. Furthermore, through music videos, the appeal for any given
dance could be spread to the fans, who would then take the lessons, buy the
videos, and want to hear the song in their night clubs in order to put their newly
learned dance steps to use. The one-to-one correspondence between a song and
its own choreographed line dance meant there was an endless supply of new
dances, continually renewing the commercial viability of this business model.

The most overtly orchestrated implementation of this model was the release of Billy Ray Cyrus's hit, "Achy Breaky Heart," in 1992.[13] The single was accompanied by a music video, which featured footage of screaming fans participating in a line dance choreographed by industry insider Melanie Greenwood specifically for that song; instructional videos were available to teach the footwork to anyone interested; and local dance instructors held special workshops to spread the dance. This marketing strategy worked so successfully for Cyrus's team because the dance climate at the time expected and allowed one official version of each line dance, and the public was willing to go to some effort to seek out that standardized version.

The television show that offered itself up as both a representation of and a model for country dance practice illustrates the gulf between the prepackaged dance traditions and the more complicated, and gendered, interactions in actual night clubs. In 1991, The Nashville Network launched a show that came to be known as *Club Dance*, filmed in Knoxville, Tennessee at a television studio and set in the fictitious White Horse Café (at Cinetel Studios).[14] Local unpaid dancers were the principle cast for the show, supplemented with visiting dance groups and individuals from across the country. The show gathered an immensely loyal viewership, and the regular dancers were viewed not only as performers but also as celebrities who shared their personal lives on the show in candid conversational moments with the hosts. By the producers' design, the dancers were granted freedom to behave and engage with the music as if the studio were merely their own local dance venue.[15]

The dances performed on the show represented the range of standard country dance repertoire: lead/follow partner dances, choreographed partner dances, and line dances. On the one hand, *Club Dance* was perceived by the greater viewing population as the representative ideal of a country dance venue. On the other hand, *Club Dance* was, in fact, an artificial construct of the world of television, and was not representative of any single real country dance venue or dance practice. By mixing and merging dance traditions from all over the country through their guest dancers, the show created an atmosphere that could not exist outside its sound studio.

Three dance practices in evidence on the show are worth noting: first, to any one song that was played, different groups of people would perform different dances at the same time. Some couples would be Two-Stepping while others line danced, and still others performed a West-Coast Swing in a different space. While there was typically a majority participating in one dance, there was significant strength of independent choice and personal expression in the dancers' responding to any song with a variety of dances. Second, the dancers who were regulars on the show performed with a recognizable amount of professional dance training, most visibly in the West-Coast Swing performances, that was not echoed in the nightclub atmosphere and social dancing in real venues.[16] The chance to perform on television inspired some of the regulars to take lessons from swing dance coaches, thereby importing a level of professionalism and even a different dance style entirely into the show.[17] The results were dance styles that social dancers in country night clubs could not echo. Third, the dancers on the show became TV stars, which brought a completely different set of motivations to their performances than those experienced by fans in a night club: their interpersonal interactions were as collaborators on a show, not individuals in a bar. Thus, the dancing presented on that show and broadcast around the country was completely void of the tensions and communications between dance partners that are part of the nightclub dance hall scene. As a result, the most widely distributed "model" for a country dance hall failed to demonstrate dancing that could be echoed by the general country fan population, and lacked the essence of interpersonal communication that governs much of the behavior in a country night club.

Formal attempts to standardize dance practices came from a number of newly created professional associations. The Country Western Line Dance Association, the United Country Western Dance Council, and the National Teachers Association for Country Western Dance were just a few of the groups that appeared on the national scene in the late 1980s, including on their agenda various intentions such as "to promote Country Western dancing, establish communication among dance teachers, develop *standardized terminology and step patterns* . . . , maintain high standards for teachers, and to more effectively instruct others in the art and practice of Country Western dancing."[18] Officially sanctioned competitions, sponsored by these organizations, also bespoke the strong push for conformity and centralized control over the way fans were dancing: promotion of these competitions publicized the specific dances that were selected for use in them.[19] All of these efforts were directed toward standardization of dance practices and support of new dances, which kept the dance instructors busy and generated new content for videos and books. Had these organizational efforts been entirely successful, their presence, combined with the nationally uniform country radio market and the ease with which fans traveled from one region of the country to another, would have fostered uniformity in the country dance hall practices and traditions that emerged from this time period. Instead, a remarkable community-based independence in dance practices remained intact in spite of these efforts.

Country Dance Practice

Country dancing thrives in a variety of types of settings within the regions of North Carolina and Tennessee, including the family-oriented and alcohol-free barn dance, the historically loosely related gatherings for square dancing and contra dancing, and specially scheduled dance events at dance studios, universities, and community centers, to name just a few. Even within the country night club scene—specifically a large venue serving alcohol and functioning primarily as a socializing avenue for the general adult population—different audience segments are served by different styles of clubs, and both fan behavior and dance practices are extremely diverse. For this study, I chose to focus only on one style of country dance hall, those venues that subscribe to the traditions most often drawn upon in mainstream commercial country music: an audience of mainly heterosexual, working-class country fans for whom the music is part of their regular entertainment selection and for whom their country identity is one that extends beyond the confines of the venue.[20]

The thirteen venues that formed the core of this study (Table 1) share certain characteristics and demographics. All feature mid- to large-sized floor spaces, serve alcohol, and are recognized as one of the primary gathering places for country fans within their metropolitan areas.[21] Some feature live bands at least some nights of the week, others rely exclusively on DJs and recorded music, but in either case, the music is a device through which the fans interact and express themselves, and it makes little difference whether the performers are live or not. The richest embodiment of dance practices is represented in the ethnography of the fans rather than in any formal, recorded history of country dancing. To experience those traditions, I submerged myself in these venues and fan communities. My weekend routine was the same at each place: after a few dollars in cover charges and an admission hand-stamp in permanent ink, I located an empty bar stool with a good view of the dance floor and sat down to watch. Without exception, over the course of the evening at least a few people would approach me with conventional conversation starters. I danced a little, talked with willing patrons, and absorbed the atmosphere in each club on as many occasions as possible.

One of the most striking aspects of these venues was the evolution and generally transient quality of the fans' dance traditions during just the four years I gathered my observations. In the late 1990s, the wave of line dance popularity sparked by "Achy Breaky Heart" and sustained by dance-centered mega-hits recorded by Brooks and Dunn, Tracy Byrd, and Shania Twain, among dozens of other artists, was still quite strong. Dance halls were still opening, rather than closing, throughout the region; most venues offered dance lessons several nights a week; and TNN still regularly aired new episodes of *Club Dance*, a show that was built quite simply on watching people dance.

Four years later, several of the dance halls covered in this original research had changed locations or closed completely, TNN's *Club Dance* had faded into memories and website reminiscences, and several catalytic events had brought marked changes to the faces of both commercial country music and dance. Though that show had been extremely popular and highly visible to the country community, it left no visible lasting effect on the dancing that happened in the country bars outside of Knoxville. It seemed symptomatic of the overall waning interest in country dancing that the large neon sign over Interstate 40 boldly announcing the location of Knoxville's Cotton Eyed Joe club was recently missing key letters, a token, perhaps, of the wear and tear of the decade on one of country dancing's more glamorous venues.

Going It Alone

The southeastern United States has never housed the same dedicated country dance tradition that was the staple of dance halls in Texas, California, and Oklahoma during the middle of the twentieth century. Western Swing was born and took root in the southwest, and particularly in California, where the eminently Two-Steppable sounds of Bakersfield fueled the dancers' energies. The southeast had its own separate dance traditions, and while some of the formal partner dances like Two-Step and Waltz were done occasionally, they never garnered the same sense of indigenous ownership as in other parts of the country.

When John Travolta and Debra Winger Two-Stepped through *Urban Cowboy* in 1980, popular American culture adopted the entertainment model of the country dance hall and suddenly, participating on the dance floor was highly fashionable. However, in regions without a history of that style of danc-ing, local populations lacked the knowledge to actually walk onto a floor and Two-Step, an act that required the partnership of a leader with the requisite skills and technical dance knowledge, and a follower, similarly trained, to communicate and execute the dance steps in harmony. In regions where Two-Stepping had been part of the dance tradition for several generations, those skills were traditionally passed down through social rituals of group participation.[22] But in regions without that ingrained tradition, the younger generations had no source from which to learn. Furthermore, the Two-Step's leader/follower partnership required a relatively even number of men and women who were willing to perform those roles within the politics of a coun-try bar, and in a region without those traditions, male fans in particular were reticent to dive into the new trend of dancing.

Line dancing quickly emerged as a welcome alternative to this situation. One of the selling points that the line dancers touted was that line dancing eliminated the cumbersome social requirement of a leader/follower dance pair, as well as any communication between dancers other than starting the dance at the same time and moving in the same direction on the floor. The helpful guidance of a DJ could take care of those aspects. In its advertised form, line dancing allowed the removal of the very characteristics of dance that were most often sung about in its traditional songs: the elements of flirtation and seduction between dance partners, the use of dance as a sexual metaphor, and the communication within the dance hall environment between prospective dance partners that amounted to a negotiation of roles for the act of dancing were all eliminated. Instead, any number of men or women, or any combination, were free to learn the steps individually and then participate in the social act of line dancing without having to confront a dance partner in any way. No longer was one's opportunity to dance limited by the availability or lack of a suitably talented and knowledgeable dance partner.

This description of line dancing, and, indeed, its practice in certain venues, took on an asexual nature, more like an aerobics class. Dancers lined up on the floor together in rows, all staring at the backs of the people in front of them, and passively waited for instructions from the DJ, at which point the dancers would all begin the steps in unison.[23] Furthermore, men and women learned identical steps, removing any specific gendered behavior from the performance. The social freedom to express oneself individually on the dance floor, while still performing the dance as part of the collective, was one benefit of this dance trend. However, in the social environment of some country night clubs, the fans' behaviors altered these principles of line dancing in strongly gendered ways.

In 1994, Tracy Byrd recorded "Watermelon Crawl," and Sue Lipscomb choreographed a line dance for the song.[24] The popularity of this line dance has survived nearly a decade, and in all the clubs visited in the course of this study, it was the only song that showed up in every single club at least once during the course of an evening. Nearly every dancer in the country community knows the standard forty beats' worth of steps for the line dance, and almost a decade after its appearance, fans continue to enjoy it. At the Longbranch in Raleigh, North Carolina, a local cover band launched into the song, and approximately sixty dancers, an even mix of men and women of all ages and abilities, filled the floor. These dancers did the conventional version of the footwork, without any particular sense of coordination—one group of dancers lined up facing the stage and started their steps; another group arrived on the floor a few seconds later, lined up facing a different direction, and began the dance. The two groups each seemed to pay attention to their own group's performance, and generally went through the motions of the dance without any particular excitement. The men and the women participated with similar styling and body language, paying little attention to each other.

In some venues, however, a variation on the steps exists that involves pantomiming the song's lyrics during one brief section of the dance. In this variation, when Byrd sings, "She rocked back on her heels, dropped down to her knees / crawled across the floor then she jumped back on her feet / she wiggled and she jiggled, beat all you ever saw," the dancers do as the text describes. As "Watermelon Crawl" started to play in Cotton Eyed Joe in Cookeville, Tennessee, the dance floor filled with only women, while the men in the venue slid barstools up to the railing that surrounded the dance floor. The DJ, perched high in the converted cab of a Freightliner, waited until the song's introduction was finished and the women were lined up on the floor, obediently waiting for his instructions. He spoke in rhythm, "5-6-7-8," and the women moved in perfect unison. As they began to dance, the interplay between the female performers and the mostly male watchers began.

The song's lyrics reveal a tale of seduction, in which the local girl entices the passing stranger with the small town's festival and dance traditions, and the women on the dance floor took the prescribed line-dance steps and used them as a platform to act out the strongly gender-segregated narrative. The primarily male audience in the club called out demands to see the dancers "drop down to their knees," quoting the song's lyrics, and as the young women on the dance floor stretched out on the hardwood to the accompaniment of appreciative whistles, the act of dancing lost its role as participatory response to the music and became merely enactment of the subtext of the song.[25] In this instance, the communication and interaction between the male and female fans was not one of exchange or partnership, as would have been required in a partner-dance situation, nor was it one of ungendered communal ritual, as was the line dance done by the fans in the Longbranch. Although the club had all the trappings of country music's culture in its décor, music selections, and fan identity as expressed by wardrobe and gesture, it became an environment where line dancing separated male and female fans, assigned them specific and distinct roles, and treated their sexuality as a commodity to be displayed, nearly even marketed, on the dance floor. In this Cookeville environment, it was the distance—both physical and metaphoric—between the fans' adopted gendered roles that was most striking.

When Cotton Eyed Joe opened in Knoxville in September of 1993, it joined five other country bars in the Knoxville area.[26] Not surprisingly, since the country dance craze has passed its peak and fair-weather fans have left the scene, it is the only remaining country night club of any social significance in Knoxville, though it retains its widely known reputation as a country dance mecca.[27] On most spring Saturday nights, the club is full but not packed. The parking lot boasts a noticeable number of shined and chromed pickup trucks, external signifiers of its country format and an identity card for those attending. Inside, one finds an energy-infused southern country décor, complete with western-style facades and memorabilia, a Dixie flag, a mechanical bull, a section built like a front porch veranda, replete with wooden swings, and wooden barrels as tables. This club holds fast to some of the most iconic aspects of country dance, and given its Knoxville location, is the venue where many of the regulars from *Club Dance* tapings congregate for social dancing.

The dance traditions in this venue are supported by the establishment in ways not found at other venues, as is best signified by the presence of a large, orange five-gallon cooler and a stack of plastic cups sitting on the bar offering patrons free water. Patrons who are at any club mainly for the purpose of dancing typically view their activity as a sport and prefer water and nonalcoholic beverages, all of which potentially cuts into the bar's profit margin. As a result, many country bars reach an unspoken equilibrium between accommodating the preferences of dancers, who are a necessity in order to maintain a "country bar" feel, and catering more to patrons who spend more money.[28]

How a dance hall navigates the complex symbiotic relationship between having a thriving dance floor and running a successful business becomes one of its identifying characteristics: all over the region, the clubs claim their dance floor as part of their identity, yet most are caught in the alcohol-financed paradox between bar and dance hall—in short, from a business perspective, most clubs just don't know what to do with water-drinking dancers. The Cotton Eyed Joe solution in Knoxville has cultivated a community in which a rich and diverse dance tradition thrives: the highly trained dancers who used to perform on *Club Dance* present competition-level Two-Stepping and West-Coast Swing, which adds a flair to the venue, while local college students line dance and freestyle dance for hours on end, keeping the club packed and popular.[29]

The strongest expression of community identity in this club came not from the most elaborate Two-Stepping dancers, but rather from the way the crowd merged local sports culture with their country dance practices. When the DJ played the traditional, bluegrass version of "Rocky Top," recorded by the Osborne Brothers, the dance floor filled up immediately.[30] Even though the twang of the banjo contrasted sharply with most of the music played that night in the club, the primarily college-age crowd launched into an enthusiastic "16-Step," circling the floor with their footwork entirely in unison.[31] The "16-Step" can be danced with couples holding hands, but all the dancers face the same direction and execute a preset pattern of steps, and most dancers in this region danced it solo, with no physical contact with other dancers.

Although an alternate techno remix version of the song is popular in many of the country night clubs I visited, no crowd was as enthusiastic in their dancing as this particular community, whose unrivaled affection for the song is fueled by its use as the University of Tennessee Knoxville's fight song. In their enthusiasm, a small group of men gathered together and began to exaggerate the steps of the dance as they progressed around the floor, each one kicking higher than his neighbor, adding extra rotations to his spins, and generally entering into a contest of one-upsmanship through elaborate footwork variations. Their entire dance was performed with a swagger and masculine accentuation as they stomped louder and louder around the floor and secured their cowboy hats lower on their heads. Although the men were clearly performing for each other and not a stationary audience, their dance steps became a medium through which they could express their physical strength and prowess, community identity as loyal Tennessee Volunteer fans, and masculine embodiment of the cowboy persona. It was a ritual in which none of the female fans joined.

In Fayetteville's Palomino, it was the techno-remix version of the traditional fiddle tune, "Cotton-Eyed Joe" that elicited a similar response. In this town, most widely known as home to Fort Bragg and Pope Air Force Base, the male fans in the club performed a "16-Step" with the same style of masculine bravado as their counterparts in Knoxville, although here a group of women, sitting near the dance floor, visibly stared at the dancers through their entire performance. When the Dixie Chicks' recording of "Sin Wagon" was played, three of the men leapt onto the floor and wowed the crowd with their "16-Step" prowess, spinning, high-kicking, and nearly prancing around the floor. Their physical performance resembled an engine-rumbling drag race through the streets as they dodged other dancers and passed them at high speeds, racing one another through the forward-moving shuffle steps.

In Fayetteville in 2000, the "16-Step" was clearly a local favorite—songs that elsewhere entertained a variety of dance steps were invariably used for the "16-Step" there; three years later, that dance's popularity had faded, and other dances, most notably "Apple Jack," had become the vehicle for men to perform in front of the female fans. Several male dancers had devised elaborate variations for "Apple Jack," and each time a bluegrass breakdown was played, the men gathered in the center of the floor to show off for each other and the watching audience.

Not only do these dance practices cultivate a sense of same-sex bonding, but country music has picked up on this option in its songs' narratives. In her neofeminist country-pop hit, "Man! I Feel Like a Woman," Shania Twain sang, "The girls need a break, tonight we're gonna take / The chance to get out on the town / We don't need romance, we only wanna dance / We're gonna let our hair hang down."[32] Amplifying its gender-bending title, the song quickly became an anthem for girls' nights out and a celebration of independence in seeking entertainment. The rhythmic grooves that Twain and producer/husband Mutt Lange use on many of her recordings veer away from the patterns required for more traditional country partner dancing, but support a number of popular line dance body motions and footwork patterns quite easily.

When the cover band Chaparral played this song in Coyote Joe's in Charlotte, female fans were the only dancers who took to the floor. Not only did Twain's lyrics support their feminine sense of identity and independence, but the fans' line dancing physically asserted that same independence. The dancing itself did not forbid the male fans' participation, but the men's involvement was clearly unnecessary for the women to enjoy and interact with the song. Although the themes of feminist independence found in the songs are layered under superficial concerns (wardrobe, hair, nails, and make-up comprise the subject of some of her songs), those themes are present nonetheless. To some extent, Twain's domination as artist and businesswoman in the industry is reflected by the undercurrent and tone of her lyrics, and through the practice of line dancing, her fans can express the same embodiment of those themes.[33]

Holding Hands

In Nashville's Silverado's Saloon and Dance Hall, one of the most popular dances and part of the standard dance repertoire is the Sweetheart

Schottische, a 26-beat couple's dance done to up-tempo, rock-beat, duple-time country songs, like Kenny Chesney's "Someone Else's Hog" in this particular venue. As this song started, men asked women to dance and the floor filled with couples. Unlike Two-Step, where a dancing couple often faces each other, in this dance male and female dancers are side-by-side, facing forward, linking hands in a shadow position.[34] The dance's basic footwork pattern has evolved into a choreographed sequence from the traditional folk dance of a Schottische, combining grapevine steps to the side with forward skips. The unusual duration of the pattern (twenty-six beats) and the highly stylized sequence of footwork bespeak contemporary choreography, but the generally accepted origin of the dance is that it is anonymous and "traditional."[35] The basic pattern is sufficiently interesting in terms of body motion, and sufficiently long at twenty-six beats, that almost all dancers are content to dance an entire song without adding any variations. Furthermore, the dance is done in a progression around the dance floor, all couples dancing in unison, with each woman doing exactly what the woman in front of her is doing, and each man copying the man in front of him.

Unlike line dancing, this dance requires the social interaction off the floor of locating a suitable dance partner, and inviting that partner onto the floor for the song. The formal invitation of, "Would you like to dance?" is often used, invoking at least some small aspect of the gendered codes of chivalry in the night club. More common in Silverado's, the invitation to dance was issued through body language and gesture only, in part a concession to the noise level in the club that made conversation difficult, and in part as a general way to shortcut and circumvent any required verbal interaction. The environment was based on nonverbal communication and gesture: fans moved around the club watching each other, and physical representation, through dress and posture, was the principle means of projecting one's identity.

Once the dancers entered the floor, the structure of the Sweetheart Schottische eliminated any further need to communicate: the footwork and body movement patterns were predetermined, and as each couple entered the floor, they simply began the footwork in unison with the couple in front of them. The male dancer was not required to lead his partner through the dance—she knew what to do and in what sequence—even though their hands were connected.

To the generally younger crowd in the Tennessee venues, this dance provided a safe and comfortable middle-ground of gendered communication and interaction. The dancers did not rely on each other for the actual performance of the dance, but only for the invitation to participate. Once the men learned their own basic steps, they were released from any requirement of further technical proficiency, or from any responsibility to lead their partners through the dance, because the women could perform their footwork, or role, without guidance. On the other hand, the dance reinserted the traditional gendered roles of the western dance hall's Two-Step in terms of the man's invitation to his partner, and in the physical contact between the partners on the floor, with him holding her hands and wrapping an arm around her shoulders.

Particularly in Nashville's Denim and Diamonds, and in Knoxville's Cotton Eyed Joe, some of the dancers moved beyond the independent execution of the dance steps in the Sweetheart Schottische through the addition of variations for individual steps. Extra spins and intricate arm patterns were inserted to display technical virtuosity, as well as the occasional aerial maneuver, but these were clearly the exceptions. In each of these venues, more fans participated in this dance than in any other partner dance.

Yet across the border in North Carolina, the dance was essentially nonexistent. Rarely, a single pair of dancers would get on the floor and attempt it, but without any collective support from the rest of the fans. As wildly popular as the dance was in Tennessee, its impact was very regionally limited. Clearly, this situation did not result from a lack of exposure or transmission opportunity: the dance was performed regularly on TNN's *Club Dance*, and many of the dancers from North Carolina travel to Tennessee to dance on occasion. In fact, during conversations about their dancing in Raleigh, many men admitted that they knew the dance, but just didn't do it there. Choreographed partner dances in general, including others such as the Cowboy Cha-Cha or the Shadow, were simply not part of the standard dance repertoire in the North Carolina clubs. One of the explanations offered by the dancers was that they simply weren't as artistically interesting: the dance pattern was predetermined, unlike in Two-Step, and at the same time, the room for personally stylizing those steps was limited by the presence of a dance partner in physical contact.

Part of the experience of dancing the Sweetheart Schottische is the ritualistic repetition, following the person in front of you for the entire duration of the song, executing the same dance pattern over and over. At the clubs with an active DJ who dictated songs and dances in a predetermined cycle, the ritual and repetition of the entire dance experience, over the course of an evening, was amplified. The dancers passively responded to the DJ's instructions at Nashville's Denim and Diamonds, when he announced, "up next will be a Cowboy Cha-Cha, so find your partners and come on out onto the floor. . . . OK, here we go . . . 5-6-7-8." The roles that each of the dancers play in that setting include the superficial interaction of dance partners, but they require little or no personal initiative to perform.

Looking for a Good Partner

There was woman in the Silver Saddle in Raleigh standing on the edge of the dance floor, tugging at the arm of her date and pleading, "Come dance with me!" The man's insistent refusal was repeated in his response, "I don't know how." Far from employing a socially acceptable excuse for not wanting to participate, this fan was quite literally facing a situation for which he did not have the requisite skills or knowledge: the band was playing a Two-Step, and to dance with his partner would have required that he communicate, through his body, how she was to move to the music—literally what direction, and in what rhythms—while responding to her body motion, all through a creative process that must occur in time to the music. Thus, she was left without a partner, and could not participate.

The lead/follow partner dances, those with only a very short basic pattern (six beats in the case of the Two-Step) and the requirement of communication between the dancers in order to execute them, invoke a series of gendered roles that extend beyond the invitation to dance. For Waltz, Two-Step, West-Coast Swing, East-Coast Swing, and Cha-Cha, the act of dancing becomes a process of communication, feedback, and response through a set of technically specific codes of movement. In these particular night clubs, the men perform the role of leader, while the women perform the role of follower, both in concert with the music.

In the bodies of the most technically proficient dancers, these roles become enablers for the dancers to achieve higher levels of artistic expression.

A couple dancing a West-Coast Swing in the Longbranch deftly and flippantly emphasized each musical phrase in Toby Keith's recording of "Who's Your Daddy," and the man's communication with his partner was so complete that each indication of a lead became an invitation for her to act. The men standing off the dance floor stared at the couple, mesmerized both by her fluid spins and sensual steps, and by the skill with which her dance partner coaxed each movement from her body.[36]

But at the same time, each partner's artistic freedom within the dance is entirely dependent on the skill level of the other. Thus, stepping onto the dance floor involves a commitment to perform a role that will be judged by one's dance partner, and one that can be easily judged by the audience. I was sitting in the Palomino in Fayetteville when a man approached me, smiled, and politely asked, not the traditional question of, "Would you like to dance?" but rather, "Do you know how to Waltz?" Similarly, a woman in Nashville's Denim and Diamonds asked a male friend, "Will you lead me in a West-Coast [Swing]?" The communication off the dance floor was essentially a code telling the potential partner what would be expected, and an inquiry as to whether he or she could perform the required role on the dance floor.

Without a suitable dance partner, a fan's ability to participate in the dancing, and thereby express his or her emotional engagement with the music, is eliminated. This tension, and formality of the roles within a lead/follow partner dance environment defines much of the code of interaction between potential partners in a country night club; the need to find a suitable partner is ever-present. Yet within many of the venues, the alternatives of line dances or choreographed partner dances are not embraced. Instead, the fans in central North Carolina typically seek out the lead/follow relationships, preferring those dances that involve communication between dancers through their bodies' connections to the music. Those modes of communication on the dance floor extend off the floor into the personal interaction of fans within the venue in general.

Country Is as Country Does?

Hickory, North Carolina, houses two country bars that seem to contradict every element of the country dance tradition. At Wayneo's Silver Bullet on a Saturday night, the local band Highrize kept the audience at a nearly frenzied energy level with their version of southern rock tunes and country standards. Across town, the same scene played out at the New Country Music Bar. But in both venues, the fans were content to enthusiastically dance freestyle, only coming in physical contact during the slow songs, when they embraced and swayed in time to the music. None of the audience line danced, Two-Stepped, or partner danced in any other way during the course of the evening. In spite of the connection between country music's identity and the various forms of country dancing that are so pervasive throughout the culture, these fans eschewed any of those styles of dancing for their musical participation.

The physical signifiers of country music culture were amplified in the décor of the clubs, the consumption of food and beverages, the fans' choice of dress, topics of discussion, and vocal preference for the music of established country stars, but the codes of gendered behavior demonstrated through country dancing, in its varied forms, were absent from the club. When a song mentioned country dancing in any format, these fans lacked any empathetic connection to the experience of partnering, communicating, and moving in harmony, in all its complexities and variations. From that perspective, the clubs, and the communities of fans within them, were defining a completely different country dance identity entirely without those components. Whatever shared cultural narrative exists in country music and fan culture about dancing was absent from these fans' experiences.

Characterizing the Dance Relationship

One might find it easy to generalize about the different dance practices and conclude that each offers distinct benefits: line dancing frees the individual for greater artistic expression, the traditions and codes of chivalry required in the lead/follow partner dances connect most strongly to the country music cultural narrative, the choreographed partner dances are an artificially constructed product to market partner dancing to an audience that lacks that tradition, etc. Conversely, one might argue that the physical interaction and mutual communication required in the lead/follow partner dances like Two-Step offer the participants more artistic freedom to embody the music than do the ritualized performances of line dances like the Watermelon Crawl encountered in Cookeville. None of those conclusions, however, would do justice to the complex configuration of relationships between country fans within a given community and their modes of expression through dance.

Instead, we are left with a portrait of diverse communal identities, where roles and codes of interaction are constructed by the ways that fans choose to dance. The commonalities between these practices are that they provide both an outlet for individual expression and a medium for communication and interaction between fans. The individual expression is found in the physical movements of dancing—the way the body projects the music, whether the body is dancing alone or in contact with another person. The communication is achieved through the codes and roles of male and female fans within the dance practice. Whether acting out the lyrics in "Watermelon Crawl" or executing the correct steps when Two-Stepping as a follower, there are expectations for the role a female fan will adopt; similarly, in order to participate, a male fan is expected to lead a Two-Step or Waltz, invite a woman to dance a Sweetheart Schottische, or display his physical prowess in a "16-Step." Even with regard to line dancing, which ostensibly eliminated the need for individual gender roles, each venue's fan base has constructed some version of them around the dance.

A newcomer to any of these dance communities must learn not only the physical dance steps used in a particular venue, but also the accompanying roles that are performed through the rituals of communication and fan interaction: what is being conveyed and promised in the act of asking another fan to dance, or in performing a dance step individually. The supposedly shared understanding of "dancing to a country song" is, in fact, a commonality with a multitude of local differentiations, relating both to the footwork and body motion and to the gendered identity projected through the act of dancing. There is no centrally available guidebook, video, or lesson plan that explains these roles for all country audiences, because they are the distinct products and markers of individual communities within the geographic region examined here.

Country music is inextricably tied to a dance tradition, but within the fan culture of North Carolina and Tennessee, there is no shared means through which fans learn what that dance tradition is. Even in the clubs where the fans frequently Two-Step, any invitation to dance is issued without the assumption that the invitee is capable of participating. Instead, contemporary fans are consciously and carefully constructing their interactive roles and dance experiences, and defining and redefining what it means to participate as a dancer in a country night club. Their actions enrich the dance metaphors on which the music so frequently draws, and thereby allow the general notion of country dancing to remain a vibrant, if diversified, part of the culture.

Between Riot Grrrl and Quiet Girl

The New Women's Movement in Country Music

BEVERLY KEEL

During the last decade, the nation's attention and entertainment headlines have been captured by a fascinating movement in rock music characterized as the era of angry young females. Artists such as Alanis Morissette, Fiona Apple, and PJ Harvey burst onto the scene with an adrenaline-fueled, machismo-mimicking ferocity that equaled their testosterone-driven male counterparts. The antithesis of people-pleasing females, these women revealed raw anger, frank sexuality, and in-your-face attitudes. Meanwhile, a much more subtle but no less important (and perhaps equally as rebellious) women's movement was happening across the dial in country music. Although largely ignored by the mainstream music press, this movement has revolutionized the way women are portrayed in popular music's most conservative genre.

While it would be easy to dismiss the feminist movement in country because it is not as blatant or daring as rock music's defiant feminist stance, it has been equally as influential and undeniable. To examine the quality and effectiveness of the strides that have been made, it is important to explore the spoken and unspoken parameters that surround female country artists. Because the country music industry is far more conservative than other popular music genres, female singers have had to make feminist stands in ways that would not offend the industry's male gatekeepers at record labels, publishing companies, and radio stations, where the sexist double standard is still alive and well. In other words, they've had to play by the rules (or at least pretend to) before they could be allowed to bend them or use them to promote feminism. In addition, country fans have historically been more conservative than rock and pop devotees, so country feminists have had to soften or temper their messages to ensure that country fans wouldn't be offended or alienated. The result has been a slowly evolving feminist movement that has made its own distinct stand for the importance of equality for women.

The country feminist movement has collectively progressed steadily but quietly for seventeen years, since the release of K. T. Oslin's *8os Ladies* (1987), which took a painfully brutal look at the lives of women on the forefront of the women's lib movement.[1] Inspired by Oslin's example, other female country singers began recording songs that increasingly presented a strong female perspective that questioned some of current mainstream society's long-held beliefs, while still adhering to the genre's strict musical and social boundaries. And now this feminist message has become the rule instead of the exception in country. Today, virtually every top female artist's songs reflect a feminist stance, and if record sales are any indication, this new way of thinking has been received warmly by country record buyers. It's now the female superstars—Faith Hill, Shania Twain, the Dixie Chicks, and Gretchen Wilson— who are dominating the *Billboard* sales charts.

In 1995, Shania Twain took Oslin's efforts to the next level by leading the charge with songs that have a feisty feminist attitude and a demand for equality. In addition, Faith Hill, Martina McBride, Lorrie Morgan, Jo Dee Messina, Trisha Yearwood, Reba McEntire, Terri Clark, Kathy Mattea, Wynonna Judd, Patty Loveless, Jessica Andrews, and others are now singing of the problems and tales of the modern, independent woman. Even Le Ann Rimes, who was just fifteen years old at the time of her first hit, sings with attitude and independence. This is significant because more women than ever are incorporating feminist themes in their careers. With more songs by more female artists delivering a feminist message, the impact on the industry is undeniable. And because they are among the biggest names in country music, their individual messages are receiving important exposure in the press.

Thanks to caricatures like the one painted by Hillary Clinton during a *60 Minutes* interview regarding her husband's infidelity ("I'm not sitting here like some little woman like Tammy Wynette, standing by my man"), women in country music have been unfairly saddled throughout the decades with the reputation of being weepy doormats for men. Although songs of heartache have traditionally been associated with female country singers, strong empowered women are nothing new in country music. Long before Loretta Lynn and Patsy Cline, women were taking tough stands by painting musical pictures of the thoughts and desires of working women. For example, the earliest American labor protest songs were of the exploitation of women in factories. "The Lowell Factory Girl" dates from the 1830s, and other nineteenth-century songs such as "All the Doo Da Day" and "Factory Girls Come All-Ye" sang of horrible working conditions.[2] As early as 1915, Appalachian women were singing about promiscuity, premarital sex, and unwanted pregnancies. In 1917, Anna Chandler addressed the women's suffrage movement with her song "She's Good Enough to Be Your Baby's Mother and She's Good Enough to Vote with You."[3]

In 1925, fifteen-year-old Roba Stanley, one of the genre's first female solo recording artists, sang "Single Life," in which she says, "I am single and no man's wife / And no man shall control me," which remains perhaps one of the strongest statements made by a woman in country music even today.[4] Ironically, she only recorded nine songs before giving up her musical career for marriage and family. "Single Girl, Married Girl" (1927) emerged from the Carter Family's initial recording sessions in Bristol. This song tells the woes of a shabbily-dressed married woman with a baby on her knee. Two years later, Adelyne Hood boasted of her ability to whip men in "Calamity Jane" (1929), which included such lyrics as, "When it comes to drinkin' likker / I can take a dozen men / And drink 'em under the tables and up on their chairs again."[5]

In the 1930s, an independent-spirited cowgirl named Patsy Montana emerged as the antithesis of the wholesome country sweetheart, and in the 1950s, Texas Ruby appeared on the scene with a deep alto voice and red lips, extolling the virtues of living hard and having fun. Also during the 1950s, Texan Charline Arthur became the first country female to don pants onstage. "Charline leaped from stage amplifiers, hollered honky-tonk blues, sang lying down onstage, and cavorted wildly to entertain the tough Texas crowds. 'I was the first to break out of the [country female] stereotype and boogie-woogie,' Charline bragged to journalist Bob Allen in 1985. 'I was shakin' on stage long before Elvis even thought about it.' "[6]

A much more conservative Kitty Wells was forbidden to sing "It Wasn't God Who Made Honky-Tonk Angels" (1952) on the stage of the Grand Ole Opry because it was too outspoken.[7] The NBC radio network even banned the song for being too suggestive. The 1952 release was written in response to country singer Hank Thompson's "The Wild Side of Life" (1952), which contained the line, "I didn't know God made honky-tonk angels."[8] Wells's song described a betrayed wife's pain and contended that virtually every broken heart has been caused by a man. The married Wells, always looking prim and proper, disagreed with Thompson's assertion that it was the wild women who led the innocent men astray, singing, "Too many times married men think they're still single / That has caused many a good girl to go wrong."[9]

The 1960s brought Wanda Jackson, the most assertive cowgirl rockabilly of her era, wearing sexy skin-tight clothes and growling and screaming her lyrics.[10] However, only a few of her songs addressed women's issues, such as the threatening "My Big Iron Skillet" (1969) ("There's gonna be some changes made when you get in tonight / Cause I'm gonna teach you wrong from right / With a big iron skillet in my hand") and "A Girl Don't Have to Drink to Have Fun" (1967).[11] In the 1960s and 1970s, singers like Loretta Lynn, Melba Montgomery, Jeanne Pruett, and Norma Jean sang songs about the problems of working-class women, yet none considered themselves feminists.

Of this group, Lynn is perhaps the best known for tackling such controversial issues as birth control ("The Pill," 1975) and a wife's right to refuse her drunken husband's unwanted sexual advances ("Don't Come Home A-Drinkin' With Lovin' On Your Mind," 1966).[12] While most view Lynn as a singer/songwriter ahead of her time, Lynn merely saw herself a woman singing about what she saw and lived. In 1968, Dolly Parton's "Just Because I'm a Woman" took a jab at society's sexual double standard when she tells her fiancée that she's not a virgin: "My mistakes are no worse than yours because I'm a woman."[13] In 1969, Jeannie C. Riley sang as the quintessential everywoman in "The Rib," made by God to be "side by side . . . Not lesser than, not greater than," and definitely not "a footbone to be stepped on" or "a leg bone to be walked on.[14]

While Parton and Lynn were questioning long-held societal beliefs about women, a more conservative movement, led by Tammy Wynette, also emerged. It was this movement that cemented the general consensus that female country singers embraced traditional, if not backwards-thinking, ideals. Wynette's 1968 hit "Stand By Your Man," as well as songs like "I'll See Him Through" (1970), "The Ways To Love a Man" (1969), and "Don't Liberate Me (Love Me)" (1971), sealed the feminists' view of Wynette as the victim, a doormat for her man.[15] In her 1967 hit "Your Good Girl's Gonna Go

Tammy Wynette's signature song, 1968's "Stand by Your Man," has remained controversial for more than thirty years. It was roundly criticized by feminists in the late 1960s for encouraging women to be doormats for their wayward husbands. Hillary Clinton resurrected that debate during a *60 Minutes* interview about her husband's infidelity.

Bad," Wynette vows to change herself however necessary to please her husband. She'll paint and powder her face, buy some new clothes and even learn to love the taste of whiskey, if that's what he wants. These songs seemed to imply that a woman's identity was defined through her husband.

Singer Connie Smith viewed women's lib as something "for unhappy women," and many female singers shared country singer Helen Cornelius's view that feminism meant work and career while nonfeminism cherished motherhood and family.[16] These singers were proud of their heartache and suffering, as if they were a badge of honor.

Onstage, Christy Lane sang "Let Me Down Easy" (1977) and "I'm Gonna Love You Anyway" (1978), while backstage her husband did everything for her except sing, including providing her answers to reporters' questions.[17] Perhaps the most passive lyric to emerge from this time was Sandy Posey's 1966 song, "Born a Woman," because it included such lines as, "A woman's place in this ol' world is under some man's thumb / If you're born a woman, you're born to be . . . Treated like dirt / I was born a woman / I'm glad it happened that way." Perhaps what is most shocking about this song is that it was recorded by six other female singers, including Connie Smith, Jean Shepherd, and Jan Howard. Other songs of this era included "Your Love Made Me a Woman" (1974), and "Born to Love and Satisfy" (1974). Bobbi Martina's 1970 hit "For the Love of Him" urged women to "Make him your reason for living."[18]

Songs like Loretta Lynn's "Don't Come Home A-Drinkin' (with Lovin' On Your Mind)" have been the exception to the rule that women were supposed to sing about heartbreak and longing. In the world of country lyrics, it seemed that women were either crying because they had been dumped or were singing with glee to be back in baby's arms. Since female singers had to fight to get good songs from publishers and share the bill with men, they certainly weren't going to risk everything to sing a song of feminism. Not only would that have been a gamble within the male-dominated country music industry, but in the public arena as well. Country has historically been the music of the masses, and more specifically, the working-class masses, so women singers didn't want to alienate their audiences just to make an outspoken point. What would be accepted in the big city simply wouldn't fly in Little Rock.

However, that all changed about a decade ago, when K. T. Oslin, the pioneer of the current pro-woman movement, released her million-selling album called *80s Ladies* in 1987.[19] When Oslin appeared on the country music stage, everything about her demanded notice. A former Broadway performer, the Arkansas native signed a record deal when she was in her early forties, which was unheard of in an increasingly youth-oriented industry. With songs she penned, she spoke to a generation of women who had done everything they had been raised to do—putting themselves last as they married and raised families—but found something was missing. She sang of dreams denied and dreams that had been based in such fantasy that they couldn't have possibly come true. The album's title song sang of girls of the fifties who had seen much more than their names change. She sang, "We've been educated, we got liberated / And that's complicated matters with men / Oh we've said I do, and we've signed I don't / And we've sworn we'd never do that again / Oh we've burned our bras and we've burned our dinners / And we've burned our candles at both ends."[20]

To illustrate the drastic divergence in song themes, just three years before Oslin's release, Janie Fricke was singing "Easy to Please" (1984): "I could buy a new dress but it's OK if I don't / We could go to a movie tonight or stay at home / I'm easy to please, pleasing you pleases me." The song said she didn't need anything—certainly not the moon and the stars—except her man, with his flaws and all.

Four years after Oslin released "80s Ladies," Reba McEntire sang of yet another who had done exactly as society had expected by putting her family first, only to find feelings of emptiness instead of satisfaction. McEntire, the most influential country female of the decade, inspired thousands of women to return to college or the workforce with "Is There Life Out There" (1991), the story of a woman who married at twenty and found herself years later with nagging self-doubt of what she might have missed in life because of the traditional choices she made. The chorus says, "Is there life out there / So much she hasn't done / Is there life beyond her family and her home / She's done what she should, should she do what she dares / She doesn't want to leave, she's just wonderin' is there life out there."[21] The song was a departure from the Reba McEntire of the 1980s, who sang lyrics like "How blue can you make me," and "You'll always have a place to come back to when whoever's in New England's through with you." In an interview with the *Chicago Tribune*, she said, "Before, a lot of women identified with 'Don't Come Home a-Drinkin' (with Lovin' on Your Mind).' Now it's, 'Don't even think about coming home, 'cause I ain't gonna be here. I ain't gonna put up with that kind of carrying on.' "[22]

While McEntire took a serious look at traditional marital roles, an all-female country group called The Forester Sisters had a smash hit with the humorous song "Men" (1991), which sarcastically complained, "They'll buy you dinner, open the door / Other than that what are they good for?" And, "You can't beat 'em up cause they're bigger than you / You can't live with 'em and you just can't shoot 'em. Men."[23] The Forester Sisters, four sisters from Georgia, were among the most successful country groups of the 1980s, garnering five No.1 hits and a nod as Vocal Group of the Year from the Academy of Country Music. Singer Suzy Bogguss, an Illinois-born mainstream country singer with folk music roots, questioned a woman's stereotypical fantasy in the 1993 song, "Hey Cinderella."

> *We're older but no more the wise*
> *But we learned the art of compromise*
> *Sometimes we laugh, sometimes we cry*
> *Sometimes we just break down*
> *We're good now because we have to be*
> *We've come to terms with our vanity*
> *But sometimes we still curse gravity.*

The chorus wonders, "Hey Cinderella, what's the story all about / I got a funny feeling we missed a page or two somehow / Ooh, Cinderella, maybe you could help us out / Does the shoe fit you now?"[24]

In 1993, Mary Chapin Carpenter expressed similar discontent with traditional notions of feminine fulfillment with "He Thinks He'll Keep Her," inspired by the old Geritol commercial that ended with a man saying, "My wife. I think I'll keep her." The song is about a woman's disillusionment with her marriage and the double standard in the workplace. "She does the carpool, she PTAs / Doctors and dentists, she drives all day / When she was twenty-nine she delivered number three / And every Christmas card showed a perfect family," says one verse describing a stultifying family life. The chorus says, "Everything runs right on time, years of practice and design / Spit and polish 'til it shines, he thinks he'll keep her / Everything is so benign, the safest place you'll ever find / God forbid you'd change your mind, he thinks he'll keep her."[25] This song was just one example of the intelligence and introspection for which Carpenter became known. Carpenter, whose comfortable appearance was a departure from the typical female attire of big and man-pleasing costumes, earned rave reviews in the mainstream press and developed fan bases in large metropolitan cities. This hit was groundbreaking because it questioned virtually everything many women had been taught since they were little girls. Although marriage had usually been considered the ultimate goal for women, Carpenter showed that the often one-sided nature of this institution can become a lifelong prison for some women.

The most noticeable change in songs has been their attitude toward men's leaving. No longer clinging to the men's legs as they're striding out the door, these women are holding the door for the men to walk through, as if to say, "Don't let the door hit you on your way out." In one song she co-wrote with then-husband Bob DiPiero, "It's Lonely Out There" (1995), Pam Tillis dares her man, "It's lonely, so lonely / Go on and get your share / But believe me baby / It's lonely out there." She taunts her lover that if he thinks he can find sweeter lips or greater adventures, then just walk away because "our love is dying for you to know."[26]

Forget pining away. These women don't miss a beat in resuming their pre-relationship lives. As modern-day-cowgirl singer Terri Clark observed in her 1995 song, they have "Better Things to Do": "I could wash my car in the rain / Change my new guitar strings / Mow the yard just the same as I did yesterday / I don't need to waste my time crying over you / I've got better things to do."[27] In "You Can Feel Bad" (1996), Patty Loveless tells the story of a woman who has just been left. Not only is she not upset, she'll be painting the town in just a few hours. She sings, "You can feel bad if it makes you feel better / Picture me crying reading all your love letters / Walking around in your old sweater / You can feel bad if it makes you feel better."[28]

And quite often in Lorrie Morgan's songs, she's the one who's doing the leaving. In "Standing Tall," she says, "Tonight I'm gonna leave you / And I'm leavin' standing tall."[29] And in "Watch Me" (1992), she tells her lover that if he doesn't believe she'll leave, he should just watch as she walks away.[30] Certainly, Morgan's songs aren't always about sass and attitude; she has her tough times, her vulnerable moments, too. But even when she's down, she's not out but merely temporarily sidelined. No matter what adversity comes her way, she'll have the strength to overcome it. "I didn't know my own strength," she sang in a song by the same name, "'Til I had to pick myself up and carry on without your love / Oh, I'm gettin' back on my feet / It's been a long hard fall / but I'll make it after all."³¹ In Kathy Mattea's song "Walking Away a Winner" (1994), she walks away from a relationship with her head held high: "I'm walking away a winner / Walking away from a losing game / With my pride intact and my vision back."³²

There are still women-as-victim songs, but these women are either fighting back or leaving. Martina McBride's 1994 song "Independence Day" tells the story of a mother who escapes her marriage to an alcoholic wife beater by burning down the family home:

> *Well, she lit up the sky that Fourth of July*
> *By the time that the firemen come*
> *They just put out the flames and took down the names*
> *And sent me to the county home*
> *Now, I ain't sayin' it's right or it's wrong*
> *But maybe it's the only way*
> *Talk about your revolution*
> *It's Independence Day . . .*
> *Let the weak be strong*
> *Let the right be wrong*
> *Roll the stone away, let the guilty pay*
> *It's Independence Day³³*

McBride's 1997 hit, "A Broken Wing," is also the story of a woman who escapes an oppressive relationship by climbing out a bedroom window: "With a broken wing / She still sings / She keeps an eye on the sky / With a broken wing / She carries her dreams / Man you ought to see her fly."³⁴ Country women are clearly saying that it's better to be alone than unhappy.

In her sophomore CD, *It Matters To Me* (1995), Faith Hill addresses the female pressures of growing up to be a people pleaser in "Someone Else's Dream." Her father raises her to be a bride while her mother trains her to be a beauty queen. The chorus says, "She was daddy's little girl, momma's little angel / Teacher's pet, pageant queen / All my life I've been pleasin' everyone but me / Waking up in someone else's dream."³⁵ And in the heartbreaking "I Can't Do That Anymore," Hill sings about a woman who sacrificed everything for her husband's career. She spends countless hours on the treadmill trying to maintain a physique that he believes the wife of a top executive should have. She sings, "I used to dream about what I would be / Last night I dreamed about a washing machine."[36]

Along those same lines, Trisha Yearwood tells of the woes of being an American girl in the 1995 song "XXXs and OOOs (An American Girl)": "Slow dance, second chance / Momma needs romance / And a live-in maid / Fix the sink, mow the yard / Really isn't all that hard / If you get paid."[37] She describes the challenge of being raised to be a proper little girl, complete with hair tied up in ribbons and bows, and now trying to succeed in her father's world, an environment where balancing love and money is extremely difficult.

Although it didn't garner much media attention, this feminist revolution progressed steadily until 1995, when Shania Twain burst onto the country scene with *The Woman in Me*, which has sold more than ten million copies, setting a record as the best-selling female country album ever. Love her or hate her, she has forever changed the country music terrain for female singers, in terms of the types of acts signed, the types of songs recorded (including feminist lyrics), and the increased sexiness in photos and videos.

Twain has emerged as the unofficial but undeniable leader of this movement and represents the future of women in country—frank, original, independent, and sexy. She loves her man, but she loves herself more. She is turning the tables on men, insisting that she's the one who must be pleased. No longer are women "putting another log on the fire" for their men, as in the 1975 Tompall Glaser song; instead, it's time for the men to light their women's fires. Rather than the woman having to do all the work to keep a relationship exciting and thriving, men now share the responsibility of caressing and expressing.

With its irresistible "We Will Rock You" rhythm, her song "Any Man of Mine" quickly became an anthem for strong young women everywhere. Scott Gray, in his book *The Shania Twain Story: On Her Way*, writes, "The supercharged hook had everyone singing along, while the take-me-as-I-am-or-take-a-hike lyrics struck a chord with both guys and gals."[38] This rule-setting song says, "Any man of mine better be proud of me / Even when I'm ugly he still better love me / I can be late for a date that's fine / But he better be on time." Twain also takes charge in "If You're Not in it For Love (I'm Outta Here)": "Let me make it clear to you my dear / If you're not in it for love, I'm outta here."[39]

As Dallas Williams writes in *Shania Twain: I'm On My Way,* "a more forthright musical persona was born—Shania Twain as butt-kicking 'macho' female. In this sense, she was now a little like Courtney Love or Alanis Morissette, but the resemblance obviously ended there."[40] Twain's lyrics assumed the feminist attitudes of these rock stars, but she lacked their anger and cloaked her themes of equality in a physical package most men found extremely pleasing.

Twain's *Come On Over* (1997), which became the best-selling female album in any genre after reaching international sales of thirty-four million copies, picked up where the previous one left off. In "Honey I'm Home," it's the woman's turn to be catered to after a hard day of work. She sings, "Honey I'm home and I had a hard day / Pour me a cold one and oh, by the way / Rub my feet, gimme something to eat / Fix up my favorite treat." Twain even tells men how they can get what they want in "If You Wanna Touch Her, Ask!" "If you're lookin' for a place in her heart / First you gotta learn to listen / If you really wanna touch her, really wanna touch her, Ask!"[41]

Twain's 1995 success opened the doors for feisty feminine women, including Mindy McCready, Le Ann Rimes, Deana Carter and Mila Mason. In the title of her five-million selling 1996 debut album, Carter asks, *Did I Shave My Legs for This?* Carter's song is a humorous look at a woman's romantic, wine-and-roses notions of marriage being dashed by the harsh reality of an unappreciative husband who wants her to cater to his every beer whim. Instead of the nice home he had promised during their courtship, she now finds herself drowning in debt while living in a leaky trailer.[42] Mindy McCready put an end to the double standard in "Guys Do It All The Time" (1996): "Guys do it all the time and you expect us to understand / But when the shoe's on the other foot, you know that's when it hits the fan / Get over it honey, life's a two-way street, or you won't be a man of mine / So I had some beers with the girls last night / Guys do it all the time."[43] Her 1997 album, *If I Don't Stay the Night,* also showcases that same determination that made her debut release a million-seller. In "This Is Me," she's a strong-willed woman who refuses to change. "This is me / Take it or leave it / My own girl / You better believe it / What you see is what I am / And who I want to be / This is me," she sings. In "Oh Romeo," McCready ponders the modern-day version of the Shakespearean love story. In this analysis of the star-crossed lovers, Romeo isn't the epitome of the perfect boyfriend, but a "romantic depressive" who "becomes obsessive." The chorus says, "Oh Romeo, who would lay down her life / Swallow the poison, pick up the knife / Maybe I'd cry just a teardrop or two / I would not die for you / I would not die for you."[44]

In "Bye Bye" (1998), Jo Dee Messina gives anything but a tearful send-off to her truth-challenged lover, telling him to find the remnants of their relationship in the dust on Highway 4. She sings, "Bye bye love, I'll catch you later / Got a lead foot down on my accelerator and the rearview mirror torn off / 'Cause I ain't never lookin' back, and that's a fact."[45] In 2000, Trisha Yearwood sang "Real Live Woman," in which she refuses to accept societal pressures to be younger and thinner:

> I don't buy the lines in magazines that tell me what I've gotta be
> Don't base my life on a movie screen
> Don't fit the mold society has planned
> I don't need to be nineteen years old
> Or starve myself for some weight I'm told
> Or turn men's heads down that road
> And thank God I finally know just who I am.[46]

In 2002, Martina McBride told the story of a well-behaved, church-choir-singing woman who had finally had enough and went on a rampage. In "When God Fearing Women Get the Blues," she warns the town folk to lock up their husbands, guns, whiskey, and Neiman Marcus high-heeled shoes. The chorus says, "When God-fearin' women get the blues / There ain't no slap-dab-a-telling / What they're gonna do / Run around yellin' / I've got a Mustang / It'll do 80 / You don't have to be my baby / I've stirred my last batch of gravy."[47] That same year, Terri Clark released "I Wanna Do It All," in which her life's to-do list includes visiting Paris and a Yankee baseball game, drinking Tequila in Tijuana and catching beads at Mardi Gras, in addition to eventually settling down and rocking her babies to sleep. She proclaims, "I wanna do it all, see Niagara Falls / Fight City Hall, feel good in my skin / Beating the odds with my back to the wall / Tryin' to rob Peter without payin' Paul / I wanna do it all."[48]

Nobody's little girl, nineteen-year-old Jessica Andrews takes a self-confident approach in the 2003 hit "There's More to Me Than You," in which she kisses goodbye a controlling and emotionally abusive lover as she taunts him with,

"How do you like me now?" She sings, "I believe in myself / That makes me stronger / Things changed and so have I / I'm gonna make hay while the sun still shines / You can clip my wings, but I'm still gonna fly / I'm on my own and on my way."[49] This is in direct contrast to the country music songs of the 1960s and 1970s, when women were strictly defined by their relationships with men.

Twain's most recent release, *Up!* (2002), continues her feminist themes in at least two songs. "She's Not Just a Pretty Face" unveils a laundry list of unconventional jobs that women are now filling, from astronauts, rodeo riders, and city councilwomen, to bass players, soldiers, surgeons, parking valets, and farmers. "Juanita" describes the restless spirit that courses through women's veins, urging them to scream, flee, or just be free. One verse urges, "When someone tries to take away the freedom of your choice / To take away your voice, that's when you need her / She's there if you dare to give your broken wings a try / C'mon and take a leap and fly, and you can be her."[50]

At first glance, the "feminist" progress made by female country singers may appear to pale in comparison to female rock singers, but these rock and pop artists face very few of the constraints that have stymied progressive country women for decades. If the analogy of a race were to be applied, country singers would be forced to start several miles behind the starting gate that launched their pop peers. It appears unlikely that country will ever catch up with pop in the feminist race because country's fans and the industry gatekeepers are far more conservative.

Now, as it has always been, country music is an industry dominated by men. Unlike the pop and rock worlds, there is not one major country label run by a female, and all of the successful music producers are male. There are just a handful of successful female artist & repertoire label executives, artist managers, publishers, studio musicians, attorneys, booking agents, and radio programmers in country music now. This means female country singers have had further to travel and more obstacles to overcome in their feminist journeys than pop singers. Certainly there must be numerous pro-female country songs that have been written but not recorded after being rejected by male label or publishing executives, or recorded but not included on an album. Perhaps many female country songwriters haven't even bothered pursuing a feminist song theme they'd developed since there would have been no commercial outlets for its exploitation. "It's hard to find traditional country songs for women that say something that have lyrics that fit the times," said Martina McBride. "It's a challenge to find those kinds of songs."[51]

The country music industry still remains one of the last bastions of male chauvinism in the music industry, which means the double standard is still alive and well on Music Row. Women are still regularly referred to as "girl singers" within label conference rooms and on tours. It wasn't until the last decade that executives even realized that female artists could sell if given equal opportunity and promotion.

In 1991, when country music sales topped the $1 billion mark for the first time, only two of the twenty-two debut acts that broke country's Top 20 were women: Trisha Yearwood and Pam Tillis. Despite the nation's new interest in country, Nashville labels were still reluctant to add women to their rosters. Since they believed that women didn't sell, the rosters of Nashville labels were typically 70 percent male artists. Fortunately, the long-held conventional wisdom of Music Row began to change in the early '90s, as Tillis and Yearwood were joined in the gold and platinum winners' circle by Reba McEntire, Wynonna Judd, Tanya Tucker, Patty Loveless, Kathy Mattea, Lorrie Morgan, and K. T. Oslin.

Now male executives have no choice but to recognize the financial clout that these women have earned. For instance, the country charts in the last eight years have been dominated by women: the Dixie Chicks, Shania Twain, Faith Hill, Lee Ann Womack, and Le Ann Rimes. Twain leads the pack of all country artists during this timeframe because two of her albums have received a Diamond Certification from the Recording Industry Association of America for sales of more than ten million. The Dixie Chicks reached Diamond status in 2002 for their second album, *Fly*. For the most part, their male counterparts have trailed behind in album sales. (While Garth Brooks remains the best-selling solo artist in any genre, his sales have declined in recent years and he has released fewer albums.)

In 2002, three country artists were included in *Billboard*'s Top 10 best-selling albums in all formats: Dixie Chicks (No. 4), Alan Jackson (No. 8), and Twain (No. 10 after being in stores for only six weeks). The fourth country CD to appear in the Top 10 was the soundtrack for *Oh Brother, Where Art Thou?*, which contained songs from many acts. Shania Twain's CD *Up!* debuted at

Although Faith Hill is closely associated with feel-good, pop-country songs such as "This Kiss" and "Let's Go to Vegas," she has also addressed women who are unhappy in their lives in such songs as "Someone Else's Dream," "I Can't Do That Anymore," and "A Man's Home Is His Castle."

No. 1 on the *Billboard* 200 in November 2002, with 874,000 copies sold in one week, the most ever by a female country act. It held the No. 1 spot for four more weeks. That same year, the Dixie Chicks' *Home* made the No. 1 spot on *Billboard*'s Top 200 with one-week sales of 780,000, and Faith Hill's *Cry* took top honors with 472,000 units sold. That compares with Tim McGraw's 602,000 debut-week showing, followed by Alan Jackson's one-week sales of 423,000 units and Toby Keith's 338,000-unit weekly debut. It is interesting to note, however, that the Top 5 Most Played Songs of 2002 by both *Billboard* and *Radio & Records* were all recorded by men.

The Dixie Chicks' television special that aired in December 2002 on NBC became the highest-rated network TV concert of the season, beating those by U2 and Paul McCartney, and attracting an audience of more than eleven million. Married couple Faith Hill and Tim McGraw both aired TV specials on NBC during the long Thanksgiving weekend; Hill's special ranked No. 30 for the week, while her husband came in at No. 41.[52]

Now that country women are selling more records, they have more power within the labels' boardrooms, as evidenced by the Dixie Chicks' suing Sony Records in a successful effort to renegotiate their deal. This means they will have more artistic freedom to say what they want on their CDs without being vetoed by the label's male-dominated A & R department.

For the most part, it's the women who are buying the country women's CDs, so there's a receptive audience for these assertive lyrics. In addition, the country fan base has spread beyond its traditional rural roots into the nation's suburbs and big cities, where both corporate executives and soccer moms alike are trying to forge their way through society's evolving expectations of women. America's fifty-percent divorce rate means that a good portion of country female fans are themselves divorced, and many of them are single working moms. Unlike Madonna, who once told *American Bandstand*'s Dick Clark that she wanted to rule the world, many female country fans are just hoping to survive through another exhausting day. These female heads-of-household hunger for songs to which they can relate, songs that help them put words to their abandoned dreams, undeterred hopes, and unconditional love for their families.

For far too long, female country singers have had to create change by working within the system, by promoting music that is inspiring to their female audience while remaining appealing to the male gatekeepers in the country music industry, particularly radio music programmers and record label executives. These gatekeepers have always wanted female country singers to "know their place." Their images had to be cute, but not too sexy, because label executives feared that would drive away their female fans. Unlike male singers, a woman who exuded too much confidence was believed to be getting "too big for her britches."

Operating too far outside of those parameters would be career suicide for female artists, or at least until Twain came along. "Maybe what is wrong is who is writing the rules," said Mercury Nashville Records President Luke Lewis. "Nashville, if it wants to be successful, has to serve the public tastes. Shania seems to be doing that without ruffling any feathers except for those in Nashville who aren't used to it."[53]

Lewis said Twain has been frustrated by the fact that she faced constraints in the country genre. "She really wasn't comfortable with the barriers that are placed by the gatekeepers. I think both she and Mutt spend a lot more time thinking about what their fans would like as opposed to what a radio programmer might think fits into a particular genre."[54] Indeed, Twain herself told the *Hartford Courant* a few years earlier, "I don't listen to the industry at all. I'm much more interested in what the fans think."[55] Lewis continued, "I think there is a reluctance in this community to break with tradition."

> I think it's a Southern tendency as well as a tendency in country music, very slow to change. I don't think she and [husband/producer] Mutt [Lange] meant to come in and kick the doors down, but in a lot of ways, that is what happened. She was ahead of a lot of us in this town in that she recognized that the audience had become far more sophisticated than we seemed to recognize. People in rural communities have satellite dishes now. I credit her with figuring out before us that you can push the envelope in terms of style and music and clothing. She was much more in tune to the audience than most of us in Nashville were.

"The smartest thing all of us at this record company did was never question it," he concluded. "It might have caused us to take pause, like it did everyone else, but the best move I ever made was getting out of the way because her instincts are uncanny."[56]

Yes, Shania Twain pushed the boundaries of country further than anyone before her, but—unlike pop counterparts such as Madonna, Britney Spears, or Christina Aguilera—she was still limited in how far she could go and still be accepted within the country music arena. Quite simply, what is celebrated in the rock world wouldn't be accepted in the country arena. For instance, consider the shock and criticism Twain has received over her video wardrobe choices. In "Whose Bed Have Your Boots Been Under," the video that put Twain on the map, Twain dances in a clingy (but certainly not skintight) long red dress. The video caused quite a stir, and Country Music Television, the industry's video network, reacted "coolly" to Twain's video because it was too sexy, even though it was much less suggestive than videos aired on MTV or VH 1.[57] Her breakthrough video, "Any Man of Mine," which cemented her image, displayed a raw sensuality that hadn't been found in country videos. Country music purists gasped as they caught a glimpse of a denim pants- and vest-clad Twain dancing because she revealed her navel, heretofore a taboo in the conservative country field. However, Twain was just emulating the belly-baring styles adopted by most Hollywood actresses and millions of middle American high school girls. Except for the occasional Country Music Association Awards gown, she rarely shows any cleavage, and she never shows her legs. She may look hot in her cropped tops and hip-huggers, but her moves are PG-13.

And while Shania's pants may be tight, so are the men's. Garth Brooks has admitted that he wears his Wranglers two sizes too small when performing and several other male singers frequently don circulation-hampering jeans in hopes of drawing their fans' eyes to their private parts. Using sex to sell country music isn't unique to Shania Twain; she's just the best at it. That's why the outrage over her image becomes laughable when compared to what pop divas such as Britney Spears, Lil Kim, Madonna, and Christina Aguilera have worn onstage and in videos. It's a sure bet that you won't find a female country singer tackling the subject of masturbation like Cyndi Lauper did two decades ago in "She Bop," or simulating such an act as Madonna did onstage on numerous occasions. Unlike pop acts like Madonna and Salt-N-Pepa, country women still find that they are trapped somewhere between the sexual boundaries of "I Wanna Hold Your Hand" and "I Want Your Sex."

Country is a mainstream genre that reflects the taste of middle America, so there simply isn't room for extremism. Most working women can't relate to Courtney Love, but they understand Reba McEntire or Faith Hill. For instance, *The Rolling Stone Book of Women in Rock* called Morissette's "You Oughta Know" "the most macho song to hit the Top 10 in 1995."[58] Contributor Elysa Gardner described the "adrenaline-charged Generation X manifesto" as "crude, vitriolic and irresistibly catchy," and said Morissette could be viewed "as a post-feminist poet or as Amy Fisher with a microphone."[59] While Morissette uses the graphic phrase, "go down on you in a theater" to describe oral sex, country females still shy away from using the word "sex" in songs altogether.[60]

The raw anger, resentment and irony of Morissette, Fiona Apple, or PJ Harvey would not be accepted in the country arena. These profanity-spewing, rough-throated women would likely alienate, or even frighten, many female country fans who still have their mothers' admonition to "be a good girl" ringing in their ears. If rock singers were the cigarette smokers and biker chicks in high school, country singers would have been student council presidents or members of their church choir.

Even today, most female artists consider the word "feminism" to be the F-word. In mainstream society, the word "feminist" can still conjure up images of embittered shorthaired women devoid of makeup who wear baggy clothes and comfortable shoes. Rather than embracing their role as the flag-carriers for feminism, they often downplay their choice of lyrical themes. When *Glamour* magazine asked Shania Twain if she was a feminist, she responded, "I guess you could say that I am, but I'm not an *angry* feminist, you know? I'm a very old-fashioned person, so I enjoy it when a man opens the door for me—I'm not offended by those things. I still believe in the theory of standing by your man. As long as a man is willing to stand by his woman!"[61] Martina McBride says she feels no obligation to speak for women in her songs. "I don't even set out intellectually to do that," she says.

> I'm not thinking, "I need to have all these songs that speak for women." If I have one hundred fifty songs that come in over the course of a month, I'm just inevitably drawn to the ones that speak about women's feelings. I am a woman, so that's the natural thing. I'm not going to record [the Toby Keith hit] "Whiskey for My Men (Beer for My Horses)." I don't think, "I've got to find the next woman's anthem to be the voice for all women."[62]

As Bill Monroe suggests in *Don't Get above Your Raisin': Country Music and the Southern Working Class*, the defining themes of country music are God, Mama, and babies.[63] Malone argues that country music offers nostalgia for a simpler time, a fond remembrance of "that little cabin on the hill," which in actuality never existed. While we've left *Leave It To Beaver* forever, we still fantasize about the good old days, when everyone seemed happy and the family nucleus was strong. He writes, "Although increasingly regionless, classless, and suburban in residence and values, these young, affluent and mobile listeners wanted a music that seemed to embody the qualities in which contemporary America seemed deficient: community, family values, and down-to-earth simplicity."[64] A common thread that runs through country songs, according to Malone, is the importance of values that were indoctrinated while being raised in a Christian household.

Country is, was, and will always be more conservative than rock 'n' roll. If rock represents the open-minded, fun-loving liberal Democrats, country is the music of the conservative, reluctant-to-change Republicans who yearn for the simplicity of days gone by. In fact, it's the very values on which country music is based that rock music rebels against. "If you were to ask the average person to describe a country star, one adjective that would almost certainly come up is 'conservative,' " wrote Mary Bufwack and Robert K. Oermann in *Finding Her Voice: The Saga of Women in Country Music.* "Ever since the political upheavals of the 1960s, country music has been aligned in the popular imagination with patriotism and religious fundamentalism."[65]

Although country music romanticizes hard-drinking, love-her-and-leave-her rambling men like Waylon and Willie, it would hardly accept a whiskey-breathed, perpetually traveling promiscuous woman (Dolly Parton's "When Possession Gets Too Strong" (1973) notwithstanding). Good timin' man? Icon-making monster hit. Good timin' woman? Not a chance. Outlaws Johnny Cash, Waylon Jennings and Merle Haggard are celebrated for their hedonistic indulgences, while hard-partying behavior by such women as Tanya Tucker and Lorrie Morgan only brings harsh criticism and a loss of respect.

Therefore, country women have had to temper their social commentary, or as Juice Newton might say, break it to them gently. Unlike many rock singers, country women aren't "in your face" with their attitudes, but by your side, like an understanding best friend who is as confused, exhausted, and hurt by modern woman's travails as most American women are. Country women don't hate men; on the contrary, they love men, as Twain shows in her song, "The Woman in Me": "The woman in me needs the man in you."[66] This country movement is neither do-me nor screw-you feminism. Perhaps the closest modern cliché that would apply would be, "I'm OK, you're OK."

As Austin-based songwriter Sandy Knox notes in "I Wanna Know" (1998), today's over-thirty females (especially country music listeners) are caught "between Betty Crocker and Betty Friedan." In the song, Knox asks, "Do I bake cookies or be a CEO / Won't somebody tell me 'cause I don't know." In "Girl Talk" (1998), Knox notes that middle-class women's conversations have evolved from garden clubs and PTAs to health clubs and IRAs.[67] Instead of just cooking and cleaning, while the men work and handle all money matters, women are now making their own money and investing it as well. Devoid of the angst, irony, or pessimism found in other musical formats, the country women have emerged as a presence that is nonthreatening to both women and men. They don't hide their sexuality, but they don't shove it down your throat either. Maybe country women haven't yet shed their people-pleasing tendencies entirely.

Perhaps the greatest irony these pro-women singers confront is that despite their softened, nonthreatening lyrics, country women still face a double standard at radio and in the press. "If pressed for an answer, I would probably say there still is (a double standard)," said Wade Jessen, head of *Billboard*'s country charts. "It's probably not as pronounced. I just don't think that men get pounced on the way women do."[68]

For instance, in a 1996 survey I conducted of fifteen radio stations regarding lyrics of country music songs, several radio programmers complained that Mindy McCready's "Guys Do It All the Time" was male-bashing, when the song merely stated that women should be allowed to do anything, like drinking beer with their friends, that men can do. Other programmers initially resisted playing Martina McBride's "Independence Day" because the song depicted a woman's murderous response to an abusive husband. Although the song was recently ranked No. 50 on CMT's list of 100 Greatest Country Music Songs, it peaked at only No. 12 on the *Billboard* country charts in 1994. Yet these same programmers had no qualms about spinning Garth Brooks's upbeat "Papa Loved Mama," in which a husband kills his cheating wife: "Papa loved Mama / Mama loved men / Mama's in the graveyard / Papa's in the pen."[69] Brooks hit No. 3 in May 1992 with that song. Does this send the message that while a woman can't kill an abusive husband, it's acceptable for a man to kill his cheating wife?

Compare Brooks's No. 3 chart performance with that of the Dixie Chicks' tongue-in-cheek "Goodbye Earl" (1999).[70] The song, on their CD *Fly*, tells the tale of two long-time friends who lethally poison an abusive husband with black-eyed peas. *Radio & Records*' Lon Helton said 20 of the 149 reporting radio stations banned it outright.[71] Despite the group's overall popularity, the song peaked at No. 13 on the *Billboard* charts, meaning that not all stations put the song into heavy rotation, said *Billboard*'s Wade Jessen.[72] While the public's reaction to a song is not something tangible that can be measured or explained, it's likely that this is another case in which radio's male programmers balked at a song that seemed to celebrate female violence against men, even if they are abusive.

Jessen said another example of a double standard at radio would be the success of Tim McGraw's "Red Ragtop," in which a man is reminded of a past relationship that ended after an abortion.[73] "That was controversial for a very short period of time, two or three weeks of the song's life, but it ended up being a big hit," he said. "My gut tells me that if a woman had performed that song, or it had been where the woman was singing about terminating a pregnancy, it would be a whole different issue. My gut tells me people who are critical would be far more critical of women."[74]

Given these constraints, these country women are to be lauded for their achievements in propelling the modern woman's perspective to the forefront. Although more softly worded and pedaled than their pop counterparts, they are no less important or admirable. Given their monstrous sales figures and unavoidable exposure in today's media, these women are inspiring a younger generation to build on the foundation they've established and push it to the next level.

In the end, success and mainstream acceptance is the best way—perhaps the only way—to bring about changes in country music. There's no going back to the "woe-is-me" country woman of the 1960s and 1970s, but country women still cannot emulate their female counterparts in other genres. The anger and sexual frankness of Liz Phair and PJ Harvey simply don't have a place in country music, and they probably never will. As such, women in country music will have to continue to make their gains in subtle yet crucially important and noticeable increments.

Going Back to the Old Mainstream

No Depression, *Robbie Fulks, and*
Alt.Country's Muddied Waters

BARBARA CHING

In 1972, when Doctor Hook and the Medicine Show sang "The Cover of
the *Rolling Stone*," they cast rock critics as arbiters of stardom. By the time
Cameron Crowe used this song in his 2000 film *Almost Famous*, it held little
irony. Sex and drugs were good but they just couldn't compare to joining
the magazine's anointed. Currently, some alternative country aspirant could
sing the same tune about *No Depression*. The magazine, now in its eighth year,
invariably uses its cover to showcase an alt.country artist. It has sponsored
alt.country package tours (in which the editors indulge the fan's dream of performing with their heroes); it produces a syndicated *No Depression* radio show;
and it publishes a longstanding top 40 chart, all of which clearly mark participants and confer status in the genre. In short, *No Depression* presides at the
gates of alt.country heaven. Its surprisingly gushy feature articles break no new
ground in the field of music journalism, but at the same time the magazine
may be the only one to ever play such a crucial role in the formation of a popular music genre. *Rolling Stone* and its ilk covered relatively well-established
genres; *No Depression* helped establish alternative country as an alternative to
mainstream, Nashville-produced "hot new country." At the same time, the way
in which it has depicted the genre and its audience and the way this depiction
has moved through the culture indicates that alt.country is in many ways not
alternative at all. In particular, I will argue that *No Depression* uses a macho nostalgia to distinguish alt.country from both rock music and contemporary country music. While sociologists Richard A. Peterson and Bruce A. Beal note that

alt.country fans evince a generalized "antimodernist" politics, they do not emphasize the way the fight against modernity is associated with masculine valor and feminine corruption.[1] Alt.country discourse separates the men, not only from the women, but also from the guys in cowboy hats, now a sartorial symbol of Nashville's domination rather than wild-west independence.

Communications scholar Jason Toynbee describes the formation of popular music genres as a "social process" which allows particular groups to validate their interests by investing the music with significance. In his words, a musical genre functions within a "deeply embedded discourse which states that the validity of a musical style will be measured by the extent to which it is an expression of grass-roots values and identity."[2] Likewise, music critic and scholar Simon Frith notes that music genres also convey "ideological and social discourses. . . . It is genre rules which determine how musical forms are taken to convey meaning and value, which determine the aptness of different sorts of judgment, which determine the competence of different sorts of people to make assessments. It is through genres that we . . . bring together the aesthetic and the ethical."[3] The question, then, is not only *whose* ethical and aesthetic values and *whose* identity *No Depression* and alternative country express, but also how. The techniques of literary analysis, which uncover recurring images and narrative patterns, can begin to answer those questions. To begin, I'll discuss four features of *No Depression* discourse: its coy enforcement of "genre rules," its emphasis on (perhaps unwitting) male bonding, its belief that authenticity lies in opposition to Nashville, and its self-conscious insistence on a nostalgic visual style. Finally, I will discuss the career of Robbie Fulks to argue that *No Depression*'s portrayal of genre rules, masculinity, authenticity, and nostalgia shapes the experience and creation of other aspects of alt.country discourse, including the music itself.

If You Have to Ask . . .

No Depression's ironic subtitle, "alt.country . . . whatever that is," simultaneously seems to enfold and withhold the definition of alt.country. It flaunts a tastemaker's secret knowledge of genre rules even if it once indicated a sincere desire to leave the borders of alt.country unpatrolled. Volume I, no. 1 (Fall

1995) announced itself as "the alternative country quarterly." One year later, the magazine became "the alt.country (whatever that is) bimonthly;" in May–June 2003, it called itself the "Try a little alt.country (whatever that is) bimonthly." In their introduction to a 1998 anthology of articles from the magazine, editors Grant Alden and Peter Blackstock claim that they use the phrase "alternative country" with "gentle sarcasm;" they also complain that this tone "seems rarely to have translated."[4] But five years later they stand by their inscrutability—and why not? By refusing to define alt.country, they preserve the right to decide who shines as an alt.country star. As Alden put it in a November–December 1997 editorial, "Peter and I have been telling interviewers ever since we started this magazine that . . . *No Depression* is and hopefully always will be a magazine guided by the music which engages its two editors. As in: Stuff we like."[5] In their anthology introduction, they describe the stuff they like as "either too old, too loud, or too eccentric for country radio."[6] *No Depression*, then, competes with country radio for taste-making power, and it's simply assumed that the stuff that *No Depression* editors like *ought* to play on country radio, and since it doesn't, they are entitled to alternatives. This sarcasm, gentle or no, indicates just how important maintaining an insider's knowledge is to the genre. If you have to ask more questions about the alternatives, their sarcasm suggests, we don't want you to know. You don't share the aesthetic and ethical values of the group and aren't "competent" (to further repeat Frith) to discern the self-evident merits of the old, loud, and eccentric. In short, *No Depression* doesn't define "alternative" beyond pointing to mainstream country radio's refusal to see things the *No Depression* way. On the other hand, the *ungently* sarcastic definition offered by "The Rock Snob's Dictionary" highlights the aesthetic and ethical dimensions of the group identity under construction: "alt.country. Self-righteous rock country hybrid genre whose practitioners favor warbly, studiedly imperfect vocals, nubby flannel shirts, and a conviction that their take on country is more 'real' than the stuff coming out of Nashville. . . . Also known as the No Depression movement."[7]

. . . You're Not One of Us . . .

While women such as Lucinda Williams, Gillian Welch, and Emmylou Harris regularly grace the cover of *No Depression*, a glance at bylines on the articles and signatures on the letters to the editors indicates that *No Depression* is a magazine written by men for men. In May–June 2003, for example, not a single major article was written by a woman; the September–October 1999 issue, more or less the midway point in the magazine's current life span, also has none. Volume I, no. 1 (Fall 1995) features just one.[8] Of the thirty-seven articles in the 1998 anthology, six were written by women.[9] In this respect, *No Depression* differs little from mainstream country journalism. The semischolarly *Journal of Country Music* (published under the auspices of the Country Music Foundation) and the glossy bimonthly *Country Music* (soon to cease publication) share similar gender parity statistics. In fact, male dominance in itself is nothing new in the world of pop music journalism. As rock critic and communications scholar Kembrew McLeod has documented, rock criticism is also dominated by men who similarly valorize their own discernment by contrasting it to the supposedly corrupt commercialism of mainstream music.[10] Furthermore, *No Depression* rarely prints a negative review or critical profile, and in this respect, *The Alternative Country Bimonthly* doesn't offer much of an alternative to the star-making machinery that is glossy commercial music journalism. Some *No Depression* profile articles I've read simply paraphrase liner notes in lieu of reporting, and it's a short step from there to paraphrasing commercially inspired press kits.[11] Other profiles are star-struck and stuck in the time-honored mode of domestic reportage described by Peter La Chapelle elsewhere in this volume. For example, in the July–August 2002 issue, novelist Silas House marvels at how beautiful and polite Kelly Willis was when he interviewed her. She let him sit in her backyard and offered him a drink! She's a "deep thinker," too.[12] Her husband, Bruce Robison, songwriter for hot new country luminaries such as Tim McGraw and Faith Hill, happened to be at home during the interview, and House unironically enthuses about what a cute couple they make: "Robison is a tall and incredibly likable fellow. . . . [i]f alt.country had a prom, Willis and Robison might well be its king and queen."[13]

While *No Depression* mirrors mainstream rock and country magazines in its male-dominated writing staff and adolescent adulation, it is unique in its first-person zine-ish rantings and its coverage of local scenes. The editors regularly contribute reviews and features, and in particular, their opening column, "Hello Stranger," links the magazine to its origins in youthful enthusiasm rather than careerist self-promotion. In the seven-year stretch of this column, Alden and Blackstock have told a sketchy story: first came disillusionment with the commercial co-optation of punk and grunge after which they "fell into country music" (November–December 1997); beginning in 1994, they participated in an AOL Internet discussion group on the band Uncle Tupelo which branched out into other artists. The board called itself "No Depression–Alternative Country." *No Depression* was the title of Uncle Tupelo's 1990 album, which included a cover version of the Carter Family's song of that name; the magazine, the editors explain, took its title from the Internet community, from Uncle Tupelo, and from the Carter Family. Those roots sprawl over a seventy-year time span, so should *No Depression* continue to thrive, Alden and Blackstock still have many chapters to tell about the *No Depression* story. They haven't yet said much about why punk frustration should lead to country as opposed to another popular music genre, or about why, at the same time, it really didn't, since they need an alternative to country, too, or about why, in particular, they often seek that alternative by looking backwards.[14] The inspirational Carter Family song expressed religious faith in the future. "I'm going to where there's no depression" meant going to heaven. Is this phrase, too, now used with "gentle sarcasm?" Does *No Depression* discourse transcend economic *and* psychological gloom (as the song does), or does it, in a rigidly ironical fashion, affect deprivation and despair?[15]

In fact, commiserating with the downtrodden is an important theme in traditional country music, a.k.a. the white man's blues. Because of this association with the disgraced white south, *No Depression*'s editors frequently feel compelled to defend themselves against charges of racism and conservatism. "I do not yet—nor ever—imagine myself a conservative," Alden temporizes in his July–August 2001 opener. In January–February 2001, he argued that alt.country fandom in itself makes a political statement since it evades the "siren calls of mainstream society." In January–February 2002, *No Depression* started a regular feature called "Sittin' and Thinkin'," in which the editors "ask some of our finest writers to wrestle with the many ghosts who inhabit our music;" so far nearly half the essays, written by the usual crew, have dealt with the topic of African American influences on country music. In September–October 1996, they congratulated themselves for their cover photo of Hank Williams posing with blackface comedians Jam Up and Honey. They got few complaints, they say, so, as usual, they "have no idea what that means." In March–April 1999, as Alden attempts to answer roots-rocker Will Oldham's charge that *No Depression* is about white people's music, he juxtaposed the accusation with a quotation from *Walden:* "Who shall say what prospect life offers to another? Could a greater miracle take place than for us to look through each other's eyes for an instant?"[16] Sanctimoniously embracing the arrogance that Thoreau wards off, Alden exonerated himself with the following proof of his miraculous vision: late one night, stopped at an intersection, he notices a black man in a neighboring lane.

> We are both smiling to the music playing loudly in our cars. The beats come hard from his trunk . . . loud enough that I am reminded how far out of touch with contemporary hip-hop I have become. It is equally doubtful that he will recognize the Del McCoury band seeping through my doors but there is still an instant when our tired eyes meet and our lips barely smile.

He concludes by stating that even though he can't remember what the black man looked like, he still remembers the moment they shared. Whatever that is.

While charges of racism and conservatism clearly raise the editors' hipster hackles, they feel no compunction about the masculine bias that structures their discourse. The image of mainstream society as a seductively feminine "siren song" allows no evasive "whatever that is" answers to questions about how alt.country, mainstream's opposite, defines its gender.[17] Similarly, in May–June 1998, Grant Alden connects punk to country through a particular filial line: "one comes late to country music . . . drawn by its capacity to reveal the unvarnished truth, that joyous link between Hank Williams and Sid Vicious."[18] Peter Blackstock opens the following issue (July–August 1998) with the claim that alt.country songs can be "pure and simple folk music, made and played of the people, by the people, for the people." The experience he describes to demonstrate this populism, however, wasn't for people like me. It was purely for the college guys: a professor's bachelor party where the groom's friends, many meeting for the first time, sat in a circle with their guitars and learned that they all liked Wilco, Son Volt, Uncle Tupelo, Robert Earl Keen, and Townes Van Zant. Significantly, Blackstock claims that the shared music gave the men a "common language."

Circle sing-a-longs provide one example of *No Depression*'s "common language," and record collecting, another bachelor pad practice, further solidifies the masculine domain of what Blackstock calls "this little corner of the underground." As communications scholar Will Straw notes, the record collector tends to present himself as a hip male connoisseur, an image most widely disseminated in Nick Hornby's 1995 novel *High Fidelity* (and the movie made from it), but this characterization is tacitly accepted in most discourse about popular music. Like rock criticism, the "homosocial interaction" engendered by such collecting reinforces the tastes of the men involved, creating and confirming "a shared universe of critical judgment"—not unlike the "genre rules" described by Frith and Toynbee.[19] Indeed, so strong is the power of this image that even Hornby's skewering of its adolescent machismo has not dislocated its pretensions to hipness. The music journalists and record geeks must have been sneering at pop songs, swooning over alternatives, haunting used record bins, making compilations, working on their endless taste-making systems of lists and ratings, and avoiding women while the rest of us were laughing at *High Fidelity*. For example, upon his arrival in Nashville, Alden boastfully bemoans the "record collecting geek" part of himself that has to haul so many heavy boxes of "vinyl" into his new apartment, located near a huge used record store where he hopes to acquire still more. In July–August 2001, he displays his connoisseurship in his description of his home office, "a room filled with books and records and art and photographs and compact discs and cassettes that crunch underfoot." Gender conflicts subtly come into play here when Alden adds that his wife "will tell you I'm not a tidy fellow."[20] His discriminating eyes see "art" where she merely sees a mess.

No Depression's unvarying table of contents similarly reflects the willful obscurity and contrived authenticity of the male music connoisseur. The magazine literally focuses on the margins in "A Place to Be," a travel column which beams a spotlight on various backwater shrines such as the Carter Family home in Maces Springs, Virginia, or Buck Owens's Crystal Palace in Bakersfield, California; the articles are usually written by visitors to these places rather than by residents. Likewise, each issue includes "Town & Country: Brief Regional Features," consisting mostly of club-hopping accounts of concerts in college towns such as Madison, Iowa City, or Gainesville. Cover stories and other profiles (listed in the table of contents as "Extended Cuts") routinely engage in genealogical praise of country traditionalists. Stories on contemporary artists, nearly all of them somewhat obscure, often grow out of a conversation between record collectors: Blackstock opens his profile of Buddy Miller by confessing that he received a promotional copy of Miller's debut but set it aside since he'd never heard of this artist. He only listened after a few of the members of the *No Depression* online community posted their own rave reviews of it.[21] Likewise, Roy Kasten discovered Ray Wylie Hubbard on a compilation tape a friend gave him, and he uses this fact to start his article on the singer.[22] Ultimately, record collecting takes pride of place in the pages of *No Depression;* reviews consume roughly a quarter of each issue with special sections devoted to the historical perspective provided by reissues, tributes, and compilations. A Summer 1996 letter to the editors from Mike McAfee of Evanston, Illinois, sums up well the defensive mix of record shopping and fraternity blackballing that alt.country shares with other genre-rule enforcers:

> This is how much I value your publication: After reading about several artists and/or their recordings in the spring issue, I have acquired the following CDs [a list of 10]. . . . Speaking of Son Volt [an Uncle Tupelo off-shoot], I was driving through a very rural part of America a few days ago and I heard "Drown" sandwiched between a Van Halen and AC/DC song. I think this is great for them as they deserve the recognition and the financial rewards that come with it (although they could care less about either of those), but part of it also bothers me because now we have to share them with the masses. Of course those lame stations wouldn't dare play a song that had a fiddle or a steel guitar in them. By the way what the hell was I doing listening to that lame station? . . . [P]erhaps I was search-ing for a truer sound!

Even in McAfee's heart of the heartland, radio stations threaten alt.country purity, but, as this letter so uncomfortably admits, once the music gets shared with the heartland's masses, alt.country risks losing its identity.

... You Might Even Live in Nashville ...

When *No Depression* and alternative country tell their stories, the mainstream-versus-alternative conflict often plays out as a battle of the sexes. Nashville, a capitalist siren, attempts to lure a sincere little Ulysses who just wants to make his own kind of music. In May–June 1997, Grant Alden recounts his move there. His quest was "to learn something about country's past, and maybe to figure out how its present got so screwed up." In the next issue, he was able to explain the screwed up part: Music City's domestication. The music executives, he asserts, go home at five o'clock and don't venture back out at night to catch the club acts. This observation proves that the *No Depression* brotherhood is "still having a conversation about something which deeply matters," while the Nashville drones are simply doing their jobs and then dutifully going home to their wives. He concludes that "if the music no longer delights and inspires you enough to get off the couch a few nights each week, you're in the wrong business." The stable of freelance writers who do the *No Depression* profiles and record reviews adopt a similar "us-against-them" rhetoric to define their subjects. Profiling Elizabeth Cook in September–October 2002, Bill Friskics-Warren rails against "the narrow strictures of the Nashville hit mill."[23] A nearly identical epithet appears later in the same issue in the same writer's review of Allison Moorer's new record. Her songs, he exults, "are just too rawboned and personal" to mesh with "the hegemony of Nashville's niche-obsessed hit mill."[24] Some alt.country artists have their ritual Nashville bashing song, too, and it's here that perhaps the enemy comes most clearly into view. As *No Depression* cover boy Robbie Fulks put it in his notorious song, "Fuck This Town," Nashville doesn't produce country music; it's "soft rock feminist crap" usually sung by "a faggot in a hat."[25] Indeed, for the past decade, commercial country radio, especially the hot new country format, appeals particularly to women.[26] Fulks feminizes the city even more overtly in the record compilation he imagines in his ironic liner notes to his ironically titled *The Very Best of Robbie Fulks.* The song "White Man's Bourbon" comes from *Nashville, We Will Slice Your Putrid Cunt to Ribbons.*[27] As opposed to the feminine new country, there's the macho alt.

Fulks makes a good case study of an alternative, whatever that is. Indeed, in Alden's cryptic story about his fall into country music (November–December

1997), Fulks shines the blinding light on the road to Nashville. Unhappily "pumping the star-making machine of grunge from an editorial desk in Seattle," Alden noticed "the first two Diesel Only compilations and the first offering from Bloodshot. Enter [Bloodshot artist] Robbie Fulks." In Kevin Roe's Summer 1996 coverage of Fulks's career, *No Depression* evinces the desperate discursive groping for an enemy to be an alternative to, taking special delight in citing Fulks's radio-unready lyrics. The first Fulks song cited, "She Took a Lot of Pills (and Died)," is described as "not your typical happy-go lucky Hollywood starlet suicide tale."[28] I guess the guys know which typical songs Roe's talking about, they must be playing all the time somewhere, but once again, I'd have to ask. This profile also cites the gruesome and graphic list of pig parts that Fulks sings about in "The Scrapple Song" and goes on to devote nearly half the article to discussing the as-yet unreleased "Fuck This Town." Fulks next graced the cover of the September–October 1997 issue; that photo is captioned with a line from the anti-Nashville ditty, and on the inside, Bill Friskics-Warren devotes a full page article to the song. Linda Ray's extensive profile of Fulks in this issue revisits these songs, too.[29]

Like Alden and Blackstock, Fulks is an inscrutable master of sarcasm although he probably wouldn't claim to be gentle. He further resembles *No Depression*'s editors in his own aspirations to literary journalism. He maintains an ostentatiously literate web site with many personal essays about his life as a beleaguered alt.country artist (the "My Day" section of www.RobbieFulks.com). For example, as he describes the vicissitudes of producing Dallas Wayne's CD *Big Thinkin'*, he compares himself to a major American writer (and a woman at that!): "Willa Cather advised sacrificing twelve long stories to one good short story; today the altar is bloody with eight-bar oblations."[30] While art may be the angel he wrestles with most intensely, women bedevil him more frequently. Fulks displays such hyperbolic misogyny that he could easily plead irony if he didn't constantly cultivate this sour grapevine. A sepia photo of a weathered country bumpkin about to attack a woman with an axe graces the cover of his debut album, *Country Love Songs*—implying that the juxtaposition of those two words, "country" and "love," means "hate." As if to confirm that suspicion, on his web site he boasts of writing a scabrous song called "Hating Women" in reaction to the Music City gurus who constantly counseled him to "say

With its depiction of rustic domestic violence, this cover art implies that the juxtaposition of the words "country" and "love" means "hate."

something nice about women" (although he is not man enough to print the lyrics). He reiterates his complaints in his over-the-top profile of 1950s country diva Jean Shepard in the *Journal of Country Music*. Even as he purports to praise her as a daring pioneer, he resents the gate crashing: "Today, fifty years after Jean first stepped behind a vocal mike . . . , the male voice in country is in danger of drowning in the estrogen tide, being reduced to a timid whisper of appeasement beneath the stampede of sexy vinyl boots."[31] When he graced the cover of this journal, the profile opened with a description of Fulks in Shania Twain drag, performing her "Man, I Feel Like a Woman."[32]

Fulks's encyclopedic repertoire mirrors *No Depression*'s interest in display-
ing a mastery over country music history. His "White Man's Bourbon," an
outtake intended for *Country Love Songs*, explains how to feel like a man (and
manages to offend all around).[33] The singer claims to be on a hunting trip in
Namibia when he spies an enticing "Zulu maid" whom he seduces with his
flask. He goes on to advise his audience, presumably men, to use the same
technique, since without this liquid enticement, the white male anatomy
would only provoke laughter. "From Dakar to Durbin, it's the white man's
bourbon make a Black girl holler for more," he concludes. As he defends
himself against the "sensitive souls at the [recording] session" who "objected
to being publicly associated with such a thing," Fulks explains it as a sort of
country music research project, his "modest contribution to the canon of
amour exotique" and cites predecessors such as "Ubangi Stomp" and
"Brown Sugar."[34] In fact, he planned *Country Love Songs* as a scholarly project, hoping to include "all the kinds of songs people don't do in country
music any more—the food song, the death song, the Latin rhythm song, the
xenophobic song."[35] Fulks's 2001 release, *13 Hillbilly Giants*, similarly draws
its inspiration from his record collection and extends his didactic aspirations.
A sort of Hornby-style compilation tape, the disc features covers of forgotten
songs by Bill Anderson, Porter Wagoner and Dolly Parton, Wynn Stewart, and
more obscure country artists from the past. Fulks wants to "offer my audience, many of whom don't listen to much country, a piece of the treasure
map I've been haphazardly assembling for the last dozen years."[36] On his
website, he writes a brief critical biography of each so-called giant, replete
with references to the *Journal of Country Music* and other exhaustive compen-
dia of historical information. In order to expand his fans' record collections,
he also gives internet links to sellers who stock disks by the thirteen giants
who have anything in print.

While the record-collector's mastery and the Nashville-hater's misogyny
link Fulks to *No Depression*'s favorite subjects, Fulks approaches political
questions quite differently.

Whereas *No Depression* stays silent on gender issues even as it asserts its
political and racial liberalism, Fulks plays the role of the embattled patriarch.
His 1997 album *South Mouth* draws its name from a Florence King column in
the *National Review*: "South Mouth: or Why Liberals Hate Dixie."[37] While King

uses the term to excoriate "liberal" criticism of the South, the definition she gives seems to describe a disease that afflicts Fulks himself: "South Mouth, a recurring infection that causes its sufferers to spout criticism, drip invective, ooze sanctimony, and chew rugs." I'm not sure how *No Depression* would defend Fulks from charges of conservatism: reading the *National Review* for Florence King's "deathless coinages" strikes me as akin to reading *Playboy* for its interviews with great novelists.[38] Indeed, on the cover of *South Mouth*, Fulks portrays himself as a sort of new believer, a liberal undergoing a cure: a crude portrait features a gruesome padlock piercing Fulks's mouth. There is no title track so the disc almost certainly takes its name from this drawing. Fulks makes a similar disavowal in "Bloodshot's Turning 5," the snide ditty he wrote for his label's fifth anniversary compilation. Liberalism simply fits alt.country's marketing plan, he implies. Bloodshot, he sings, took "the twang of a steel guitar [and] a little trendy left-wing jive" to create its niche.

. . . During the 21st Century . . .

Even as the term "alt.country" handily captures the high-tech lingo of the internet, the panache of alternative rock, and all sorts of symbolic slaps at the bourgeoisie, it also conveys nostalgia for the good alt days when red-blooded he-men sang as they pleased. Thus, in its visuals, *No Depression* (and many alt.country album covers) hearkens back to the 1930s and '40s. On their web site, the *No Depression* editors specifically counsel potential contributors to observe this retro style. In September–October 2002, they claim that modern-day computer-created graphics obscure the words, while they "approached this [publishing] enterprise with a radically retrograde philosophy: words are good." Their design preference indicates their refusal of "the mainstream of American magazine publishing wisdom;" instead, they prefer older models of wisdom. As we know, they particularly like the "common language" of college guys with guitars. Similarly, on their homepage, the images that direct surfers to the relevant sections all depict men involved in publishing, except for a comely secretary who evidently handles subscription gruntwork. Still, from their first cover to their most recent, they claim, they have drawn inspiration

Robbie Fulks's
alt.country
stardom as
portrayed on
the cover of
No Depression.

from the September 1937 issue of *Better Homes and Gardens*. Their 1998
anthology was festooned with retro clip art such as old tractors, cowboy boots,
and portable record players. David Goodman, whose *Modern Twang: Alternative Country Guide and Directory* was designed by the same designer and featured similar "Americana icons," explained to interviewer Renee Dechert that
these images were chosen because alt.country "is a pretty male dominated
genre so the icons are weighted heavily toward 'guy things.'"[39] The division of
labor implied by the icons, with women in the home and gardens and men
on the range, at the record players, and writing music criticism, must be one
of the alternatives to today's mainstream country.

Even though Homes and Gardens Were Better in the Good Alt.Days

The unprecedented success of the *O Brother, Where Art Thou?* soundtrack va-lidated *No Depression*'s perspective on alternatives to commercial country music since the magazine had featured such soundtrack standouts as Gillian Welch, Allison Krauss, Ralph Stanley, and even producer T. Bone Burnett long before the film was released. The confluence of the film's and the magazine's musical preferences not only brought alt.country a new level of recognition, it also solidified the nostalgic perspective inherent to *No Depression* and thus to alt.country. In the story *O Brother* tells, white men can be officially pardoned for their crimes, they emerge safely from skirmishes with sirens, and they pretend to be black when it advances their careers. Politicians embrace integration for the same reason. But mostly, the music confirms men's place in the ruling order. The Soggy Bottom Boys become part of the governor's "Brain Trust." Similarly, in the pages of *No Depression*, Capra-esque heroes armed with guitars and grim determination fight Nashville's feminized and profit-driven innovation, exchange fleeting smiles with black men at the crossroads, and rightfully assume positions of power. Because *No Depression* portrays the battle through images of the past and the enemy as a woman, victory, too, implicitly lies in a return to the better homes and gardens of the good old days rather than the embrace of a new (and inevitably more diverse) cultural order. It seems that for those who already know what alternative country is, there was relatively little depression in the days before hot new country, before the civil rights movement in the South, and before the second wave of feminism gave women alternatives to improving homes and gardens.

At the same time, the success of *O Brother* highlights the paradox of alt.country's quest for authentic musical expression. In theory, authenticity, like alt.country itself, requires no definition. Authenticity simply is what it is. But, the story goes, Nashville has so corrupted the audience for country music that only a select fraternity resist the siren and know good music when they hear it (or read about it). Hence, in the paradoxical discourse of alt.country, the authentic figures as an artistic ideal, depicted in staged photographs and retro imagery rather than in the experiences of people who work and wander through the dislocations of the here and now—the very people who favored

country music back when it was presumably real enough to need no alternative. Hence, in the July–August 2001 issue, Alden worries over the fact that you
can hear the *O Brother* soundtrack playing while you shop in a middle-America
emporium like Target. In his online essays, Fulks is even more unrestrained in
his disdain for life as it is lived in the boondocks. On the way to a tax audit,
necessity forces him to stop at a strip mall for lunch. Since the restaurant
teems with "glassy-eyed office drones, potbellied bozos with pagers on their
Dockers, anhedonic single moms, and desperate pink-collar climbers," Fulks
pronounces that "my wife and I will have our sandwiches to go."[40]

Fulks does not exempt his fans from his scorn, either. While he complains
about Nashville's attempt to saturate a "moron market" with its tuneful feminism, he also denounces the alternative crowd. On his web site, he describes
his audience at a particular show in Houston as "a heterogeneous lot. There
are hillbilly anarchist types, a big table of refugees from some consultants'
convention, a handful of gorgeous, smartly dressed young women . . . and
quite a few others arrayed in soothing earth tones who look to have had sexual fantasies about Mother Maybelle Carter. . . . And, on the other side of the
humanoid spectrum, the five drunk young uber-hicks."[41] One Fulks song
labels his audience "Roots Rock Weirdoes" who will only be happy when every
band consists of "four white guys." The singer fears the cultural agenda of
these wannabes who affect a black accent even as they worship a "fat dead
cracker king" and poison the air with three-chord songs and "self-regard." He
further underscores (and mocks) the retrograde sensibility in the song's fade-
out, adopting the voice of a crazed Viennese psychoanalyst who insists that "I
prefer your earlier verk [work]." This song, he jokes in his *Best of* liner notes,
first appeared on a "limited-release 45" entitled *I Loathe My Fans*.

While Fulks may have led *No Depression*'s editors to alt.country, *No
Depression* led him to the dreaded mainstream. It turns out that David Geffen,
of Joni Mitchell's "Free Man in Paris" and original operator of the "star-
making machinery behind the popular song," wanted to send Fulks down his
assembly line. Geffen's representatives were reading the alternative 'zine to do
their scouting, and the brief *No Depression* profile of Fulks in Summer 1996
inspired them to offer alt.country's hero an alternative to dissing the mainstream. Paradoxically, Linda Ray's subsequent cover story trumpets this turn
of events in its subtitle, a banner that spans two pages: "Robbie Fulks bids

adieu to Bloodshot and gets ready for the big leagues." The big leagues weren't yet ready for Fulks, though. Shortly after Geffen Records released *Let's Kill Saturday Night* (1998), the label was bought and all but the top-selling artists released from their contracts. Fulks returned to Bloodshot but he's chafing at the limitations of their formula. Paradoxically, the Geffen executives let him do what he wanted, he says, and the songs on *Let's Kill Saturday Night* indicate that Fulks sometimes likes to sound like a pop singer.[42] For that matter, even *The Very Best of Robbie Fulks* has a tear-soaked cover of John Denver's "Leavin' on a Jet Plane" and a jingly ode to pop singer Susanna Hoffs, "That Bangle Girl." *Couples in Trouble*, Fulks's 2001 release, resolutely abandons country song scholarship and Fulks's assertively offensive earlier verk. Heartbreak, rather than genre rules, holds this album together.

Conclusion
"I'm Going to Where There's No Depression"

While *No Depression* long ago settled into a preference for earlier work, I keep listening to Fulks in the hope that his quick wit and high-powered alienation can craft something new. Even as he engages in the forms of connoisseurship he detests in his fans, he seems to want to break free of the "aesthetic and ethical" dictates of "genre rules." He characterizes alt.country musicians as "a bunch of thirtysomethings who sound exactly like old country stars except that they can't write songs and can't really sing the songs they can't write."[43] Alt.country's particular credos, he repeatedly implies, have infected him with "South Mouth." In a moment of self-loathing, just before he plays a show in the city of the Siren, he notes his symptoms:

> I guess because it's Nashville and it's me, I can't stop slamming contemporary country music between songs. . . . How easy to go around tearing down, tearing down, tearing down; how superior and discerning one must be to jeer at mass-market entertainment; how very canny of oneself to secure a small but comfortable niche in the roots-cracker-fringe-roadhouse-Western-Beat firmament with crude ideological invective rather than honest musical labor.[44]

Even more searing is the moment when Fulks calls himself a "hat whore." Given the chance to pose for a *GQ* fashion spread featuring alt.country stars, Fulks can't summon the courage to reject a cowboy hat the stylists want him to wear. He posts his shame on the worldwide web: "let's be perfectly honest, and I don't care how shallow it sounds: I am thrilled to be in *GQ*." As he does an interview with a *GQ* staffwriter, Fulks again finds himself fulminating against Nashville, offering witty epigrams and "pithy concoction[s] . . . that should play pretty well in the august pages of *GQ*."[45] When one of his heroes, Buck Owens, rewrote "The Cover of the *Rolling Stone*" as "The Cover of the *Music City News*" (1974), he celebrated his exclusion from the critically anointed elite. It's too late for Fulks to offer up "The Cover of *No Depression*," but he needs a similar aesthetic populism. Like Owens on *Hee Haw*, Fulks has cast himself as the incurable rustic, too rude even for Nashville. As his stories reveal, he repeatedly falls from the sublime to the ridiculous. Even his *No Depression* canonization saps his power, subjecting him to the "left-wing jive" of alt.country's entrepreneurs. In fact, his most objectionable songs, whether I like them or not, portray a simultaneously comic and violent impotence. White men have nothing but bourbon to offer: like his hard-country predecessors Hank Williams and Buck Owens, Fulks self-consciously burlesques the role of the powerful white man while *No Depression* offers its readers a fantasy of regaining the old mainstream.[46] Fulks's anguished genre-rule bending allows him to say almost anything. It seems quite possible that one day he'll say something new—whatever that would be. Alt.country's taste-makers could once again be struck from their high horses, but at this point, only their slogans flirt with innovation and authenticity. Their media send another message.

Postlude

CHARLES WOLFE

The remarkable essays in *A Boy Named Sue* represent some of the ongoing research by a new generation of country music scholars, and reflect a variety of new directions in the study of country music. Just how dramatic these new approaches are can only be appreciated by seeing them in perspective of earlier, more traditional efforts to understand one of our culture's most complex—and misunderstood—art forms.

Country music is often grouped with two other musical genres that developed out of the folk tradition and which defined themselves through the new mass media emerging in the 1920s: jazz and blues. All three forms began to break out of their Southern home and find their own audiences at about the same time, yet most of the perceptive analyses of them was focused on jazz and blues. By World War II, country had a substantial radio, concert, and recording presence, and had given birth to a number of subgenres such as western swing, close-harmony singing, Hollywood cowboy songs, and what later became honky-tonk. Yet country had attracted no serious chroniclers, as had jazz with Sheldon Brooks, Ramsey and Smith, and Charles Delaunay, or blues with the works of Newman I. White or Dorothy Scarborough. It wasn't until 1968, when Bill C. Malone wrote his still-definitive *Country Music USA*, that country music began to receive the serious study its companion genres had garnered twenty or thirty years before. From there on, it was a matter of country music scholars playing catch-up ball.[1]

There are reasons why scholars were slow to appreciate the significance of country music, many of them too complex and problematical to go into here. One that might be relevant to this collection, however, is that country music was, in a sense, a victim of its own success. The audience, the venue, and the aesthetic for classic jazz and blues developed into a tight, well-defined cadre of fans who generally shared the same expectations from the music. Many of the great blues singers, such as Robert Johnson, sold relatively few records, were seldom heard on radio, and were not well known out of their own region. A jazz player like Bix Beiderbeck had to bury his work in lumbering pop orchestras like Paul Whiteman's, where those few cognoscenti who appreciated his cornet work had to listen to a record with three minutes of mush in order to hear an eight-bar break by their hero.

Country music, on the other hand, expanded into dozens of venues and substyles, spread across radio, records, and through almost daily concerts. It became amoeba-like in its complexity and undirected growth, and attracted a number of different audiences; with each audience came a different set of expectations and values. Some fans got satisfaction from the nostalgia and sentiment of Chicago's *National Barn Dance*; others cherished the hot fiddle improvisation of a Bob Wills western swing record; others took solace in the tough hard times white blues of Jimmie Rodgers, or in the mountain imagery of the Carter Family. A writer attempting to analyze or explain classic country music might well ask, "Which country music?" or, more to the point, "Which country audience?" The fans of country music crossed gender, class, geographical, age, ethnic, and occupational lines—they were far from the monolithic southern rural audience that early writers assumed. As a result, there were few writers brave enough to define or explain the subject: there were no Ralph Ellisons to comment intelligently on this music, no Amiri Barakas to offer a country music counterpart to *Blues People*. Until Bill Malone wrote *Country Music USA*, there was not even a map of the territory for later students to follow.[2]

The first generation of country music scholars thus followed basically an historical approach—either expanding on a section of development Malone had defined, or creating conventional biographies of artists like Jimmie Rodgers, Bob Wills, Patsy Cline, Pee Wee King, Rose Maddox, the Stoneman Family, Hank Williams, and the Louvin Brothers. A handful—Cecilia Tichi, Dorothy Horstman, and Malone's later *Don't Get Above Your Raisin': Country Music and the Southern Working Class*—experimented with basing their analyses on the content of song lyrics, and a few others explored the role of cultural geography in the scope of the music, focusing on a city or region. Mary Bufwack and Robert Oermann's *Finding Her Voice: Women in Country Music* offered a Malone-like map to the hitherto unappreciated role of women in the music, and opened up dozens of avenues for further research. As important as these later studies were, though, they served primarily to add to the database about the music, to fill in the terra incognita spaces of the country music map.[3]

Thus, beginning in the 1990s, several things happened that encouraged a new generation of country music students to take the next step in exploring the music. They began to understand something of how a commercial art form like country really worked, and that to understand it one had to take into account not only the traditional knowledge of singers and songs, but the merchandizing techniques, the complex nature of the audience, the various ways the music found its consumers, the role of image and the ways images were constructed, and the stereotypes that have for generations obfuscated a clear picture of the complex dynamics of the music. The increasing archive of materials relating to the music, past and present, offered to trained researchers a rich database from which fresh interpretations of the music could be drawn. No longer were country historians drawn from the ranks of traditional history, folklore, and literature, but now from a battery of new specialties like gender studies, media studies, industrial sociology, musicology, cultural geography, genre integrity, and cultural consumption. With this variety of specialized tools, the full story of the complex dynamic that is the country music experience is starting to be written. This present collection is one of its first chapters.

Notes

Foreword
Muddying the Clear Water: The Dubious Transparency of Country Music

1. Joli Jensen, *The Nashville Sound: Authenticity, Commercialization, and Country Music* (Nashville: Country Music Foundation/Vanderbilt University Press, 1998), 40.

2. Mary A. Bufwack and Robert K. Oermann, *Finding Her Voice: Women in Country Music 1800–2000* (Nashville: Country Music Foundation/Vanderbilt University Press, 2003.

3. David Sanjek, "Can A Fujiyama Mama Be The Female Elvis? The Wild, Wild Women of Rockabilly," in *Sexing the Groove, Popular Music and Gender*, ed. Sheila Whiteley (London: Routledge, 1997); David Sanjek, *Always on My Mind: Music, Memory and Money* (Middletown, Ct.: Wesleyan University Press, forthcoming).

4. Richard Peterson, *Creating Country Music: Fabricating Authenticity* (Chicago: University of Chicago Press, 1997).

5. Nicolas Dawidoff, *In the Country of Country: People and Places in American Music* (New York: Pantheon, 1997); Paul Hemphill, *The Nashville Sound: Bright Lights and Country Music* (New York: Simon & Schuster, 1970).

6. Dawidoff, *In the Country of Country*, 310.

7. *Ibid.*, 309.

8. *Idem.*

9. *Ibid.*, 212.

10. Barbara Ching, *Wrong's What I Do Best: Hard Country Music and Contemporary Culture* (New York: Oxford University Press, 2001), 5.

11. *Ibid.*, 15.

12. Jensen, *The Nashville Sound*, 15.

Introduction

1. Teresa Ortega, " 'My name is Sue! How do you do?': Johnny Cash as Lesbian Icon," *South Atlantic Quarterly*, 94 (Winter 1995), 267.

2. Joan Wallach Scott, *Gender and the Politics of History* (New York: Columbia University Press, 1988), 31.

3. Barbara Ching, *Wrong's What I Do Best: Hard Country Music and Contemporary Culture* (New York: Oxford University Press, 2001); Richard A. Peterson, "Class Unconsciousness in Country Music," in *You Wrote My Life: Lyrical Themes in Country Music*, ed. Melton A. McLauren and Richard A. Peterson (Philadelphia: Gordon and Breach, 1992).

4. Andreas Huyssen, *After the Great Divide: Modernism, Mass Culture, and Postmodernism* (Bloomington: Indiana University Press, 1986), 44–62.

"Bury Me Beneath the Willow": Linda Parker and Definitions of Tradition on the *National Barn Dance*, 1932–1935

1. Karl and Harty with the Cumberland Ridge Runners, [no date], Old Homestead Records.
2. WLS *Family Album*, 1934, Country Music Foundation, Nashville, TN.; Mrs. James F. Victorin to the Listeners' Mike, *Stand By!*, 1:28 (1935), 5.
3. O. W. to the Listeners' Mike, *Stand By!*, 1:28 (1935), 2.
4. Dave Samuelson, "Linda Parker: The WLS Sunbonnet Girl," *Journal of the American Academy for the Preservation of Old-Time Country Music*, 30 (1995), 16–17.
5. Richard A. Peterson, *Creating Country Music: Fabricating Authenticity* (Chicago: University of Chicago Press, 1997); Bill C. Malone, *Country Music, USA* (Austin: University of Texas Press, 1985).
6. Malone, *Country Music, USA*.
7. Robert Coltman, "Sweetheart of the Hills: Women in Early Country Music," *John Edwards Memorial Foundation Quarterly* (no. 52, 1978), 161–81.
8. David Sanjek, "Can A Fujiyama Mama be the Female Elvis?: The Wild, Wild Women of Rockabilly," in *Sexing the Groove, Popular Music and Gender*, ed. Sheila Whiteley (London: Routledge, 1997), 137–67.
9. Mary Bufwack, "The Feminist Sensibility in Post-War Country Music," *Southern Quarterly*, 22 (Spring 1984), 135–44; Mary Bufwack and Robert K. Oermann, *Finding Her Voice: The Saga of Women in Country Music* (New York: Crown Publishers, 1993); Robert K. Oermann and Mary Bufwack, "Songs of Self-Assertion: Women in Country Music" (Somerville, Mass.: New England Free Press, 1979).
10. Barbara Welter, "The Cult of True Womanhood: 1820–1860," *American Quarterly*, 18 (Summer 1966), 151–74; Nancy F. Cott, *The Bonds of Womanhood: "Women's Sphere" in New England, 1780–1835* (New Haven: Yale University Press, 1977); Linda Kerber, "Separate Spheres, Female Worlds, Woman's Place: The Rhetoric of Women's History," *Journal of American History*, 75 (June 1988), 9–39.
11. Ardis Cameron, *Radicals of the Worst Sort: Laboring Women in Lawrence, Massachusetts, 1860–1912* (Urbana: University of Illinois Press, 1993).
12. Peterson, *Creating Country Music*, 256, fn. 11.
13. Henry Shapiro, *Appalachia On Our Mind: The Southern Mountains and Mountaineers in the American Consciousness, 1890–1920* (Chapel Hill: University of North Carolina Press, 1978); Jane S. Becker, *Selling Tradition: Appalachia and the Construction of an American Folk, 1930–1940* (Chapel Hill: University of North Carolina Press, 1998).
14. Dorothy Scarborough, *A Songcatcher in the South* (New York: Columbia University Press, 1937), 4.
15. Emma Bell Miles, *Spirit of the Mountains* (Knoxville: University of Tennessee Press, 1975).
16. Loyal Jones, *Radio's "Kentucky Mountain Boy" Bradley Kincaid* (Berea College: Appalachian Center, 1980).
17. Bradley Kincaid, WLS Radio Address, "The First Evening: A Close-up Of the Mountaineers" [ca. 1929], Bradley Kincaid Papers, Southern Appalachian Collection (Hutchins Library, Berea College, Berea, Ky.).
18. Kincaid, WLS Radio Address, "The Third Evening: America's Debt to the Mountains," [ca. 1929], Kincaid Papers.
19. Kincaid, "America's Debt to the Mountains."
20. Kincaid, "A Close-up of the Mountaineers."
21. Kincaid, "America's Debt to the Mountains."
22. Kincaid, "To My Radio Friends, Songbook #2," 1929, Kincaid Papers.
23. Emma Riley Akeman to Our Dear Bradley?, April 9,1935, Kincaid Papers.

24. Lisa Yarger, "Banjo Pickin' Girl: Representing Lily May Ledford" (M.A. thesis, University of North Carolina, Chapel Hill, 1997).

25. Radio Script, WLS [ca. early 1930s], John Lair Papers, Southern Appalachian Collection.

26. Radio Script, WLS [ca. 1930–1931], Lair Papers.

27. Radio Script, *Aladdin Barn Dance Frolic*, Dec. 20, 1930, Lair Papers.

28. "Cousin Emmy," *Time*, Dec. 6, 1943, p. 62.

29. *Alka Seltzer Barn Dance Program*, 1936, Bayer Corporation Papers (Elkhart, Ind.).

30. Souvenir Program, *WLS National Barn Dance*, Lair Papers.

31. Radio Script, *Monday Night in Renfro Valley*, Oct. 14, 1940, Lair Papers.

32. Radio Script, *Monday Night in Renfro Valley*, Aug. 5, 1940, Lair Papers.

33. Radio Script, WLS, Eleven o'clock . . . Sat. Night, Oct. 3, 1931, Lair Papers.

34. Radio Script, WLS, [ca. 1930–1931], Lair Papers.

35. William Carson Ellis, "The Sentimental Mother Song in American Country Music, 1923–1945" (Ph.D. diss., Ohio State University, 1978).

36. See, for example, the published research of folklorist Scarborough, *A Song Catcher in the Southern Mountains;* Cecil Sharp & Maud Karpeles, *Eighty Appalachian Folk Songs* (Winchester, MA: Faber & Faber, 1968).

37. WLS Interview with John Lair, [broadcast 1930s], Lair Papers.

38. Radio Script, WLS, [ca. early 1930s], Lair Papers.

39. Radio Script, WLS, untitled, [ca. early 1930s], Lair Papers.

40. Radio Script, *Aladdin [sic] Barn Dance Frolic, no. 2*, Dec. 20, 1930, Lair Papers.

41. Ann Lair Henderson, *On the Air with John Lair* (Mt. Vernon, KY: Polly House Productions, 1998).

42. John Lair interview by Reuben Powell, Oct. 26, 1967, audiotape (Southern Appalachian Collection).

43. Samuelson, "Linda Parker."

44. Kathy Peiss, *Hope in a Jar: The Making of America's Beauty Culture* (New York: Metropolitan, 1998).

45. Faye Dudden, *Women in American Theater: Actresses and Audiences, 1790–1870* (New Haven: Yale University Press, 1994).

46. Radio Script, *Thursday Noon*, Feb. 25, 1932, Lair Papers.

47. Henderson, *On the Air with John Lair.*

48. Radio Script, *Thursday Noon Program*, Feb. 25, 1932, Lair Papers.

49. *Ibid.*

50. Radio Script, *Hamlin*, Feb. 24, 1934, Lair Papers.

51. *Ibid.*

52. Radio Script, WLS *Play–Party Frolic, 7:45–8:15*, May 7, 1932—8th St, Lair Papers.

53. W. Demont Wright to The Prairie Farmer Station, Feb. 18, 1934, Lair Papers.

54. Victorin to the Listeners' Mike, 5.

55. Mrs. E. E. Muenich to John Lair, Dec. 28, 1935, Lair Papers.

56. Art Janes was a singer with the Barn Dance band Maple City Four, named for La Porte, Indiana.

57. Kristine M. McCusker, "Dear Radio Friend: Listener Mail and the *National Barn Dance,* 1931–1941," *American Studies*, 39 (no. 2, 1998), 173–95.

58. Lois Almy, to the Listeners' Mike, *Stand By!*, 1:28 (1935), 2.

59. Radio Script, *Bunk House and Cabin Songs*, Jan. 18, 1936, Lair Papers.

60. *Ibid.*

61. Mrs. E. E. Muenich to John Lair, Feb. 18, 1936, Lair Papers.

62. Charles Baker to Friend, Feb. 1, 1936, Lair Papers.

"Spade Doesn't Look Exactly Starved": Country Music and the Negotiation of Women's Domesticity in Cold War Los Angeles

1. Catherine Winston, "Musically Inclined Spade Cooley Family Enjoys Valley Life," *Antelope Valley Press*, 6 (November 6, 1960), p. 8.

2. Spade Cooley envelope, *Los Angeles Examiner* files, Hearst Collection, East Library (Regional History Center, University of Southern California, Los Angeles, Calif.); *Los Angeles Times*, April 5, 1961, pp. A1, A26. Cooley spent most of the rest of his life in prison.

3. Historians who study women's roles in the family and in society during the early cold war have tended to associate themselves with two general schools of thought. The more pessimistically inclined—a group whose sentiments have been most popularized by Elaine Tyler May in her seminal book *Homeward Bound: American Families in the Cold War Era* (New York: BasicBooks, 1988)—have argued that the Eisenhower era was a time in which women's opportunities were severally curtailed. Although careful to point out that this curtailment was often negotiated and that her work explored only middle-class white women, May consulted a variety of social and sexological studies of the era to argue in the parlance of the cold war bureaucrat that women's occupational, familial, and sexual desires were largely "contained."

On the other end of the debate, stands a group of scholars, many of whom contributed to *Not June Cleaver: Women and Gender in Postwar America, 1945–1960* (Philadelphia: Temple University Press, 1994), a volume edited by women's labor historian Joanne Meyerowitz. The school that has grown up around *Not June Cleaver* has spent much of its time identifying the divergences in women's experiences in the 1950s and highlighting the agency of working-class, ethnic, and African American women. While cognizant of the conservative character of Eisenhower-age gender roles, such scholars highlight the "ambivalence, contradiction and self parody of gender ideals" in the popular culture of the age and point to "pockets of resistance" significant groups of women "questioned and loosened postwar constraints" (p. 4).

My own research indicates that the processes highlighted by May and Meyerowitz might be occurring simultaneously, within different though overlapping subsections of a single social group's cultural milieu. By incorporating both the messages of the mass culture industry as they are mediated through recorded music, broadcasting, and fan magazines and the actual community of women fans and performers who took part in the subculture, a study of postwar country music culture in Los Angeles suggests that while the publicity pulps of the local country music industry lionized docility and domesticity in women, some women artists and fans used the same subculture to contest constraints and push the boundaries of women's accepted roles.

4. Fordist wage structures got their name from carmaker Henry Ford's efforts in the 1930s to bolster employee consumer power by guaranteeing his auto workers five dollars a day, a reasonably high wage for the time. Ford had originally hoped such wages would prompt workers to buy his cars. As a general term, Fordism has come to mean any manufacturing wage system that offers workers a relatively substantial wage in return for labor peace (i.e., no-strike pledges). Fordism is also used today to connote a specific period in American economic history (the 1940s to 1960s) that has gradually been replaced by a new "Post-Fordist era" (the 1970s on) marked by outsourcing, overseas plant relocations, workforce "flexibility," less job stability, and lower wages.

5. Richard P. Stockdell, "The Evolution of the Country Radio Format," *Journal of Popular Culture*, 16 (Spring 1983), 146–47; Cal Worthington interview by Peter La Chapelle, Aug. 28, 2001, audio tape (in Peter La Chapelle's possession); "Sammy Masters," *Country Music Report* (Orange, California), 1 (Dec. 1963), 24; "Cal Worthington," *Country Music Report*, 1 (Dec. 1963), 23; John Lomax, III, "The Center of Music City: Nashville's Music Row," *The Encyclopedia of Country Music*, ed. Paul Kingsbury (New York: Oxford University Press, 1998), 386–87; "Capitol Records' Fast Rise Belies Early Turbulence," Feb. 22, 1955, *Los Angeles Examiner* files, Hearst Collection.

6. Runs—both complete and incomplete—of these fan journals can be found in the John Edwards Memorial Foundation (JEMF) archive in the Southern Folklife Collection, Wilson Library (University of North Carolina, Chapel Hill, N.C.); the Country Music Foundation Library and Media Center, Nashville, Tenn.; and in the personal collection Thomas Sims, San Diego, Calif. *Western and Country Music*, in fact, was so adamant about its Western identity that the magazine was originally titled with a singular adjective, *Western Music*.

7. Runs of some of these magazines are located in Country Music Foundation Library and Media Center, but the JEMF collection is particularly strong on Southern California periodicals of this era.

8. Specifics on Ciesla were gleaned from "Miss Sunny Ciesla: 'Round-up in Hollywood' News Editor," *National Hill-Billy News*, 3 (Sept.–Oct. 1947), 4–5; and Sunny Ciesla, "Round-Up in Hollywood," *National Hill-Billy News*, 3 (Jan.–Feb. 1948), 6. Dusti Lynn, "The Trail Dreamer," *National Hill-Billy News*, 5 (Nov.–Dec. 1949), 22; "Western Palisades Cops *Top Hand*," 5; "Western Palisades" advertisement, *Top Hand*, 1 (April 1946), 10; "Grace Purdy Joins Tophand Staff," *Top Hand*, 1 (April 1946), 1; "Nat Vincent Pens a Poem," *Top Hand*, 1, (April 1946), 3.

9. Bill A. Wheeler, "At Home with Doye O'Dell," *Country Music Report*, 1 (Nov. 1963), 14–15, 37; Bill A. Wheeler, "A Home That Talks: It Speaks of Cash," *Country Music Review* (Anaheim, formerly *Country Music Report*) (May 1964), 12–13; Bill A. Wheeler, "At Home with Joe and Rose Lee Maphis," *Country Music Review First Annual Yearbook* (Anaheim, California: Cal-Western Publications, 1965), n.p.; Jim Harris "West Coast Notes," *Country Music Life* (Aug. 1966), 4; Jim Harris, "West Coast Notes," *Country Music Life* (Sept. 1966), 5; Carolina Cotton, "Bits 'n Pieces from Carolina Cotton's West Coast Treasure Chest," *Rustic Rhythm*, 1 (July 1957), 4. On Devvy Davenport see 1963 issues of *Country Music Report* and 1964 issues of *Country Music Review*.

10. "Doorman Fillips Country Barn Dance" cartoon, *Top Hand*, 1 (Sept. 1946), 10; photographic collage, *Top Hand*, 1 (Dec. 1946), 31; *Country Music Life* (Nov. 1965), 4.

11. "Meet the Mrs." columns appeared in *Country Song Roundup* while "At Home with . . ." columns were regular features of *Country Music Report* and its successor *Country Music Review*.

12. Winston, "Musically Inclined Cooley," 8; "Meet the Mrs.: Ruth O'Dell," *Country Song Roundup*, 1 (Oct. 1953), 13.

13. Compare, for instance, information presented in Ken Griffis, "The Beverly Hill Billies," *John Edwards Memorial Foundation Quarterly*, 16 (Spring 1980), 3–16; Maxine (Crissman) Dempsey interview by Richard Reuss, June 14–June 18, 1968, field notes, Richard Reuss Papers (Indiana University, Bloomington, Ind.), 4; and *The Carter Family: Old Time Music Booklet 1*, ed. John Atkins (London: Old Time Music, 1973) with those of the cold war era such as "Dear John: Ferlin Huskey and Jean Shepard," *Country Song Roundup*, 7; "At Home with Stuart Hamblen," *Country Music Report*, 1 (Oct. 1963), 14–15, 33; Wheeler, "At Home with Doye O'Dell," 14–15, 37; Wheeler, "A Home That Talks," 12–13; and Wheeler, "At Home with Joe and Rose," n.p.

14. Winston, "Musically Inclined Cooley," 8; "At Home with Stuart Hamblen," 14–15, 33. This movement into whiter, more prosperous neighborhoods is discussed in greater detail in author's dissertation, " 'That Mean Ol' Oakie Boogie': Country Music, Migration, and the Construction of Whiteness in Southern California, 1936–1969," (Ph.D. diss., University of Southern California, 2002), 219, 220, fig. 2.

15. "Meet the Mrs.: Ruth O'Dell," 13; "At Home with Stuart Hamblen," 14–15, 33.

16. Wheeler, "At Home with Joe and Rose," n.p.; Andy Mosely, "Mr. and Mrs. Country Music: Joe and Rose Lee Maphis," *Country Music Life* (March 1968), 38–40.

17. Woody Guthrie and Maxine "Lefty Lou" Crissman, *Woody and Lefty Lou's Favorite Collection of Old Time Hill Country Songs: Being Sung for Ages, Still Going Strong* (Gardena, California: Spanish American Institute Press, 1937), 22; *Spade Cooley's Western Swing Song Folio* (New York: Hill and Range Songs, 1945), 18–19; Bea Terry, "Folk Music and Its Folks: Carolina Cotton," country music

publication clipping (*Hoedown?*), ca. 1950, Carolina Cotton name file, Country Music Foundation Library and Media Center.

18. Songs sampled were recorded by these artists between 1950 and 1965 and were obtained through the Center for Folklife and Cultural Heritage (Smithsonian Institution, Washington, D.C.); the Library of Congress's Performing Arts Reading Room; and author's personal collection. Compare with Woody Guthrie, "Songs of Woody Guthrie" [n.d., ca. 1937–1940], carbon copy of typescript, pp. 17, 197, box 2, Writings, Woody Guthrie Manuscripts, American Folklife Center (Library of Congress, Washington, D.C.). Thompson, a Texas-based artist, called Los Angeles the "bread and butter" of his performance tour. Frizzell settled in the San Fernando Valley by the late 1950s.

19. Joanne Meyerowitz, "Beyond the Feminine Mystique: A Reassessment of Postwar Mass Culture, 1946–1958," in *Not June Cleaver: Women and Gender in Postwar America*, ed. Joanne Meyerowitz (Philadelphia: Temple University, 1994), 246–52.

20. May, *Homeward Bound*, 114–34; Bill C. Malone, "Honky-tonk," in *Encyclopedia of Country Music*, ed. Kingsbury, 246; Carolina Cotton, "Carolina's Cotton Pickin' News," *Rustic Rhythm*, 1 (May 1957), 32–33; Joe Maphis and Rose Lee, "Dim Lights, Thick Smoke (And Loud, Loud Music)," Various Artists, *Swing West!: Volume 1: Bakersfield* (compact disc; Razor & Tie 7930182197-2; 1999).

21. Patsy Montana, radio interview, KXLA Studios, Pasadena, California, June 25, 1959, audio-cassette, Field Recording Collection no. FT2682, JEMF archive; Chris Comber, "Patsy Montana: The Cowboy's Sweetheart," newsclipping, *Old Time Music*, 4 (1972), 10.

22. "Maddox Bros. and Rose," Four Star publicity materials, ca. 1954, Rose Maddox name file, Country Music Foundation Library and Media Center; "Maddox Brothers and Rose: Most Colorful Western and Hillbilly Band in America," *Western Music*, 1 (July 1951), 14; George Sanders, "Hollywood Hoedown Lowdown," *Country Song Roundup*, 1 (Oct. 1952), 8; "Bill Price's Ranch Roundup," *Rustic Rhythm*, 1 (July 1957), 54; Maddox Brothers and Rose, "I Wish I Were a Single Girl Again" (78 rpm disc; Four Star 1586); Maddox Brothers and Rose, "Philadelphia Lawyer" (78 rpm disc; Four Star 1289); Johnny Whiteside, "Cowgirl in a Cadillac," *LA Weekly*, April 27–May 3, 1990, pp. 16–17. Also see Whiteside's excellent biography of Maddox, *Ramblin' Rose: The Life and Career of Rose Maddox* (Nashville: Country Music Foundation Press/Vanderbilt University Press, 1997).

23. "Dear John: Ferlin Huskey and Jean Shepard," *Country Song Roundup*, 1 (Jan. 1954), 7; Chris Skinker, liner notes to Jean Shepard, *The Melody Ranch Girl* (compact disc set; Bear Family Records BC 15905 EI; 1996), 4–7; Jean Shepard, "A Real Good Woman" and "The Trouble with Girls," audio recording, SFC 45–377 P21, JEMF.

24. Jean Shepard, "Two Hoops and a Holler," "Girls in Disgrace," "The Root of All Evil (Is a Man)," and "Second Fiddle (to an Old Guitar)," *The Melody Ranch Girl*; Skinker, liner notes, 11, 28.

25. Mary A. Bufwack and Robert K. Oermann, *Finding Her Voice: The Illustrated History of Women in Country Music* (New York: Henry Holt and Company, 1993), 178–79; C. Phil Henderson, " 'Ritin' th' Range," *Top Hand*, 1 (April 1946), 3; Sunny Ciesla, "Round-Up in Hollywood," *National Hill-Billy News*, 4 (March–April 1949), 12–13; Lulu Bell Errett, "Speakin' of the 'Squeakin' Deacon,' " *National Hill-Billy News*, 4 (Nov.–Dec. 1948), 20; Biff Collie, "What Is a Disc Jockey," *Country Music Life* (Jan. 1968), 41; George Sanders, "Hollywood Hoedown Lowdown," *Country Song Roundup*, 1 (Oct. 1952), 8; Bea Terry, "Folk Music and Its Folks: Carolina Cotton," newsclipping [n.d., ca. 1950], Carolina Cotton name file, Country Music Foundation Library and Media Center; KFOX advertisement, *Country Music Report*, 1 (Dec. 1963), 17; Hugh Cherry, "The KFOX Story."

26. Ben Townsend, "The Magic Wanda," *Hoedown* (Denver), 1 (May 1966), 8–12; Robert Medley, authorized biography synopsis, typed manuscript, May 1, 1991, Oklahoma City, Oklahoma, Wanda Jackson Artist File, JEMF archive; Kurt Wolff, "Q & A with Wanda Jackson,"

The San Francisco Chronicle, Nov. 5, 1995, p. 34; Alison DeBrucque, "The Queen of Rockabilly," *Oklahoma Gazette*, April 24, 1991, p. 21; Bob Garbutt, *Rockabilly Queens* (Ontario, Canada: Duck Tail Press, 1979), 15, 21; Wanda Jackson, "I Gotta Know," "Hot Dog! That Made Him Mad," "Cool Love," "This Should Go On Forever," "Fujiyama Mama" and "Let's Have a Party," *Vintage Collection Series* (compact disc; Capitol 7243-8-36185); Rich Kienzle, liner notes to Jackson, *Vintage Collections;* Nick Tosches, *Unsung Heroes of Rock 'n' Roll* (New York: Charles Scribner's Sons, 1984), 128–32; "Town Hall Party," program 11, reel 2, Nov. 29, 1959, video recording, Country Music Foundation Library and Media Center; Randy Fox and Michael Gray, "Hillbilly Boogie: All Mama's Children Are Doin' the Bop," *Journal of Country Music*, 20 (no. 2, 1999), 21.

27. Barbara Mandrell with George Vecsey, *Get to the Heart: My Story* (New York: Bantam Books, 1990), 256.

28. Shirley Desy interview by Peter La Chapelle, Aug. 7, 2001, audiotape (in Peter La Chapelle's possession); Shirley Desy to Peter La Chapelle, July 29, 2001 (in Peter La Chapelle's possession).

29. Desy interview by La Chapelle.

30. James Gregory, *American Exodus: The Dust Bowl Migration and Okie Culture in California* (New York: Oxford University Press, 1989), 139–71. Although Gregory is the most recent and by far the most eloquent exponent of this conservatism thesis, the origins of such thinking originate in the rural sociology of the 1930s. See, for instance, Walter Goldschmidt, *As You Sow: Three Studies in the Social Consequences of Agribusiness* (1947; Montclair, N.J.: Allanheld, Osmun & Co., 1978), 70–74, 185; Stuart M. Jamieson, "A Settlement of Rural Migrant Families in Sacramento Valley, California," *Rural Sociology*, 7 (March 1942), 59–60.

Charline Arthur: The (Un)Making of a Honky-Tonk Star

1. Paul Kingsbury, "Women in Country: A Special Report," *Journal of Country Music*, 15 (no. 1, 1992), 22.

2. *Country and Western Jamboree*, 1 (Aug. 1955), 4.

3. Bob Allen, "Charline Arthur," *Journal for the Society of the Preservation of Old Time Country Music* (1991), 19.

4. Charline Arthur, *Welcome to the Club* (compact disc; Bear Family BCD 16279; 1998).

5. Mary A. Bufwack and Robert K. Oermann, *Finding Her Voice: The Saga of Women in Country Music* (New York: Crown, 1993), 173.

6. *Ibid.*, 169.

7. Bob Pinson, Richard Weize, and Charles Wolfe, *The Golden Years of Kitty Wells* (Germany: Bear Family Records, 1987), 16.

8. Bob Allen, liner notes, Arthur, *Welcome to the Club.*

9. Curtis W. Ellison, *Country Music Culture: From Hard Times to Heaven* (Jackson: University Press of Mississippi, 1995), 69.

10. Nicholas Dawidoff, *In the Country of Country: A Journey to the Roots of American Music* (New York: Vintage Books, 1997), 64.

11. Catharine Saxberg, *Good-Hearted Women and Honky-Tonk Angels: Women's Voices in Country Music* (Toronto: University of Toronto, 1991), 29.

12. Bufwack and Oermann, *Finding Her Voice*, 178.

13. Ruth A. Banes, "Dixie's Daughters: The Country Music Female," in *You Wrote My Life: Lyrical Themes in Country Music*, ed. Melton A. McLaurin and Richard A. Peterson (Philadelphia: Gordon and Breach, 1992), 95.

14. Bufwack and Oermann, *Finding Her Voice*, 173.

15. *Idem.*

16. George H. Lewis, "Tension, Conflict and Contradiction in Country Music," in *All That Glitters: Country Music in America*, ed. George H. Lewis (Bowling Green, Ohio: Bowling Green State University Popular Press, 1993), 214.

17. John Buckley, "Country Music and American Values," in *All That Glitters*, ed. Lewis, 199.

18. Allen, "Charline Arthur," 19.

19. *Country and Western Jamboree*, 1 (Sept. 1955), 20.

20. "You're Not Easy to Forget," performed by Kitty Wells, *Queen Of Country Music 1949–1958* (compact disc; Bear Family BCD 15638; 1993).

21. Pinson, Weize and Wolfe, *Golden Years of Kitty Wells*, 14.

22. Allen, liner notes.

23. Mary Bufwack and Robert Oermann, "Rockabilly Women," *Journal of Country Music*, 8 (no. 1, 1979), 69.

24. Bufwack and Oermann, *Finding Her Voice*, 174.

25. *Billboard*'s June 20, 1953, issue reported that after Kitty's "Honky-Tonk Angels" and Goldie Hill's hit, "I Let the Stars Get in My Eyes," record labels were "scouring the hinterlands for additional girl country singers. . . . While the recording execs are not yet willing to predict a major trend toward girl singers in the country market, they all agree that the spark lit by Misses Wells and Hill seems to have fired some additional enthusiasm for the fem singers" (Bufwack and Oermann, *Finding Her Voice*, 181–82).

26. Kitty Wells, *After Dark* (album; Decca DL8888; 1959).

27. Mary A. Bufwack, "Girls with Guitars—and Fringe and Sequins and Rhinestones, Silk, Lace and Leather," *South Atlantic Quarterly*, 94 (Winter 1995), 190.

28. Cecilia Tichi, *High Lonesome: The American Culture of Country Music* (Chapel Hill: University of North Carolina Press, 1994), 72.

29. *Country Song Roundup*, 1 (Jan. 1955), 15–16.

30. *Country and Western Jamboree*, 1 (July 1955), 2.

31. *Country and Western Jamboree*, 1 (Aug. 1955), 21.

32. Elaine Tyler May, *Homeward Bound: American Families in the Cold War Era* (New York: BasicBooks, 1998), 119.

33. *Country Song Roundup*, 1 (Oct. 1950), 24.

34. *Country Song Roundup: The Official Year Book* (Poughkeepsie: Country Song Roundup, 1957), 49.

35. *Ibid.*, 61.

36. *Country Song Roundup*, 1 (May 1954), 20.

37. *Country Song Roundup*, 1 (July 1955), 11.

38. Jimmie N. Rogers, *The Country Music Message: Revisited* (Fayetteville: University of Arkansas Press, 1989), 17.

39. Allen (1986).

40. *Ibid.*

I Don't Think Hank Done It That Way: Elvis, Country Music, and the Reconstruction of Southern Masculinity

1. Bob Luman's description can be found in Paul Hemphill, *The Nashville Sound: Bright Lights and Country Music* (New York: Simon and Schuster, 1970), 272–73.

2. *Rock 'n' roll: The Early Days*, dir. Patrick Montgomery and Paula Page (Archive Film Production, 1984) (videotape; RCA/Columbia Pictures Home); Jimmy Snow, *I Cannot Go Back* (Plainfield, New Jersey: Logos International, 1977), n. p.

3. Herb Abramson, "Rock 'n' Roll: Seen in Perspective," *Cashbox*, July 28, 1956, p. 78.

4. Bill Simon, "Boundaries between Music Types Fall; Deejays Spin 'Em All," *Billboard*, Nov. 12, 1955, 34. The term "rockabilly" is one that folklorist D. K. Wilgus claims to have originated, although he cannot remember where it was first published. In May of 1956, *Cashbox* used the designation to describe a "rock and roll country style" show in Missouri. In July, *Cashbox* mentioned in passing the term "rock-a-billy" in discussing the merger between country and rhythm and blues. An October 1956 *Billboard* review of Warren Smith's (borderline racist) "Ubangi Stomp" predicted that it would be "another disk to keep the Sun label near the top of the rock-a-billy heap." In using the term "rockabilly," Memphis journalist Robert Johnson erroneously claimed that *Billboard* had coined a new word. Several months later, pop crooner Guy Mitchell, in an obvious attempt to exploit the popularity of southern and country-based rock 'n' roll, recorded an inane ditty entitled "Rock-a-Billy" for Columbia Records. See D. K. Wilgus, "Country-Western Music and the Urban Hillbilly," *The Urban Experience and Folk Tradition*, ed. Americo Paredes and Ellen J. Stekert (Austin: University of Texas Press, 1971), 164; "The Cashbox Country Roundup," *Cashbox*, May 26, 1956, p. 38. "The Cashbox Rhythm and Blues Ramblings," *Cashbox*, July 28, 1956, p. 76; "Review Spotlight on . . . C&W Records," *Billboard*, Oct. 6, 1956, p. 80. "New Memphis Rock-A-Billy Recording Star Rising," *Memphis Press-Scimitar*, Oct. 12, 1956, p. 25.

5. Bill Sachs, "Growth of C&W Field an Industry Phenomenon," *Billboard*, March 3, 1956, p. 53. For influence on youth on country music industry, see Paul Ackerman, "Diskeries in Race for RnR Country Talent," *Billboard*, May 12, 1956, pp. 12, 14; "Teenage Music Survey Has Diskery Heads Reeling," *Cashbox*, May 28, 1955, p. 19; "Teenage Market!" *Cashbox*, Jan. 28, 1956, p. 3.

6. Mary A. Bufwack and Robert K. Oermann, *Finding Her Voice: The Saga of Women in Country Music* (New York: Crown, 1993), 216; George Lipsitz, *Rainbow at Midnight: Labor and Culture in the 1940s* (Urbana: University of Illinois Press, 1994), 11.

7. William E. Leuchtenburg, *A Troubled Feast: American Society since 1945* (Boston: Little, Brown and Company, 1983), 65–66.

8. 8 On Presley and country music, see Bill Malone, "Country Elvis," *In Search of Elvis: Music, Race, Art, Religion*, ed. Vernon Chadwick (Boulder: Westview Press, 1997), 3–18.

9. For a contemporary view of Presley as a country artist, see "Sun's Newest Star," *Country Songs Magazine* (June 1955), 7; "Folk Music Fireball," *Country Song Roundup*, 1 (Sept. 1955), 14; Frieda Barter, "Overnight Stardom Comes to Elvis Presley," *Country and Western Jamboree*, 1 (May 1956), 10–11. For Presley's rise to the most promising male country artist, see "Annual Disk Jockey's Poll," *Billboard*, Nov. 13, 1954, p. 80; "Artists Receive Awards at Festival," *Cashbox*, Nov. 26, 1955, p. 41; "Annual Disk Jockey's Poll," *Billboard*, Nov. 12, 1955, pp. 98–105.

10. The "boy next door" reference is found in John Wilson, "How No-Talent Singers Get 'Talent,'" *New York Times Magazine*, June 21, 1959, p. 16. The "jug" analogy can be located in "Hillbilly on a Pedestal," *Newsweek*, May 14, 1956, p. 82. Also see James and Annette Baxter, "Man in the Blue Suede Shoes," *Harper's* (Jan. 1958), 45–47.

11. On "Horatio Alger in Drawl," see Linda Ray Pratt, "Elvis, or the Ironies of a Southern Identity," *Southern Quarterly*, 18 (1979), 41.

12. For good oral accounts on various aspects of Presley's early life and career, see Michael Donahue, "'That's All Right, Mama,': The Project Years," *Memphis Commercial Appeal Mid-South Magazine*, Aug. 11, 1986, pp. 5–6, 12–15; Peter Cronin, Scott Isler, and Mark Rowland, "Elvis Presley: An Oral Biography," *Musician* (Oct. 1992), 50–67; Joseph Lewis, "Elvis Presley Lives," *Cosmopolitan* (Nov. 1968), 92–95; John Morthland, "An Oral History of Elvis," *Country Music*, 7 (1977), 46–56, 79–82; Rose Clayton and Dick Heard, eds., *Elvis Up Close: In the Words of Those Who Knew Him Best* (Atlanta: Turner Publishing Inc., 1994).

13. Wilbur J. Cash, *The Mind of the South* (Garden City, New York: Doubleday Anchor, 1941), 62. Charles S. Johnson, *Shadow of the Plantation* (Chicago: University of Chicago Press, 1934), 182. W. E. B. DuBois, *Dusk of Dawn: An Essay toward an Autobiography of a Race Concept*

(New York: Schocken Books, 1968 [1940]), 181. On the tendency of African American males to adhere to Southern patriarchy, see David Goldfield, *Still Fighting the Civil War: The American South and Southern History* (Baton Rouge: Louisiana State University Press, 2002), 154.

14. Carl Degler, *The Other South: Southern Dissenters in the Nineteenth Century* (New York: Harper and Row, 1974), 1–10. "New York Beat," *Jet*, Aug. 12, 1954, p. 65. For the "cat-minded" appellation, see June Bundy, "R&B Disks Sock Pop Market; Major Firms Jump into Ring," *Billboard*, Jan. 29, 1955, p. 56.

15. Greil Marcus, *Mystery Train: Images of America in Rock 'n' Roll Music* (New York: E.P. Dutton & Company, 1982), 169. The model of the hipster was popularized by Norman Mailer, "The White Negro: Superficial Reflections on the Hipster," *Advertisements for Myself* (New York: G.P. Putnam's Sons, 1959), 337–75. See also Patrick Mullen, "Hillbilly Hipsters of the 1950s: The Romance of the Rockabilly," *Southern Quarterly* 22 (Spring 1984), 79–92.

16. Cash, *The Mind of the South*, 62. On the issue of race and southern history, see Joel Williamson, *The Crucible of Race: Black-White Relations in the American South since Emancipation* (New York: Oxford University Press, 1984).

17. Nathan I. Huggins, *Harlem Renaissance* (New York: Oxford University Press, 1971), 253. For the origins of southern racial attitudes, see Winthrop Jordan, *Black over White: American Attitudes Toward the Negro, 1550–1812* (Chapel Hill: University of North Carolina Press, 1968). For a more contemporary view, see Thomas Waring, "The Southern Case against Desegregation," *Harper's* (Jan. 1956), 39–45.

18. "The B.B. King Story," *Tan* (June 1956), 82; "From Ring to Rock 'n' Roll," *Sepia* (Aug. 1958), 63; "Wynonie Harris, "Women Won't Leave Me Alone," *Tan* (Oct. 1954), 29.

19. Ralph Ellison, "Editorial Comment," *Negro Quarterly*, 1 (1943), 301. See also Robin D. G. Kelley, "The Riddle of the Zoot: Malcolm Little and Black Cultural Politics during World War II," in *Race Rebels: Culture, Politics, and the Black Working Class* (New York: The Free Press, 1996), 161–81.

20. Williamson, *Crucible of Race*, 59, 212–13.

21. Ibid., 59, 212–13; Lawrence Levine, *Black Culture and Black Consciousness: Afro-American Folk Thought from Slavery to Freedom* (New York: Oxford University Press, 1978), 102–33, 367–445; Charles Kreil, *Urban Blues* (Chicago: University of Chicago Press, 1991), 26.

22. Robin D. G. Kelley, *Yo' Mama's Disfunktional!: Fighting the Culture Wars in Urban America* (Boston: Beacon Press, 1997), 41.

23. Hortense Powdermaker, *After Freedom: A Cultural Study in the Deep South* (New York: Atheneum, 1969), 20; F. N. Boney, "The Redneck," *Georgia Review*, 25 (1971), 333; Cheryl Harris, "Whiteness as Property," *Harvard Law Review* 106 (June 1993), 1709–91.

24. 24 William Alexander Percy, *Lanterns on the Levee: Recollections of a Planter's Son* (New York: Alfred A. Knopf, 1941), 149; I. A. Newby, *Plain Folk in the New South: Social Change and Cultural Persistence 1880–1915* (Baton Rouge: Louisiana State University Press, 1989), 13. Louis Rubin, "An Image of the South," *The Lasting South: Fourteen Southerners Look at their Home*, ed. Louis Rubin and James Kilpatrick (Chicago: Henry Regeny, 1957), 6.

25. Cash, *Mind of the South*, 62; William B. Hesseltine and David L. Smiley, *The South in American History* (Englewood Cliffs: Prentice-Hall, 1960), 195; Mikhail Bakhtin, *Rabelais and His World*, trans. Helene Iswolsky (Cambridge: M.I.T. Press, 1968), 10, 7; Johnson, *Shadow of the Plantation*, 182; Florence King, *Southern Ladies and Gentleman* (New York: Bantam Books, 1981), 106; Newby, *Plain Folk*, 330.

26. Bill C. Malone, *Don't Get Above Your Raisin': Country Music and the Southern Working Class* (Urbana: University of Illinois Press, 2002), 119–20.

27. Eric Lott, *Love and Theft: Blackface Minstrelsy and the American Working Class* (New York: Oxford University Press, 1993), 52; Charles Joyner, "A Single Southern Culture: Cultural

Interaction in the Old South," *Black and White Cultural Interaction in the Antebellum South*, ed. Ted Ownby (Jackson: University Press of Mississippi, 1993), 6.

28. Charles Joyner, *Shared Traditions: Southern History and Folk Culture* (Urbana: University of Illinois Press, 1999).

29. Powdermaker, *After Freedom*, 29; Gunnar Myrdal, *An American Dilemma: The Negro Problem and Modern Democracy* (New York: Harper, 1944), 582; Ulrich B. Phillips, "The Central Theme of Southern History," *American Historical Review*, 34 (Oct. 1928), 43.

30. Percy, *Lanterns on the Levee*, 299. See also David Goldfield, *Black, White, and Southern: Race Relations and Southern Culture, 1940 to the Present* (Baton Rouge: Louisiana State University Press, 1990); Leon Litwack, *Trouble in Mind: Black Southerners in the Age of Jim Crow* (New York: Vintage Books, 1998).

31. Ralph Ellison, *Invisible Man* (New York: Vintage Books, 1989), 302. According to Joel Williamson, "It was possible in the South for one who was biologically pure white to become black by behavior. A white person could cross over to blackness. Blackness and whiteness became a matter not just of color or even blood, but of inner morality reflected by outward performance." Williamson, *Crucible of Race*, 467.

32. Richard Wright, *Black Boy* (New York: Harper, 1993, [1945]); Charles S. Johnson, *Growing Up in the Black Belt: Negro Youth in the Rural South* (Washington, D.C.: American Council on Education, 1941).

33. Kyle Chichton, "Thar's Gold in Them Hillbillies," *Collier's*, April 30, 1938, pp. 24–25; "Hillbilly Boom," *Downbeat*, May 6, 1949, p. 1; "Corn of Plenty," *Newsweek*, June 13, 1949, p. 76; Don Eddy, "Hillbilly Heaven," *America* (March 1952), 28–29, 119–23.

34. On the interchange between black and white in country music, see George Pierson, *Black Legacy: America's Hidden Heritage* (Amherst: University of Massachusetts Press, 1993).

35. Tony Russell, *Blacks, Whites, and Blues* (New York: Stein and Day, 1970), 59–77, 81–85, 102.

36. Russell, *Blacks, Whites, and Blues*, 43, 85.

37. On the "bulldozer revolution," see C. Vann Woodward, "The Search for Southern Identity," *The Burden of Southern History* (New York: Mentor Books, 1969), 29.

38. For the best historical approach to honky-tonk, see Bill C. Malone, "Honky-Tonk: The Music of the Southern Working Class," *Folk Music and the Modern Sound*, ed. William Ferris and Mary L. Hart (Jackson: University Press of Mississippi, 1982), 119–28.

39. For a more detailed discussion on this post–World War II Southern generation and the issue of race, see Michael Bertrand, *Race, Rock, and Elvis* (Urbana: University of Illinois Press, 2000).

40. "Rockabilly: A Fusion of Country and Rock 'n' Roll," *Billboard*, Nov. 2, 1963, p. B40; "Letters to the Editor," *Country and Western Jamboree*, 1 (Sept. 1956), 4; "Letters to the Editor," *Country and Western Jamboree*, 1 (Aug. 1956), 34.

41. Randy Blake, "Disk Jockey Urges Return to Spinning Only Country Music," *Downbeat*, Jan. 26, 1956, p. 1; "C&W Talent Hits Spots in B.S. Pop Chart," *Billboard*, March 10, 1956, p. 57. "Letters to the Editor," *Country and Western Jamboree*, 1 (Sept. 1956), 4; "Letters to the Editor," *Country and Western Jamboree*, 1 (May 1956), 17.

42. Horace Logan with Bill Sloan, *Elvis, Hank, and Me: Making Musical History on the Louisiana Hayride* (New York: St. Martin's Press, 1998), 3, 135; Paul Ackerman, "What Has Happened to Popular Music," *High Fidelity* (June 1958), 37. The term "rockabilly" seems to have conveyed a negative racial connotation for many people. See Craig Morrison, *Go Cat Go: Rockabilly Music and Its Makers* (Urbana: University of Illinois Press, 1996), 3–4.

43. Bill Malone, "Elvis, Country Music and the South," *Southern Quarterly*, 18 (Fall 1979), 123; Malone, *Don't Get Above Your Raisin'*, 9; Paul Ackerman, "Rhythm and Blues Notes," *Billboard*, Nov. 5, 1955, p. 47.

44. Eldridge Cleaver, *Soul on Ice* (New York: Dell, 1968), 195.

45. Kreil, *Urban Blues*, 27.

"I Wanna Play House": Configurations of Masculinity in the Nashville Sound Era

1. Patrick Carr, "Will the Circle Be Unbroken: The Changing Image of Country Music," in *Country: The Music and the Musicians*, ed. Paul Kingsbury and Alan Axelrod (New York: Abbeville Press, 1988), 504, 508; John Morthland, *The Best of Country Music* (New York: Doubleday, 1984); John Morthland, "Changing Methods, Changing Sounds: An Overview," *Journal of Country Music*, 12 (no. 2, 1987).

2. Michael Kimmel, *Manhood in America: A Cultural History* (New York: Free Press, 1996); Pamela Fox, "Recycled 'Trash': Gender and Authenticity in Country Music Autobiography," *American Quarterly*, 50 (June 1998), 236; Bill Malone, "Honky-Tonk: The Music of the Southern Working Class," in *Folk Music and the Modern Sound*, ed. William Ferris and Mary L. Hart (Jackson: University Press of Mississippi, 1982), 120–21; Barbara Ching, *Wrong's What I Do Best: Hard Country Music and Contemporary Culture* (New York: Oxford University Press, 2001), 47–64; Steve Waksman, *Instruments of Desire: The Electric Guitar and the Shaping of Musical Experience* (Cambridge: Harvard University Press, 1999), 75–112.

3. "Country Stations: Fatter and Happier," *Sponsor*, Aug. 8, 1966, p. 43; Kimmel, *Manhood in America*, 223–66.

4. Lizabeth Cohen, *A Consumer's Republic: The Politics of Consumption in Postwar America* (New York: Knopf, 2003); John E. Bodnar, *Blue-Collar Hollywood: Liberalism, Democracy and Working People in American Film* (Baltimore: Johns Hopkins University Press, 2003).

5. Cecilia Tichi, *High Lonesome: The American Culture of Country Music* (Chapel Hill: University of North Carolina Press, 1994), 19–50; Bill C. Malone, *Don't Get above Your Raisin': Country Music and the Southern Working Class* (Urbana: University of Illinois Press, 2002), 53–88.

6. Jack Stapp, typescript speech, Country Music Association Sales and Marketing Programs (microfiche: fiche 2 of 3), Country Music Association Papers (Country Music Foundation Library and Media Center, Nashville, Tenn.), p. 1.

7. *Ibid.*, 10.

8. Elaine Tyler May, "Cold War—Warm Hearth: Politics and the Family in Postwar America," in *The Rise and Fall of the New Deal Order, 1930–1980*, ed. Steve Fraser and Gary Gerstle (Princeton: Princeton University Press, 1989), 153–84.

9. Robert L. Griswold, *Fatherhood in America: A History* (New York: Basic Books, 1993), 195, 198, 187; Kimmel, *Manhood in America*, 242, 246.

10. Chet Atkins with Bill Neely, *Country Gentleman* (New York: Ballantine, 1974); Bob Allen, "The Prime of Chet Atkins," *Journal of Country Music*, 10 (no. 3, 1985), 8.

11. Atkins with Neely, *Country Gentleman*, 106, 120, 133, 181; Allen, "Prime of Chet Atkins," 7. Eddy Arnold's autobiography tells a similar, though more upbeat, story of childhood poverty and recurring insecurity about being able to provide for his family. Eddy Arnold, *It's a Long Way from Chester County* (Old Tappan, NJ: Hewitt House, 1969), 38–40, 49, 72–74, 89–90, 102.

12. Biff Collie quoted in Richard Price Stockdell, "The Development of the Country Music Radio Format" (M.A. thesis, Kansas State University, 1973), 38; Joe Allison interview by John Rumble, March 15, 1994, audio tape, side 1, tape 1, Country Music Foundation Oral History Collection (Country Music Foundation Library and Media Center).

13. Stapp, typescript speech, 5; Paul Ackerman, "WSM DJ Festival Public Relations Coup," *Billboard*, Nov. 28, 1953, p. 42; Joe Allison, "Country Music Fans Not Easy to Fool," *Pickin' &* *Singin' News*, Feb. 15, 1954, p. 2.

14. Atkins with Neely, *Country Gentleman*, 172; Jo Walker-Meador interview by John Rumble, July 30, 1997, side 1, tape 2, Country Music Foundation Oral History Collection; Diane Pecknold, "The Selling Sound: Country Music, Commercialism, and the Politics of Popular Culture, 1920–1974" (Ph.D. diss., Indiana University, 2002), 105–10.

15. Joe Allison interview by Diane Pecknold, March 26, 1999, audiotape (in Diane Pecknold's possession), side 1, tape 2; Betty Carson, "Who Said 'Too Many Fans in Nashville?' " *K-Bar-T Country Roundup*, Dec. 1969, p. 23.

16. "Jo Walker: CMA's Lucky Accident," *Billboard*, March 18, 1978, CMA-3, CMA-8.

17. Roger Schutt, "Den Mother of Country Music," *Music City News*, 1 (Nov. 1963), 5; "Just Plain Jo Is a Dynamo," *Billboard*, Oct. 28, 1967, p. 74.

18. Joe Allison, typescript script, "A Visit with Tex and Roy," p. 10, Country Music Association Sales and Marketing Programs (microfiche: fiche 3), Country Music Association Papers.

19. John Rumble, "Wesley Rose," in *The Encyclopedia of Country Music*, ed. Paul Kingsbury (New York: Oxford University Press, 1998), 459–60; "Profiles: Ken Nelson," *Close-Up* (Oct. 1964), 1, 2; Joe Sasfy, "The Hick from Lizard Lick," *Journal of Country Music*, 12 (no. 1, 1987), 16–24, 33; "Our Respects to Connie Barriot Gay," *Broadcasting*, Feb. 2, 1959, p. 27.

20. Allison interview by Pecknold, side 1, tape 2.

21. Daniel Horowitz, *American Social Classes in the 1950s: Selections from Vance Packard's The Status Seekers* (Boston: Bedford, 1995), 16, 83.

22. Jo Walker-Meador interview by Diane Pecknold, Aug. 2, 1999, audiotape (in Diane Pecknold's possession), side 1, tape 1. In fact, the removal of *Hee Haw* and other shows with rural settings was part of a larger re-orientation at CBS toward urban audiences because of the changing demographics of rural and urban populations. As the rural population aged, the network turned its attention to younger and, from the advertiser's perspective, more desirable urban viewers.

23. Joe Allison, "The Sound of Country Music, Presented for the Sales-Marketing Executives of Chicago, Monday, June 7, 1965," pp. 8, 13–17, Country Music Association Sales and Marketing Programs (microfiche: fiche 1, 2).

24. *Ibid.*; Joe Allison, "Presentation to the Nashville Chamber of Commerce," Country Music Association Sales and Marketing Programs (microfiche: fiche 2).

25. Paul Hemphill, *The Nashville Sound: Bright Lights and Country Music* (New York: Simon and Schuster, 1970), 33.

26. Allison, "Presentation to the Nashville Chamber of Commerce," 2.

27. J. W. Williamson, *Hillbillyland: What the Movies Did to the Mountains and What the Mountains Did to the Movies* (Chapel Hill: University of North Carolina Press, 1995), 1–20, 62–64, 167–72; Bodnar, *Blue Collar Hollywood*, 133–75.

28. George Lipsitz, *Time Passages: Collective Memory and American Popular Culture* (Minneapolis: University of Minnesota Press, 1990), 39–77; James N. Gregory, "Southernizing the American Working Class: Post-war Episodes of Regional and Class Transformation," *Labor History*, 39 (no. 2, 1998), 149.

29. "Country Is Spelled with '$' not 'Cents,' " *Sponsor*, Aug. 8, 1966, p. 40.

30. Bill Malone, *Singing Cowboys and Musical Mountaineers: Southern Culture and the Roots of Country Music* (Athens: University of Georgia Press, 1993); Richard Slotkin, *Gunfighter Nation: The Myth of the Frontier in Twentieth-Century America* (Norman: University of Oklahoma Press, 1992).

31. "Eddy Arnold: The Tennessee Plowboy," *Country Song Roundup*, 1 (March 1955), 8–9; Mrs. Eddy Arnold, "The Arnolds at Home," *ibid.*, 10.

32. "Ferlin on the Farm," *Country Song Roundup*, 1 (Aug. 1956), 18.

33. WJJD Aircheck, May 13, 1965, 8:00 a.m.–9:00 a.m. (audio cassette), master 1326, Marvin Bensman Collection (University of Memphis Library, Memphis, Tenn.); WJJD Aircheck, May 7, 1965, 1:00 p.m.–2:00 p.m. (audio cassette), master 1325, *ibid.*; WJJD Aircheck, Feb. 15, 1965, 10:00 a.m.–11:00 a.m. (audio cassette), master 1438, *ibid.*

34. "Country Music: A Gold Mine for City Broadcasters," *Sponsor*, Aug. 8, 1960, p. 76; "C&W Sound Captures U.S. Heart and Purse," *Sponsor*, May 20, 1963, p. 32; "New Appeal of Country Music," *Broadcasting*, Aug. 1, 1966, p. 56.

35. "C&W Pulse Published for 24 U.S. Markets," *Close-Up* (Sept. 1965), 1; "Growing Sound of Country Music," *Broadcasting*, Oct. 18, 1965, p. 70.

Patsy Cline's Crossovers: Celebrity, Reputation, and Feminine Identity

1. I spent six weeks in Nashville during the summer of 1979, where I did archival research and conducted interviews with the invaluable help of staff members of the Country Music Association's Hall of Fame Library and Media Center, especially Robert K. Oermann, Ronnie Pugh, and Don Roy.

2. Patsy Cline then had an imaginative location in popular culture memory much like the once widely known, but now relatively obscure, pop singer Connie Francis has today (at least for now).

3. Joli Jensen, "Patsy Cline's Recording Career: The Search for a Sound," *Journal of Country Music*, 9 (no. 2, 1982), 34–46; Don Roy, "Patsy Cline's Recording Career: The Search for a Sound [Discography]," *Journal of Country Music*, 9 (no. 2, 1982), 34–46.

4. Ellis Nassour, *Patsy Cline* (New York: Tower Publications, 1981).

5. Joli Jensen, "Genre and Recalcitrance: Country Music's Move Uptown," *Tracking: Popular Music Studies*, 1 (Spring, 1988), 30–41; Joli Jensen, *The Nashville Sound: Authenticity, Commercialization and Country Music* (Nashville: Vanderbilt University Press, 1998).

6. Margaret Jones, *Patsy: The Life and Times of Patsy Cline* (New York: Harper Collins, 1994).

7. Janet Maslin, "Jessica Lange in 'Sweet Dreams,' " *New York Times*, Oct. 2, 1985.

8. Pauline Kael, "Sweet Dreams," *New Yorker*, Oct. 21, 1985.

9. Jim White, "Is Charlie Making Patsies of Lesbians?" *The Independent*, April 16, 1993, p. 18.

10. For how scholars can be compared with fans, see Joli Jensen, "Fandom as Pathology: The Consequences of Characterization," in *Popular Culture: Production and Consumption*, ed. C. Lee Harrington and Denise D. Bielby (New York: Blackwell Publishers, 2000).

11. Kennedy Wilson, "Still 'Crazy' . . . for Queen of the Heartbreak Ballad," *The Herald, Caledonian Newspapers Ltd.*, March 31, 1994, p. 15.

12. Nick Kimberley, "Tears of a Cline," *The Independent*, Dec. 16, 1991, p. 15.

13. Bill Carey, "Gone 30 Years, Fans Still Crazy for Patsy Cline," *Atlanta Journal-Constitution*, Oct. 10, 1993, p. M-1.

14. Teal Ferguson, "Country Tuneup Time," *Washington Times*, Aug. 23, 1992, p. E1.

15. Mary Harron, "Is She Lonesome Tonight?" *Independent: The Sunday Review*, Feb. 28, 1993, p. 23.

16. Carey, "Gone 30 Years."

17. *Ibid.*

18. Wilson, "Still Crazy . . . For the Queen of the Heartbreak Ballad."

19. Paul Kingsbury, liner notes, *Patsy Cline Collection*, 5.

20. This is Hannah Arendt's argument in the 1950s mass culture debate. See Hannah Arendt, "Society and Culture," in *Mass Culture Revisited*, ed. Bernard Rosenberg and David Manning White

(New York: Van Nostrand Reinhold, 1971), 93–101. It is also the argument of the New Humanists during the early part of the century. See, for example, Norman Foerster, *Humanism and America: Essays on the Outlook of Modern Civilization* (Port Washington, NY: Kennikat Press, 1976).

21. Wilson, "Still Crazy . . . For the Queen of the Heartbreak Ballad," 15.

22. Geoffrey Himes, "How Patsy Cline Put the Pieces Together," *Washington Post*, Nov. 15, 1991, p. N-17.

23. Kimberly, "Tears of a Cline," 15.

24. *Ibid.*

25. Himes, "How Patsy Cline Put the Pieces Together," N-17.

26. Ferguson, "Country Tuneup Time," E1.

27. White, "Is Charlie Making Patsies of Lesbians?" 18.

28. *Ibid.*

29. Rosanne Cash, "Patsy Cline, Honky Tonk Angel," *New York Times Magazine*, Nov. 24, 1996, pp. 66–67.

30. Robert Sandall, "The Big Country," *The Times* (London), March 19, 1995, sec. 10, p. 29.

31. White, "Is Charlie Making Patsies of Lesbians?" 18.

32. *Ibid.*

33. Cash, "Patsy Cline, Honky Tonk Angel," 66.

34. *Ibid.*, 67.

35. Harron, "Is She Lonesome Tonight?" 23.

36. *Ibid.*

37. *Ibid.*

38. Joli Jensen, "Taking Country Music Seriously: Coverage of the 1990s Boom," in *Pop Music and the Press*, ed. Steve Jones (Philadelphia: Temple University Press, 2002), 183–201.

39. *Ibid.*

40. Sandall, "The Big Country," 29.

41. Jones, *Patsy*, 48.

Dancing Together: The Rhythms of Gender in the Country Dance Hall

1. Thirteen country dance halls were visited between May 1999 and August 2003: Carolina Stampede (closed), 3091 Waughtown St., Winston-Salem, NC 27107; Coyote Joe's, 4621 Wilkinson Blvd., Charlotte, MC 28208; Cotton Eyed Joe, 11220 Outlet Dr., Knoxville, TN 37932; Cotton Eyed Joe, 106 E. Broad St., Cookeville, TN 38501; Denim & Diamonds, 950 Madison Sq. N. Gallatin Rd., Madison, TN 37115, Longbranch Saloon, 608 Creekside Dr., Raleigh, NC 27609; New Country Music Bar, 1822 10th Ave. SW, Hickory, NC 28602; New Country USA (closed), 5523 Oleander Dr., Wilmington, NC 28412; Palomino Club, 210 Owen Dr., Fayetteville, NC 28304 (New location: 2869 Owen Dr., Fayetteville, NC 28306); Palomino Club (closed), 4514 High Point Rd., Greensboro, NC 27407; Silver Saddle (closed), 3210-131 S. Wilmington St., Raleigh, NC 27603; Silverado's Saloon & Dance Hall, 1204 Murfreesboro Pike, Nashville, TN 37217; Wayneo's Silver Bullet, 5172 NC Highway 127 S, Hickory, NC 28602.

2. Judith Lynne Hanna, *To Dance Is Human* (Austin: University of Texas Press, 1979), 5. Hanna's writings on dance span more than two decades and include seminal foundations, ideas, and definitions on the relationship between music and dance.

3. Hillary Rodham Clinton highlighted one of the most famous of these stereotypes with a politically charged reference in 1992 to Tammy Wynette's 1968 recording, "Stand by Your Man." Kitty Wells's 1952 recording of "It Wasn't God Who Made Honky-Tonk Angels" (by J. D. Miller) opened the answer-song category with he-said/she-said versions of a song; since the 1970s,

artists and authors alike have been discussing gender stereotypes both in songs and in print. Tammy Wynette and Billy Sherrill, "Stand by Your Man," performed by Tammy Wynette, *Stand by Your Man* (compact disc; Epic/Legacy EK 66018; 1999); J. D. Miller, "It Wasn't God Who Made Honky-Tonk Angels," performed by Kitty Wells, *Country Music Hall of Fame Series* (compact disc; MCAD-10081; 1991).

4. The notion of shared cultural stories as a means for constructing meaning within the genre has been discussed elsewhere. Aaron A. Fox, "The Jukebox of History: Narratives of Loss and Desire in the Discourse of Country Music," *Popular Music*, 11 (Jan. 1992), 53–72; especially 54, 60.

5. Jimmie Rogers discusses the sexual tension in Glenn Sutton and Billy Sherrill's 1966 song "Almost Persuaded," memorably performed by David Houston, including the line, "then we danced and she whispered I need you." In another song, Conway Twitty's recording of "Tight Fittin' Jeans" allows no indiscretion in the protagonist's retelling of the evening's events, but the full extent of the encounter is recorded in "we danced every dance, and Lord, the beer that we went through . . . ," leading to the conclusion, "in my mind she's still a lady, that's all I'm gonna say . . ." Jimmie N. Rogers, *The Country Music Message (Revisited)* (Fayetteville: University of Arkansas Press, 1989), 128, 88.

6. Mary Chapin Carpenter's recording of "Down at the Twist and Shout" nostalgically portrays a typical Saturday night routine with her two-step partner. Chely Wright sings "I'm dancing in a sea of cowboy hats . . . / Two-steppin' fools as far as the eye can see" in her self-penned "Sea of Cowboy Hats" as a means of validating her country-ness for the listener. Shane Minor's song "Slave to the Habit" opens with him hollering over the introduction, "Hey, here's a little song you can do the twelve-step to . . . ," lest the listener need some instructions on how to dance to the song. Mary Chapin Carpenter, "Down at the Twist and Shout," performed by Mary Chapin Carpenter, *Shooting Straight in the Dark* (compact disc; Columbia 046077; 1990); Chely Wright, "Sea of Cowboy Hats," performed by Chely Wright, *Woman in the Moon* (compact disc; Polygram 314-523 225-2; 1994); Kostas, Toby Keith, and Chuck Cannon, "Slave to the Habit," performed by Shane Minor, *Shane Minor* (compact disc; Mercury 314-538346-2; 1999).

7. The music video for Garth Brooks's song "The Dance," expounded on this philosophical perspective by including footage of American heroes whose contributions extended beyond the conventional bounds of country music's interest—Martin Luther King, Jr., John F. Kennedy, Jr., and the crew of the Space Shuttle Challenger, among others. Garth Brooks and Tony Arata, "The Dance," performed by Garth Brooks, *Garth Brooks* (compact disc; Capitol CDP 7-90897-2; 1989); Troy Johnson and Marshall Morgan, "Some Days You Gotta Dance," performed by Dixie Chicks, *Fly* (compact disc; Monument NK 69678; 1999); Mark D. Sanders and Tia Sillers, "I Hope You Dance" performed by Lee Ann Womack, *I Hope You Dance* (compact disc; MCA 088-170-099-2; 2000).

8. Larry Gorick interview by Jocelyn Neal, Oct. 5, 2000. Gorick is General Manager at radio station WQDR, 312 High Woods Boulevard, Suite 201, Raleigh, North Carolina 27604.

9. According to the *New York Times*, Clear Channel Communications, Inc. owns more than 1,200 stations and captures 25% of the nation's listeners. In many markets, the only available country stations are owned by Clear Channel. Jennifer Lee, "Radio Giant Defends Its Size at Senate Panel Hearing," *New York Times*, Jan. 31, 2003, sec. C, p. 4.

10. Journalists and columnists have touted this viewpoint in many articles; for a pointed example, see Neil Strauss, "The Country Music Country Radio Ignores," *New York Times*, March 24, 2002, sec. 2, p. 1. Strauss highlights the controlling factors of advertising demographics that govern song style, content, and diversity within the country radio industry.

11. There have been extremely successful movements to organize lead/follow partner dancing for purposes of competition: dance studios have official syllabi that outline both the

options for steps and dance figures, and governing organizations for the competitions have guidelines about what dancers can and cannot do, and what proper execution of each figure involves. However, these movements have not had as potent an effect on the social dancers who frequent the dance halls.

12. Line dancing certainly predates disco in several forms: the tradition of swing dancing from the 1920s and '30s in the New York City ballrooms included various forms of line dancing from lindy-hop footwork, for instance, one of the best-known being the "Shim-Sham." However, only the most tenuous connections link contemporary line dance practice in the country night clubs to these, and earlier, origins. Mr. "Hillbilly" Rick Meyers recalls line dancing in the Indiana area in 1980–1981, when the dancing was done to pop and disco music. Mr. Meyers has become a central figure in country DJ consulting. Rick Meyers to Jocelyn Neal (n.d.; 1999) (in Jocelyn Neal's possession).

13. Don Von Tress, "Achy Breaky Heart," performed by Billy Ray Cyrus, *Some Gave All* (compact disc; Mercury 314-510635-2; 1993); Bill Malone, *Country Music, USA* (Austin: University of Texas Press), 429.

14. The Nashville Network, or TNN, first aired in 1983 and was an established part of the Gaylord Entertainment holdings in country music media. TNN was made over by MTV Networks during the summer of 2003, emerging as "The New TNN, The First Network for Men." The original name of the show was "Club Dance at the White Horse Café."

15. Anecdotes and interviews with the producers are catalogued in Nancy Rubin Stuart, *Club Dance Scrapbook: The Show, the Steps, the Spirit of Country* (Knoxville: Knoxville Entertainment Publishing, 1998).

16. Practical considerations played into the presence of west-coast swing on the show. First, the dance can be done in relatively small spaces, and dancers report that the studio where the show was filmed was deceptively small. The lack of floor space made the dances that move around the floor (like the two-step) much more difficult to do, and indeed, excerpts from the show with significant amounts of two-stepping look like a bad traffic jam with limited mobility. West-coast swing is a partner dance that involves intricate leading and following patterns. Danced primarily to blues or R&B-influenced music, the leader and follower work in a rectangular space (the "slot") with plenty of eye contact and flirtatious body motion layered with elaborate spins and turns. The "slot" used by west-coast swing dancers could fit between tables or in odd corners. Furthermore, the dancers who became regulars on the show visibly enjoyed performing for the cameras, and the showy nature of the west-coast swing let them display their dance talents and more flamboyant techniques. Many of the dance descriptions of "Club Dance" are courtesy of Gary Cox, a regular dancer on the show for many years. Gary Cox interview by Jocelyn Neal, May 8, 2000.

17. David Holden interview by Jocelyn Neal, May 16, 2000. Mr. Holden was a regular on Club Dance.

18. Emphasis added. "What Is the NTA?" *The National Teachers Association for Country Western Dance: An Organization of Teachers Helping Teachers*, http://www.apci.net/~drdeyne/nta.htm (May 15, 2000). National Teachers Association for Country Western Dance was established in 1986; the United Country Western Dance Council (UCWDC) was established two years later. The NTA has since faded, although the UCWDC remains a significant participant in the scene, controlling the most widely respected country dance competitions worldwide.

19. Note that at the same time country music was leaving behind its most rural, hillbilly, and cowboy roots in newer, more "hip" pop-influenced music and dance styles adopted from disco, the dance organizations were clinging to the phrase "country western," an artificial appropriation of an older and more tradition-affiliated identity.

20. Obviously, there is no absolute consistency in the populations that attend these dance halls. However, for purposes of studying the gendered roles within these communities it was

necessary to limit the scope of the venues. In some cities, there is a thriving scene of queer country dancing, which has been studied by several scholars and is easy to locate on the internet. Amy R. Corrin, "Queer Country, Line Dance Nazis, and a Hollywood Barndance: Country Music and the Struggle for Identity in Los Angeles, California," in *Country Music Annual 2000*, ed. Charles K. Wolfe and James E. Akenson (Lexington: University Press of Kentucky, 2000), 141–50. The recent resurgence of interest in old-time and "traditional" forms of country music has given rise to different types of clubs and entertainment venues. There are also some clubs that feature a "country night," more as a costumed theme party than as full subscribers to the tradition. These and other types of clubs have not been included here merely for reasons of scope of the investigation.

21. Of some significance, the Wild Horse Saloon, located in downtown Nashville on Second Avenue, is missing from this venue list. When I visited the Wild Horse Saloon in 1997, it was still a country dance venue of some significance and the filming location of a popular TNN dance show. The presence of the show helped maintain the local dancers' interest in the club. By the time I formally began this research, however, it was no longer the site of any local dancing. TNN had cancelled its show, the entire face of country tourism in Nashville had changed with the closing of the Opryland theme park, and the management of the Wild Horse Saloon had placed dining tables on the beautiful hardwood dance floor. A steady stream of out-of-town tourists prevented any communal dance traditions from taking root. Also, both Fayetteville, North Carolina, and Charlotte, North Carolina, were included, although they lie some distance from the I-40 corridor through the state. Both cities have a thriving country nightclub scene and are part of the urban geography of the state.

22. The country dances in New Mexico and Texas where I first experienced the tradition were often multigenerational affairs. Parents taught their children to dance, and young teens developed their skills by dancing with each other.

23. The instructions from the DJ usually comprised telling the dancers when to begin the pattern.

24. Buddy Brock and Zack Turner, "Watermelon Crawl," performed by Tracy Byrd, *No Ordinary Man* (compact disc; MCA MCAD-10991; 1994).

25. This actualization of role and text through dance is one of the six devices Judith Lynn Hanna writes about as a means of communicating meaning through dance. Judith Lynn Hanna, *Dance, Sex, and Gender* (Chicago: University of Chicago Press, 1988), 15. What makes this performance noteworthy is that country dance typically eschews actualization in its practice—country dance relies not on realizing a text but on metaphoric communication as response to musical impulse.

26. Melonee McKinney, "Country before Country Was Cool, Knoxville Now Is the Coolest Spot of All," *Knoxville News Sentinel*, Sept. 24, 1993, sec. 4, pp. 8–10.

27. Since the country music craze peaked in the early- to mid-90s, country bars across the nation have closed their doors or changed formats.

28. In personal email correspondence DJ consultant and country dance consultant Rick Meyers writes, "Top seven reasons for the decline in dancers and places to dance!: 1. Dancers Don't Drink! 2. Dancers Don't Drink! 3. Egos and competitive spirits of the instructors. 4. Failure to teach enough of the same dances in the same area. . . . 5. Too many dance clubs opened at once. . . . 6. Dancers Don't Drink! 7. Failure by some clubs to play music that their dancers want to hear." Rick Meyers to Jocelyn Neal, May 22, 2000 (in Jocelyn Neal's possession).

29. One of the techniques used by the DJs at this club (and others) is a predetermined cycle of dances, selected to "turn the floor," or maximize the flow of the crowd onto the dance floor for a short time, then off, and, presumably, to the bar. The DJ will play a sequence of a few two-steps, each one increasing in speed, then a few choreographed partner dances, announcing each dance prior to the start of the song, followed by a set number of line dances, again

preannounced, a few freestyle or pop-rock numbers, and a few slow dances, at which point the cycle repeats.

30. Felice Bryant and Boudleaux Bryant, "Rocky Top," performed by the Osborne Brothers, *The Osborne Brothers, 1956–1958* (compact disc; Bear Family Records BCD 15-598-4; 1995 [1968]).

31. The "16-Step" is also called "Rebel Strut" in some regions—the two dances are occasionally distinguished by the replacement of two pivot steps with two rocking steps, but most dancers consider them individual options within the same dance and use the dance names interchangeably. It is worth noting as an aside that the "16-Step" dance pattern is actually 24, not 16, beats long.

32. Shania Twain and Mutt Lange, "Man! I Feel Like a Woman!" performed by Shania Twain, *Come On Over* (compact disc; Mercury 314-536003-2; 1997).

33. Although Twain's exploitation of her own sex appeal has been widely used to disparage any social importance of her lyrics' message, throughout the songs on *The Woman in Me, Come On Over*, and *Up!* is a continual repetition of subtly gender-reversed situations and lyrics. Her most recent album, *Up!*, features the up-tempo (and line-danceable) "In My Car, I'll Be the Driver" in this same vein, for instance. "In My Car, I'll Be the Driver," performed by Shania Twain, *Up!* (compact disc; Mercury 314-088170-2; 2003).

34. The woman stands to the right of the man. They join left hands near her left shoulder, and right hands with the man reaching behind her neck and over her right shoulder.

35. The dance showed up in the footage of the Full Moon Dance sequence in *The Thing Called Love* (Paramount Pictures, 1993), although, oddly, in that scene, it was not done by all the dancers in unison, but rather, by a scattered few. The published dance steps in the *Club Dance Scrapbook* claim that "although the Sweetheart Schottische has roots in faraway places, it has been the most popular couples dance (other than the two-step) in many areas down south for the past few years." Stuart, *Club Dance Scrapbook*, 57. One of the most comprehensive country dance-step libraries on the web lists it as "Choreographer: Unknown," and many dance studios include it in their syllabi without any historical explanation. "Sweetheart Schottische—With Options," *Country Western Dance Library*, http://www.ibiblio.org/schools/rls/dances/unknown/sweetheart_schottische.html (September 16, 2003).

36. It is worth noting that within the microcosm of the dance partnership, the relationship was quite similar to that of the women performing to "Watermelon Crawl" and the men catcalling from the bar railings: the leader's instructions, communicated through his body and his dance leads, were for the follower to express her sexuality and display her physical grace and enticements through her dance movements. The difference between the two situations was in the individual nature of the relationship—a single partnership—and in the subtly and technically advanced means of communication inside the dancing itself.

Between Riot Grrrl and Quiet Girl: The New Women's Movement in Country Music

1. K. T. Oslin, *80s Ladies* (compact disc; RCA 5924-2-R; 1987).

2. Mary A. Bufwack and Robert K. Oermann, *Finding Her Voice: The Saga of Women in Country Music* (New York: Crown Publishers, 1993), 63.

3. *Ibid.*, 44.

4. *Ibid.*, 68.

5. *Ibid.*, 48.

6. *Ibid.*, 172.

7. *The Encyclopedia of Country Music*, ed. Paul Kingsbury (Oxford University Press, 1998), 577.

8. Arlie A. Carter and William Warren, "The Wild Side of Life," performed by Hank Thompson, *All-Time Greatest Hits* (compact disc; Curb D2-77329; 1990).

9. J. D. Miller, "It Wasn't God Who Made Honky-Tonk Angels," performed by Kitty Wells, *Country Music Hall of Fame Series* (compact disc; MCAD-10081; 1991).

10. Bufwack and Oermann, *Finding Her Voice*, 234.

11. B. Creswell and W. Creswell, "My Big Iron Skillet," performed by Wanda Jackson, *Tears Will Be Chaser for Your Wine* (compact disc box set; Bear Family BCD 16114; 1997); "A Girl Don't Have to Drink to Have Fun," performed by Wanda Jackson, *ibid.*

12. Lorene Allen, Don McHan, and T. D. Bayless, "The Pill," performed by Loretta Lynn, *The Country Music Hall of Fame* (compact disc; MCA MCAD-10083; 1991); Loretta Lynn and Peggy Sue Wells, "Don't Come Home a-Drinkin' (with Lovin' on Your Mind)," performed by Loretta Lynn, *ibid.*

13. Dolly Parton, "Just Because I'm a Woman," performed by Dolly Parton, *Just Because I'm a Woman: Songs of Dolly Parton* (compact disc; Sugar Hill Records SUG-CD-3980; 2003).

14. Bufwack and Oermann, *Finding Her Voice*, 325.

15. *Ibid.*, 333.

16. *Ibid.*, 343.

17. *Ibid.*, 349.

18. *Idem.*

19. Oslin, *80s Ladies*.

20. K. T. Oslin, "80s Ladies," performed by K. T. Oslin, *80s Ladies.*

21. Susan Longacre and Rick Giles, "Is There Life Out There," performed by Reba McEntire, *For My Broken Heart* (compact disc; MCA MCAD-10400; 1991).

22. Jack Hurst, "Reba McEntire Feeling Right at Home with Toughest of Audiences," *Chicago Tribune*, May 18, 1986, 30.

23. Robert Byrne and Alan Schulman, "Men," performed by The Forester Sisters, *Talkin' 'bout Men* (compact disc; Warner Brothers 9-26500-2; 1991).

24. Suzy Bogguss, Matraca Berg, and Gary Harrison, "Hey Cinderella," performed by Suzy Bogguss, *Something Up My Sleeve* (compact disc; Liberty CDP-7-89261-2; 1993).

25. Mary-Chapin Carpenter and Don Schlitz, "He Thinks He'll Keep Her," performed by Mary-Chapin Carpenter, *Come On, Come On* (compact disc; Columbia CK-48891; 1992).

26. Bob DiPiero and Pam Tillis, "It's Lonely Out There," performed by Pam Tillis, *All of This Love* (compact disc; Arista; 18799-2; 1991).

27. Tom Shapiro, Terri Clark, and Chris Waters, "Better Things to Do," performed by Terri Clark, *Terri Clark* (compact disc; Polygram 314-526991-2; 1995).

28. Matraca Berg and Tim Krekel, "You Can Feel Bad," performed by Patty Loveless, *The Trouble with the Truth* (compact disc; Epic E 67269; 1996).

29. Larry Butler and Ben Peters, "Standing Tall," performed by Lori Morgan, *To Get to You: Greatest Hits Collection* (compact disc; BNA 07863-67919-2; 2000).

30. Tom Shapiro and Gary Burr, "Watch Me," performed by Lorrie Morgan, *Watch Me* (compact disc; BNA 07863-66047-2; 1992).

31. Rick Bowles and Robert Byrne, "I Didn't Know My Own Strength," performed by Lorrie Morgan, *To Get to You.*

32. Bob DiPiero and Tom Shapiro, "Walking away a Winner," performed by Kathy Mattea, *Walking away a Winner* (compact disc; Mercury 314-518852-2; 1994).

33. Gretchen Peters, "Independence Day," performed by Martina McBride, *The Way That I Am* (compact disc; RCA 66288-2; 1993).

34. James House, Sam Hogin and Phil Barnhart, "A Broken Wing," performed by Martina McBride, *Evolution* (compact disc; RCA 67516-2; 1997).

35. Craig Wiseman and Trey Bruce, "Someone Else's Dream," performed by Faith Hill, *It Matters to Me* (compact disc; Warner Bros. 9-45872-2; 1995).

36. Alan Jackson, "I Can't Do That Anymore," performed by Faith Hill, *It Matters to Me.*

37. Matraca Berg and Alice Randall, "XXXs and OOOs (An American Girl)," performed by Trisha Yearwood, *Thinkin' about You* (compact disc; MCA MCAD-11201; 1995).

38. Scott Gray, *The Shania Twain Story: On Her Way* (New York: Ballantine Books, 1998), 130.

39. Robert John, Mutt Lange, and Shania Twain, "Any Man of Mine," performed by Shania Twain, *The Woman in Me* (compact disc; Mercury 314-522886-2; 1995); Mutt Lange and Shania Twain, "(If You're Not in It for Love) I'm Outta Here!" performed by Shania Twain, *ibid.*

40. Dallas Williams, *Shania Twain: On My Way,* ECW Press, 1997, p. 130.

41. Mutt Lange and Shania Twain, "Honey, I'm Home," performed by Shania Twain, *Come On Over* (compact disc; Mercury 314-536003-2; 1997); Mutt Lange and Shania Twain, "If You Wanna Touch Her, Ask!" performed by Shania Twain, *ibid.*

42. Deana Carter and Rhonda Hart, "Did I Shave My Legs for This?" performed by Deana Carter, *Did I Shave My Legs for This?* (compact disc; Capitol 8-37514-2-6; 1996).

43. Bobby Whiteside and Kim Tribble "Guys Do It All the Time," performed by Mindy McCready, *Ten Thousand Angels* (compact disc; BNA 07863-66806-2; 1996).

44. Sunny Russ, Tim Johnson, and David Malloy, "This Is Me," performed by Mindy McCready, *If I Don't Stay the Night* (compact disc; BNA 07863-67504-2, 1997); Matraca Berg and Gary Harrison, "Oh Romeo," performed by Mindy McCready, *ibid.*

45. Phil Vassar and Rory Michael Bourke, "Bye Bye," performed by Jo Dee Messina, *I'm Alright* (compact disc; Curb D2-77904; 1998).

46. Bobbie Cryner, "Real Live Woman," performed by Trisha Yearwood, *Real Live Woman* (compact disc; MCA Nashville 088-170102-2; 2000).

47. Leslie Satcher, "When God-Fearin' Women Get the Blues," performed by Martina McBride, *Greatest Hits* (compact disc; RCA 07863-67012-2; 2001).

48. Tim Nichols, Rick Giles, and Gilles Godard, "I Wanna Do It All," performed by Terri Clark, *Pain to Kill* (compact disc; Mercury 088-170325-2; 2003).

49. Marcel, James Thomas Slater, and Jessica Andrews, "There's More to Me Than You," performed by Jessica Andrews, *Now* (compact disc; DreamWorks 0044-50356-2; 2003).

50. Shania Twain and Mutt Lange, "She's Not Just a Pretty Face," performed by Shania Twain, *Up!* (compact disc; Mercury Nashville 088-170314-2; 2002); Shania Twain and Mutt Lange, "Juanita," performed by Shania Twain, *ibid.*

51. Martina McBride interview by Beverly Keel, Sept. 6, 2003.

52. All country-music related sales and ratings figures provided by the Country Music Association.

53. Luke Lewis interview by Beverly Keel, May 13, 1999.

54. *Ibid.*

55. Roger Catlin, "Pop and Country: The Twain Meet with Shania," *Hartford Courant,* August 13, 1998, 20.

56. Lewis interview by Keel.

57. Clark Parsons, "Twain of Command," *Journal of Country Music,* 18 (no. 3), 16.

58. Elysa Gardner, *Trouble Girls: The Rolling Stone Book of Women in Rock* (New York: Random House, 1997), 359.

59. *Ibid.,* 359.

60. Alanis Morissette and Glen Ballard, "You Oughta Know," performed by Alanis Morissette, *Jagged Little Pill* (compact disc; Maverick/Reprise 45901-2; 1995).

61. Jill Herzig, "Shania the Crusader, *Glamour* (Oct. 2003), 249.

62. McBride interview by Keel.

63. Bill Malone, *Don't Get above Your Raisin': Country Music and the Southern Working Class* (Urbana: University of Illinois Press, 2002).

64. *Ibid.,* 86.

65. Bufwack and Oermann, *Finding Her Voice*, 326.
66. "The Woman in Me," performed by Shania Twain, *The Woman in Me.*
67. "I Wanna Know," performed by Sandy Knox, "Girl Talk."
68. Wade Jessen interview by Beverly Keel, June 16, 2003.
69. Garth Brooks and Kim Williams, "Papa Loved Mama," performed by Garth Brooks, *Ropin' the Wind* (compact disc; Capitol Nashville, CDP 7-96330-2; 1991).
70. Dennis Linde, "Goodbye Earl," performed by Dixie Chicks, *Fly* (compact disc; Monument NK-69678; 1999).
71. Lon Helton, Reporting in an E! on-line story, April 3, 2000.
72. Jessen interview by Keel.
73. Tim McGraw, "Red Ragtop," performed by Tim McGraw, *Tim McGraw and the Dancehall Doctors* (compact disc; Curb D2-78746; 2002).
74. *Ibid.*

Going Back to the Old Mainstream: *No Depression*, Robbie Fulks, and Alt.Country's Muddied Waters

1. Richard Peterson and Bruce Beal, "Alternative Country: Origins, Music, Worldview, Fans, and Taste in Genre Formation—A Discographic Essay," *Popular Music and Society*, 25 (Spring/Summer 2001), 237. Compare their conclusions to those of Trent Hill, who argues that "alternative country is not particularly nostalgic." Trent Hill, "Why Isn't Country Music 'Youth' Culture?" in *Rock Over the Edge: Transformations in Popular Music Culture*, ed. Roger Beebe, Denise Fulbrook, and Ben Saunders (Durham: Duke University Press, 2002), 183.
2. Jason Toynbee, *Making Popular Music: Musicians, Creativity and Institutions* (New York: Oxford University Press, 2000), 110. Musician Charlie Daniels exemplifies the link between popular music genres and social groups when he gives his definition of southern rock: "The genre was a *genre of people* that were all basically raised the same way. . . . Everybody was raised in a blue collar situation, came up listening to the same music, eating the same food, going to the same type of churches. We were all street people." Cited in Lee Ballinger, *Lynyrd Skynyrd: An Oral History* (New York: Spike, 1999), 2.
3. Simon Frith, *Performing Rites: On the Value of Popular Music* (Cambridge: Harvard University Press, 1996), 95.
4. Grant Alden and Peter Blackstock, *No Depression: An Introduction to Alternative Country Music. Whatever That Is* (Nashville: Dowling, 1998), 7.
5. "Hello Stranger," *No Depression*, 12 (Nov.–Dec. 1997), 2. Unless otherwise noted, all citations from *No Depression* come from this regular page two feature.
6. Alden and Blackstock, *No Depression*, 8.
7. Steven Daly, David Kamp, and Bob Mack, "The Rock Snob's Dictionary," in *Da Capo Best Music Writing 2001: The Year's Finest Writing on Rock, Pop, Jazz, Country & More*, ed. Nick Hornby and Ben Schafer (New York: Da Capo, 2001), 8.
8. In fact, *No Depression*'s extensive coverage of women performers leads Trent Hill to conclude that it "reflects, in part, the strength of feminist politics in postpunk culture in general." Trent Hill, "Why Isn't Country Music 'Youth' Culture?" 190, n. 93.
9. I once proposed an article to them that was rejected although in retrospect my idea seems lame enough to have merited that response.
10. Kembrew McLeod, " '★½': A Critique of Rock Criticism in North America," *Popular Music*, 20 (no. 1, 2001), 47–60.
11. Baker Maultsby, "Drive-by Truckers," *No Depression*, 35 (Sept.–Oct. 2001), 72–80.

12. Silas House, "Nothing to Fear," *No Depression*, 40 (July–Aug., 2002), 74.

13. House, "Nothing to Fear," 76.

14. *No Depression* hero Ryan Adams (erstwhile lead singer in Whiskeytown) gives a similar genealogy and nonexplanation in "Faithless Street," the title cut from Whiskeytown's first album: "I started this damn country band / 'cause punk rock was too hard to sing." "Faithless Street," performed by Whiskeytown, *Faithless Street* (compact disc; Outpost OPRD-30002; 1998).

15. Peterson and Beal also note the disjunction between the adoption of the Carter Family's hopeful song and the nostalgic imagery of alt.country. Peterson and Beal, "Alternative Country," 235.

16. Perhaps Oldham was seeking to exonerate himself after playing the self-absorbed artiste in Allison Stewart's profile of him. Allison Stewart, "Palace," *No Depression*, 4 (Summer 1996).

17. Germanicist Andreas Huyssen notes that this critical inclination has a long history: "the notion . . . gained ground in the 19th century that mass culture is somehow associated with woman while real, authentic culture remains the prerogative of men." Andreas Huyssen, *After the Great Divide: Modernism, Mass Culture, Postmodernism* (Bloomington: Indiana University Press, 1986), 47.

18. Grant Alden, review of Bruce Feiler, *Dreaming Out Loud: Garth Brooks, Wynonna Judd, Wade Hayes, and the Changing Face of Nashville*, *No Depression*, 15 (May–June 1998), 93.

19. Will Straw, "Sizing Up Record Collections: Gender and Connoisseurship in Rock Music Culture," in *Sexing the Groove, Popular Music and Gender*, ed. Sheila Whiteley (London: Routledge, 1997), 5.

20. Grant Alden, "Hello Stranger," *No Depression*, 34 (July–Aug., 2001), 2.

21. Peter Blackstock, "Buddy Miller," in *No Depression*, ed. Alden and Blackstock, 64.

22. Roy Kasten, "Ray Wylie Hubbard," in *No Depression*, ed. Alden and Blackstock, 44.

23. Bill Friskics-Warren, "You Don't Have to Call Her Darlin,'" *No Depression*, 41 (Sept.–Oct. 2002), 53.

24. Bill Friskics-Warren, review of Allison Moorer, *Miss Fortune*, *No Depression*, 41 (Sept.–Oct. 2002), 121.

25. For other examples of the anti-Nashville song, hear Jason and the Scorchers, "Greetings from Nashville" on *Still Standing* (compact disc; EMI Capitol 72435-41210-2-9; 2002); Charlie Robison's "Molly's Blues" on *Life of the Party* (compact disc; Sony 69327; 1998); and Dale Watson, "Nashville Rash," on *Cheatin' Heart Attack* (compact disc; Hightone HCD 8061; 1995).

26. "Contemporary country radio is targeting young adult females," said Paul Allen, the executive director of the Country Radio Broadcasters, a trade association. "Now, why would you want to target them? Because that's what advertisers want. The young female adult is often-times a mom. She influences 90 percent of all the buying decisions in the household; she's a generation X or Y consumer, and not brand loyal. That's a very influenceable and key demographic to go after." Neil Strauss, "The Country Music Country Radio Ignores," *New York Times*, March 24, 2002, sec. 2, p. 1.

27. Robbie Fulks, liner notes, Robbie Fulks, *The Very Best of Robbie Fulks* (compact disc; Bloodshot Records BS 059; 1999).

28. Kevin Roe, "Robbie Fulks: He Took a Lot of Scrapple (and Lived)," *No Depression*, 4 (Summer 1996), 21.

29. Bill Friskics-Warren, "Leaving NashVegas," *No Depression*, 11 (Sept.–Oct. 1997), 57; Linda Ray, "It Drawled from the Mouth," ibid., 52–56.

30. Robbie Fulks, "Overdubs of the Gods," *RobbieFulks.Com*, http://robbiefulks.com/myday/index.html?id=00009 (March 8, 2000).

31. Robbie Fulks, "Jean Shepard: The Woman in the Asbestos Suit," *Journal of Country Music*, 22 (no. 3).

32. Peter Margasak, "Robbie Fulks: Country without Borders," *Journal of Country Music*, 21 (no. 3), 6.

33. Like many of Fulks's Bloodshot odds and ends, this song ended up on the sarcastically titled *The Very Best of Robbie Fulks*.

34. Robbie Fulks, liner notes, Fulks, *The Very Best of Robbie Fulks*.

35. Joel Bernstein, "Just Plain (Robbie) Fulks," *Country Standard Time*, http://www.countrystandardtime.com/robbiefulks4FEATURE.html (Jan. 14, 2000).

36. Robbie Fulks, liner notes, Robbie Fulks, *13 Hillbilly Giants* (compact disc; Bloodshot Records BS 084; 2001).

37. Florence King, "South Mouth: or Why Liberals Hate Dixie," *National Review*, April 21, 1997, pp. 65–67.

38. Robbie Fulks, liner notes, Robbie Fulks, *South Mouth* (compact disc; Bloodshot Records BS 023; 1997).

39. S. Renee Dechert, "An AMP EXCLUSIVE! Interview with Modern Twang Author David Goodman," *AMP [Alt.Music.Press]*, 1 (Sept. 1999), http://www.geocities.com/SunsetStrip/Gala/4092/second_issue/moderntwanginterview.html (April 28, 2000).

40. Robbie Fulks, "Audits and Heaven, Too," *RobbieFulks.com*, http://robbiefulks.com/myday/index.html?id=00050 (Aug. 30, 2000).

41. Robbie Fulks, "Country & Wrestlin' " *RobbieFulks.com*, http://robbiefulks.com/myday/index.html?id=00007 (April 28, 2000).

42. Bernstein, "Just Plain (Robbie) Fulks," *Country Standard Time*.

43. Robbie Fulks, "Busking for Medicine," *RobbieFulks.com*, http://robbiefulks.com/myday/index.html?id=00051 (June 8, 2000).

44. Fulks, "Busking for Medicine," *RobbieFulks.com*

45. Robbie Fulks, "Hat Whore," *RobbieFulks.com*, http://robbiefulks.com/myday/index.html?id=00058 (Jan. 30, 2001).

46. For a full discussion of this hard country theme, see Barbara Ching, *Wrong's What I Do Best: Hard Country Music and Contemporary Culture* (New York: Oxford University Press, 2001).

Postlude

1. Frederic Ramsey, Jr., and Charles Edward Smith, *Jazzmen* (1939; New York: Proscenium, 1985); Charles Delaunay, *Hot Discography* (New York: Commodore Music Shop, 1940); Newman I. White, *American Negro Folk-Songs* (Cambridge: Harvard University Press, 1928); Dorothy Scarborough, *On the Trail of Negro Folk-Songs* (Cambridge: Harvard University Press, 1925); Bill C. Malone, *Country Music* (Austin: American Folklore Society/University of Texas Press, 1968).

2. Ralph Ellison and Robert G. O'Meally, *Living with Music: Ralph Ellison's Jazz Writings* (New York: Modern Library, 2001); Imamu Amiri Baraka, *Blues People: Negro Music in White America* (New York: William Morrow, 1963).

3. Nolan Porterfield, *Jimmie Rodgers: The Life and Times of America's Blue Yodeler* (Urbana: University of Illinois Press, 1979); Charles R. Townsend, *San Antonio Rose: The Life and Music of Bob Wills* (Urbana: University of Illinois Press, 1976); Ellis Nassour, *Patsy Cline* (New York: Dorchester, 1985); Wade H. Hall, *Hell-Bent for Music: The Life of Pee Wee King* (Lexington: University Press of Kentucky, 1996); Jonny Whiteside, *Ramblin' Rose: The Life and Career of Rose Maddox* (Nashville: Country Music Foundation/Vanderbilt University Press, 1997); Ivan M. Tribe, *The Stonemans: An Appalachian Family and the Music That Shaped Their Lives* (Urbana: University of Illinois Press, 1993); Roger M. Williams, *Sing a Sad Song: The Life of Hank Williams* (1970; Urbana: University of Illinois Press, 1981); Charles K. Wolfe, *In Close Harmony: The Story of the*

Louvin Brothers (Jackson: University Press of Mississippi, 1996); Cecelia Tichi, *High Lonesome: The American Culture of Country Music* (Chapel Hill: University of North Carolina Press, 1994); Dorothy Horstman, *Sing Your Heart Out, Country Boy* (New York: Dutton, 1975); Bill C. Malone, *Don't Get above Your Raisin': Country Music and the Southern Working Class* (Urbana: University of Illinois Press, 2002); Wayne W. Daniel, *Pickin' on Peachtree: A History of Country Music in Atlanta, Georgia* (Urbana: University of Illinois Press, 1990); Charles K. Wolfe, *Kentucky Country: Folk and Country Music of Kentucky* (Lexington: University Press of Kentucky, 1982); Charles K. Wolfe, *Tennessee Strings: The Story of Country Music in Tennessee* (Knoxville: University of Tennessee Press, 1977); Joe Carr and Alan Munde, *Prairie Nights to Neon Lights: The Story of Country Music in West Texas* (Lubbock: Texas Tech University Press, 1995); Mary A. Bufwack and Robert K. Oermann, *Finding Her Voice: Women in Country Music, 1800–2000* (Nashville: Country Music Foundation/Vanderbilt University Press, 2003).

Contributors

MICHAEL BERTRAND is assistant professor of history at Tennessee State University. His first book, *Race, Rock & Elvis* (Illinois, 2000) has been widely acclaimed for its re-evaluation of white Southern working-class culture and the emergence of rockabilly in the 1950s. He is also a contributor to the *Encyclopedia of Tennessee History and Culture* (Rutledge Hill, 1998).

BARBARA CHING is associate professor of English and director of the Marcus W. Orr Center for the Humanities at the University of Memphis. She has written extensively on country music and rural culture, including essays in *White Trash* (Routledge, 1997), *Soundtrack Available* (Duke, 2002), and *Whiteness: A Critical Reader* (New York University, 1997). She is co-editor of *Knowing Your Place: Rural Identity and Cultural Hierarchy* (Routledge, 1997) and author of *Wrong's What I Do Best: Hard Country Music and Contemporary Culture* (Oxford, 2001).

JOLI JENSEN is professor of communication at the University of Tulsa. Her publications include *Is Art Good For Us? Beliefs about High Culture in American Life* (Rowman & Littlefield, 2002); *The Nashville Sound: Authenticity, Commercialization, and Country Music* (Vanderbilt, 1998); and *Redeeming Modernity: Contradictions in Media Criticism* (Sage, 1990). She is coeditor (with Steve Jones) of *Afterlife as Afterimage* (Lang, forthcoming), a collection of essays on posthumous fame, and is currently completing *Media in Society*, an upper-division undergraduate textbook for Bedford/St. Martin's Press (with Richard Campbell and Douglas Gomery). She has served on the editorial boards of *Country Music Annual*, the *Journal of Communication,* and *Journalism Monographs* and, along with Steve Jones, Will Straw, and Anahid Kassabian, is co-editor of the Peter Lang book series, Music/Meaning.

BEVERLY KEEL is a freelance music journalist and associate professor in the Department of Recording Industry at Middle Tennessee State University.

She serves as entertainment editor of *American Profile* magazine and Nashville correspondent for *People* magazine. She has written for such publications as *USA Today, Entertainment Weekly, Country Music Magazine, EQ*, and *Guitar World*, as well as *RollingStone.com* and is the Entertainment Editor for *American Profile Magazine*. She has been featured on VH 1, CMT, and Bravo TV networks, as well as the *Charlie Rose Show.*

PETER LA CHAPELLE is assistant professor of mass communications at Wilson College. He received his Ph.D. from the University of Southern California in 2002 and is currently completing a manuscript on the Dust Bowl migration and the cultural politics of Los Angeles country music (University of California, forthcoming). A recent Smithsonian Postdoctoral Fellow, his articles have appeared in *Moving Stories: Migration and the American West* (University of Nevada, 2001) and *Dress: The Annual Journal of the Costume Society of America.*

KRISTINE M. McCUSKER is assistant professor of history at Middle Tennessee State University. She has published articles on women and barn dance music in *American Studies* and *Southern Folklore* and contributed articles on Renfro Valley and John Lair to the *Encyclopedia of Appalachia* (Tennessee, forthcoming). She has presented her research at the Berkshire Conference on the History of Women, the American Studies Association, and the International Country Music Conference, where she has also been an invited panelist for sessions on the Carter Family and old-time country music. She is currently revising her dissertation, "It Wasn't God Who Made Honky-Tonk Angels: Women, Work, and Barn Dance Radio, 1920–1960," for publication.

JOCELYN R. NEAL is assistant professor of music theory at the University of North Carolina at Chapel Hill, where she teaches music theory and analysis of popular music. Dr. Neal received her Ph.D. from the Eastman School of Music in 2002 with a dissertation on the music of country music pioneer Jimmie Rodgers. Her articles on contemporary country music and dance, music-text relations, and rhythm and meter have appeared in such publications as *Country Music Annual* (Kentucky, 2000) and *Reading Country Music* (Duke, 1998).

EMILY C. NEELY is a graduate student in folklore at the University of North Carolina. Her research on Charline Arthur has appeared in *Southern Cultures*, and her multimedia research projects on North Carolina's coastal fishing industry and artisanal pottery can be viewed online at http://www.unc.edu/ ~ecneely/.

DIANE PECKNOLD is an independent scholar and instructor of American history. She received her Ph.D. from Indiana University and is currently revising her dissertation, "The Selling Sound: Country Music, Commercialism, and the Politics of Popular Culture," for publication (Duke, forthcoming). She is also co-editor, with Michael McGerr, of *"This Is My Country": Popular Music and Modern American History* (Indiana, forthcoming), a primary source reader on popular music in the twentieth century. Her articles and review essays have appeared in *Country Music Annual* and the *Journal of American History*.

DAVID SANJEK is director of the BMI (Broadcast Music Inc.) Archives. Along with his late father, Russell Sanjek, he is co-author of *Pennies from Heaven: The American Popular Music Business in the 20th Century* (Da Capo, 1996) and is completing *Always On My Mind: Music, Memory, and Money* (Wesleyan, forthcoming). Recent publications include essays in *American Studies, Quarterly Review of Film & Video, American Quarterly*, and the *Journal of Popular Music Studies* as well as essays in the collections *The Aesthetics of Cultural Studies: Form, Function, Fashion* (Blackwell, 2004), *Music & Technoculture* (Wesleyan, 2003) and *This Is Pop: In Search of the Elusive at the Experience Music Project* (Harvard, 2004). He has been the chair of the U.S. chapter of the International Association for the Study of Popular Music and serves as a member of the editorial boards of *Popular Music and Society, American Studies*, and the *Journal of Popular Music Studies*.

CHARLES K. WOLFE is professor of English at Middle Tennessee State University. He has written more than fifteen books on country and roots music, including biographies of Deford Bailey, the Louvin Brothers, and Leadbelly. His most recent books include *Classic Country* (Routledge, 2000) and the authoritative history of the *Grand Ole Opry, A Good Natured Riot* (1999). He is co-editor of *Country Music Annual* and editor of *Tennessee Folklore Society Quarterly* and served as a historical consultant for the documentary series *American Roots Music*.

Index